POET McGONAGALL

POET McGONAGALL

A Biography

Norman Watson

BIRLINN

First published in 2010 by
Birlinn Limited
West Newington House
10 Newington Road
Edinburgh
EH9 1QS

www.birlinn.co.uk

ISBN: 978 1 84158 884 1

British Library Cataloguing-in-Publication Data
A catalogue record for this book is available from the British Library

Designed and typeset by Iolaire Typesetting, Newtonmore
Printed and bound by MPG Books Ltd, Bodmin

CONTENTS

LIST OF ILLUSTRATIONS

ACKNOWLEDGEMENTS

No project of this nature could have been accomplished without the support of Dundee Central Libraries and access to their collection of McGonagall poems, letters, broadsides and books. It was a pleasure to work with the library staff, notably Eileen Moran, Deirdre Sweeney, Ida Glendinning, Carol Smith and Maureen Reid. I am also grateful to Head of Reference Services, David Kett, for his help with images.

Remaining in Dundee, I owe thanks to Ian Flett, Richard Cullen and staff at Dundee City Archives and Pat Whatley and staff at Dundee University's Centre for Archives and Information Studies. In particular I am indebted to Gwen Kissock and Anne Swadel of DC Thomson & Co. Ltd, Dundee, for their valuable assistance, and to the directors of that firm for continuing to support my writing activities.

Librarians and archivists across Scotland and beyond were generous with time and help, including those at the National Library of Scotland, the 'Edinburgh Room' at Edinburgh City Libraries, the National Archives of Scotland and the British Library. Sarah Maclean of Orkney Archives and Pamela McIntyre of Ayrshire Archives deserve special mention for their assistance.

Several individuals helped with this work. Special thanks are due to Carol Moonie and the family of the late William Smith for access to their family archive. Dundee author and playwright Gordon Douglas frequently offered support. Others who assisted included Linda Caston, Frank McGonigal, Mary McGonigal, Bill Crabb, Steve Cromar, Forbes Inglis and Dick Levin.

Shirley Elizabeth Blair, as usual, scrutinised the text on my behalf and I thank her once again for her diligence and expert guidance.

Finally, I am grateful for the inspirational help from those who shared their thoughts on Poet McGonagall and helped to bring his story to life. Clearly he was not the only purveyor of bad verse to come out of Scotland.

INTRODUCTION

E XTRAORDINARY. Here we are in the twenty-first century reconstructing the life of a victimised Victorian poet who died in obscurity more than 100 years ago.

His verses began with 'Beautiful' this or that, or ' 'Twas on' such-and-such a date, or 'All hail to' so-and-so, and wandered along their tortuous paths without recourse to rhythm and metre. They have been criticised for their lack of poetic merit and for their abandonment of literary rules. Hamish Henderson said McGonagall's work was 'a sort of frowsy doss-house in which every wooden phrase, every gormless anti-climax was sure to find a bed'. To Hugh MacDiarmid his productions knew 'nothing of grammar, the rubrics and the accepted devices of versification'. William McIlvanney noted that McGonagall was responsible for 'excruciating scansion and rhymes of such numbing impact they could give you cauliflower ears just from silent reading'.[1]

And so William McGonagall endured three decades as Scotland's national joke. He strode Dundee's streets 'a weird drab figure' with long hair sheltered by a wide-brimmed hat, peddling penny poem sheets and pamphlets and winning a reputation as a fool. He became a figure of fun, a target of malice and cruelty, pelted with rotten fruit and bags of flour. And for half a century he endured hunger, debt and humiliation, eventually dying as he had lived, in poverty.

Yet no other Dundonian has enjoyed such fame or acclaim. Today the verses of the worst poet who ever lived are loved the world over. McGonagall is on film, CD and DVD and his poetic gems are sprinkled across countless books and websites. He has been parodied and popularised by the Goons, the Pythons and the Muppets, Spike Milligan, Peter Sellers, JK Rowling, Terry

Pratchett and Philip Pullman. There are McGonagall societies and dinners, plaques and portraits. The tell-tale terrible rhymes of one of the greatest Victorian eccentrics still make the headlines.

Thus Poet McGonagall was not just any poet. He was the country's greatest, he claimed. Or its worst, as his legacy suggests. There are no in-betweens. Either confront thudding couplets like 'dumb and mausoleum' or 'grief and Crieff' from this unchallenged prince of doggerel – or duck and make a run for the decent stuff. Whichever, the awfulness is what makes McGonagall's poetry madly unforgettable.

Sadly, though, the man *The Times* called 'the only truly memorable bad poet in our language' has largely escaped the biographer's pen. Collections of his work have been in print since the year after his not-to-be-denied vision to become a poet in 1877. Yet apart from David Phillips' part-fictional account in 1971, described by its author as an imaginative study, no adequate telling of his story has been attempted.

The omission is partly explainable. Until now no one has said with certainty where William McGonagall was born, where and how he grew up or, indeed, exactly where he is buried. Little is known about the first three-quarters of his life before his body was inflamed on a summer's morning and he was seized with a strong desire to write poetry . . . 'So strong, in fact, that in imagination I thought I heard a voice crying in my ears, "Write! Write".' Indeed, it is yet to be properly established how many poems he wrote, the number of broadsides he printed and when and where his pamphlets were published.

McGonagall obscured his story in autobiographical ramblings by offering two dates for his birth, various options for his upbringing and a maze of possibilities over his pre-poet public appearances. His confused accounts place him in Edinburgh or Glasgow, in Paisley or Ayrshire – even on Orkney – prior to arriving in Dundee. So no one has unpicked his frustrating first 50 years, rather concentrating on his output as a poet in the third quarter of the nineteenth century, when the habit of traducing his flow of verse became a pastime. Modern collections of his poetry are limited to listing his curious odes and addresses, only adding the briefest of biographical notes from his muddled memoirs. Thus hitherto bypassed from histories, or dismissed in a meagre quota of words, much of William McGonagall's story remains a mystery.

This work therefore seeks to reconstruct his life. In doing so it uses an extensive range of sources to examine his pathway to Dundee, schooling, work, marriage and family. It scrutinises his beginnings as an actor and raconteur, which pre-dated his poetry phase by two decades. It sets out to unstitch his transformation from impoverished weaver to howling-voiced performance poet. And it shows how, inadvertently but gloriously, Scotland's literary history was rewritten . . . badly.

As the chapters demonstrate, McGonagall's daily life was always a struggle, the pennies he made from pamphlets and public appearances barely keeping the bailiffs at bay. Yet the response to his creative dedication was ridicule and physical mishandling. He was baited unmercifully as he flogged his poems. He was invited to Rotary-type functions with the sole purpose of making him look ludicrous or to perpetrate a hoax upon him. He was conferred with bogus honours praising – if you read between the lines – his banality. And eventually, it is said, he fell under the spell of his own invention as he desperately tried to secure a paying clientele for what he considered and admired as the fruits of his own superior talent.

So this book also seeks to answer why McGonagall endured such hostility with straight-faced magnanimity. Did he implicitly believe his genius, or was his deafness to insults and laughter a sly ruse? Was his unparodiable eccentricity real – or was he, as one contemporary reported, 'actually fooling his baiters'?[2] Could it have been a carefully-planned leg-pull, one in which McGonagall was aware that the first show of intelligence on his part would threaten his livelihood? The alternative may, after all, have been starvation and a place in the poorhouse.

Many difficulties arose in charting this extraordinary story.

McGonagall left several 'autobiographies' – all entertainingly, but infuriatingly, different. Official records relating to him are missing or are sometimes equally vague. Some of his poems are known by fragments only and dating them can be problematic. Thus, Appendix II provides the first comprehensive, chronological listing of his known output, including details of many unpublished works. As poems are shown only in part in the text, it is recommended that *William McGonagall Collected Poems*, with an introduction by Chris Hunt (Birlinn 2006), should be consulted.

Such historical idiosyncrasies added to the challenge of research, though hardly diminished the enjoyment of writing.

Norman Watson, July 2010

ONE

THE IRISH QUESTION

Nailing down William McGonagall's early years is a biographer's nightmare.

Into this broiling broth of a bard can be added half a dozen divergent autobiographies written perhaps in 1878, possibly in 1880, probably in 1885, again in 1887, doubtless in 1890 and unquestionably in 1901 – the cooked-up stories his only consistency. Mix in irreverent obituaries in 1902 and a slandering spoof 'autobiography' banned in 1885 but published vindictively three years after his death; season with the unflattering jottings of pooh-poohing poets and lampooning literary critics, and bring to a boil with the smattering of documentation from official sources which took the trouble to mention him. The ingredients are all there, though, and with spoonfuls of contemporary evidence and anecdote, this work moves the life of William McGonagall from the back burner of history and brings it to the boil of a biographer's scrutiny.

To be untangled are the country of McGonagall's birth, where it took place, where he was brought up, even where he was ultimately laid to rest. Requiring scrutiny are his extraordinary ambition and unshakeable self-belief – but also the bizarre appearance and head-in-the-clouds eccentricity which met with indulgent smiles and made him a household name for all the wrong reasons. Hitherto unresolved are the number of poems he wrote and publications he printed. History is vague over where he lived in Dundee and uncertain as to when he spent time in other places. Little wonder that countless editions of his poetry lazily ignore the man in favour of a cut-and-paste capture of his tumbled-over wordplay.

The neglect is explainable if not defendable. Official records are lean where William McGonagall is concerned. It is not helpful that his name transmogrifies from McGonegal on a marriage register to

MacGonagall in the census to McGonigal on his death certificate –
with various maddening oddities popping up in between. His story
is also concealed behind a maze of possibilities over his birth and
upbringing. It is thus little wonder no serious attempt has been
made to place him in his life and times.

The starting point for this reconstruction requires analysis of the
six contrasting life stories William McGonagall left to the world. His
'autobiographies' comprise two undated manuscripts, one undated
printed pamphlet and three memoirs published in dated poetry
collections. In likely order of composition they are:

1. *A Summary History of Poet McGonagall*, undated manuscript, four
   pages, *c* 1878.
2. *Original Manuscript of an Autobiography by William McGonagall*,
   undated manuscript, 15 pages, *c* 1880. (This document is
   untitled, but is bound in a folder labelled 'Original Manuscript of an Autobiography by William McGonagall'.)
3. *The Authentic Autobiography of the Poet McGonagall, Written by
   Himself*, Luke, Mackie & Co., 115 Murraygate, Dundee,
   undated pamphlet, *c* 1885. 20 pages.
4. *The Autobiography and Poetical Works of William McGonagall*,
   Charles Mackie & Co., 13 & 15 Peter Street, Dundee,
   1887. 40 pages, 10 devoted to autobiography.
5. *Brief Autobiography*, included as frontispiece to *Poetic Gems,
   Selected from the Works of William McGonagall, Poet and Tragedian,
   Dundee*, Winter, Duncan & Co., Dundee, 1890. 96 pages, 9
   devoted to autobiography.
6. *The Autobiography of Sir William Topaz McGonagall, Poet and
   Tragedian, Knight of the White Elephant, Burmah*, published in
   parts by the *Weekly News* in 1901 and reissued as an 18-page
   pamphlet the same year.

These will be referred to throughout this text as *Summary History*
(*c* 1878), *Original Manuscript* (*c* 1880), *Authentic Autobiography* (*c* 1885),
The Autobiography and Poetical Works (1887), *Brief Autobiography* (1890)
and *The Autobiography of Sir William Topaz McGonagall* (1901). It is clear,
however, that McGonagall overlapped versions of his life story and it

will not be required, nor sensible, to add to his confusing story by referring in detail to all six versions of his memoirs.

In conceptual shorthand, William McGonagall's first autobiography, *Summary History, c* 1878, contains one version of his life. *Brief Autobiography*, No. 5 in 1890, combines elements of Nos 2, 3 and 4 and takes his story into the 1880s. His final and longest work, No. 6, in 1901, expands on his poetry output and public performances. McGonagall being McGonagall, the reminiscences offer exasperating alternatives for his early life.

Summary History is four pages in length and written in pencil on coarse paper measuring 385mm by 500mm. There has been speculation that the document was an invention of a former Dundee librarian and is not genuine. The handwriting matches other writings known to be McGonagall's, however. McGonagall also provides the names of his brothers Charles and Thomas, information that appears in no other version of his life, but now corroborated in official records open to the public. *Summary History*, therefore, appears to be an authentic 'autobiography'.

Summary History is undated. Matching the eight poems mentioned in the text against those contributed by McGonagall to the *Weekly News* confirms composition before the end of 1878. That *Summary History* does not extend beyond his trek to Balmoral in 1878 helps to confirm its origin to that year. Indeed, McGonagall erroneously entered '1878' for his date of birth on the document before amending it to '1825' with a stroke of his pencil.

Summary History was rediscovered in 2009 bound with a manuscript of McGonagall's sole surviving play, 'Jack o' the Cudgel'. It is uncertain why he sketched out this brief account of his life so soon after his first poem was published in 1877. Most likely it was intended to feature in a collection of verse under consideration at that time as, after discussing the eight poems, McGonagall ends *Summary History* with the comment that there are 'a host of others too numerous to mention, which will be publish'd shortly'. Curiously, it does not appear in his first-ever printed offering, a four-poem pamphlet titled *Poems and Song* issued in May 1878. Neither is it included in *The Complete Works of the Poet William McGonagall*, published as a booklet in June 1879 with 17 poems. Thus it remains a mystery as to why *Summary History* never appeared in print until it was reproduced in *Last Poetic Gems* in 1968, almost a century after it was written.

Summary History offers a glimpse of what William McGonagall wanted to record of the pre-poet period of his life. The manuscript opens with a statement that he was born in Edinburgh in March 1825. He tells his 'dear readers' that his parents were Irish and came to Scotland 'shortly after their marriage.' He does not refer to his parents, Charles and Margret, by name and there is no mention of his grandparents, Charles McGonagall and Nancy Baxter. In this version of his life, his family settled for 10 years in Maybole in Ayrshire, where his father worked as a cotton weaver. It was common for large numbers of immigrant workers to be employed or laid off, depending on the peaks and troughs of the cyclical industry and, come the downturn, he says his family travelled to Edinburgh where his father 'got settled down again to work cotton fabrics which there was a greater demand for than in Maybole.'

McGonagall recalls in *Summary History* that the family lived in Edinburgh for more than eight years, again until cotton weaving began to fail, before moving to the Orkney Islands. There, he says, his father purchased a living as a pedlar on South Ronaldsay and supported his wife and children by selling hardware among the scattered island community, 'returning home every night to his family, when circumstances would permit him'. After 'about three years' on Orkney the family moved to Dundee to enable his father to take up weaving again. No dates are provided for the transition between these various locations.

The first gleanings as to William McGonagall's family are also provided in *Summary History*. He notes: 'William, The Poet, was the youngest, and was born in Edinburgh. And the rest of the family was born in Maybole and Dundee.' He says Charles, his elder brother, tended cows for a farmer on South Ronaldsay. His eldest sister, Nancy, also worked 'in service' on the farm. But both William and his second brother, Thomas, were sent to school in South Ronaldsay under 'the pariah' schoolmaster James Forbes. From a later poor law application it appears another sibling was a girl, Agnes. It seems likely that Nancy, named after her grandmother, was the eldest, followed by Agnes, Charles, Thomas and William. The age span between the five was about ten years. Three brothers are confirmed, but no record survives of a third sister mentioned by McGonagall in the text. Curiously, there is no reference in *Summary History* to William's six younger siblings, documented after the family's arrival in Dundee.

Thus, according to the first known version of his life, William McGonagall's parents arrived from Ireland, say around 1815, lived in Ayrshire for 10 years, where presumably the first of their children was born, moved to Edinburgh around 1825, where William was born, and after eight years in the capital moved to Orkney for three years. This would provide an approximate date of entry to Dundee of 1836, when William was aged around 10.

McGonagall's second and third autobiographies – *Original Manuscript* (*c* 1880) and *Authentic Autobiography* (*c* 1885) – are unquestionably related.

Original Manuscript runs to 15 pages and small sections of its text appear incomplete. It is written in black ink on hand-made paper and measures 265mm by 360mm. Approximately five years after it was created the manuscript was supplied to Luke, Mackie & Co. to be used for the 20-page pamphlet *Authentic Autobiography*. This is proved by printers' corrections on McGonagall's text which were subsequently incorporated into the printed transcript.

Both manuscript and printed pamphlet are undated, but neither takes McGonagall's story beyond his Balmoral journey in 1878. As with *Summary History* they include poems and comments on his life to that year only. What appears to have occurred is that the manuscript was prepared some years in advance of the printed tract. The pamphlet can be dated to 1885 at the earliest, however, when Luke, Mackie & Co. was established at 115 Murraygate.[1]

The year 1885 was also when John Willocks produced an uncompromising attack on McGonagall in a spurious and cruelly-exaggerated 'autobiography'. It seems plausible that when Willocks' sixpenny booklet was announced and later withdrawn under threat of legal action, McGonagall required a genuine riposte – a factual account of his background and beginnings as a poet. Thus in 1885 he handed Luke, Mackie & Co. the version in longhand which he had penned for whatever purpose several years earlier. It is probably no coincidence that *Authentic Autobiography* carried the subtitle *Written by Himself,* presumably as counterblast to Willocks' damaging text.

In this second account of his life, McGonagall says he was born in Edinburgh in 1830, five years later than the date provided in *Summary History*. Again, it seems he initially wrote '1825' before, perhaps after giving it some thought, scratching in a '30' on top of the '25' in heavier black ink. He reveals that his mother and father were 'both born in Ireland' where they spent the 'greater part of their lives after their marriage'. This, too, contradicts *Summary History*. He relates that his parents were poor, 'but honest, sober, and God-fearing'. Without providing a date, McGonagall says they left Ireland for Scotland and 'never returned to the Green Isle'. His father, he adds, was a handloom weaver who 'wrought at cotton fabrics during his stay in Edinburgh' where he says the family remained for two years. Thereafter, 'owing to the great depression in the cotton trade in Edinburgh, he removed to Paisley with his family, where work was abundant for a period of about three years'. When depression blighted Paisley – or the 'crash' as McGonagall puts it – the family moved to Glasgow in the hope of securing work there. The move was essential for his father 'to support his young and increasing family, as they were all young at that time, your humble servant included'.

According to *Original Manuscript* and *Authentic Autobiography*, his father found work as a weaver in Glasgow for two years, and it was in that enlarging manufacturing monolith McGonagall was sent to school for the first time, 'where I remained about eighteen months'. In the next downturn, however, 'my poor parents were compelled to take me from school, being unable to pay for schooling through adverse circumstances; so that all the education I received was before I was seven years of age'. Forced to leave Glasgow, the family finally set foot in Dundee, 'where plenty of work was to be had at the time'.

Thus, according to this version of his life, only seven years – not the 21 stated in *Summary History* – were spent in Scotland before the McGonagalls settled in Dundee. These were in Edinburgh, Paisley and Glasgow. There is no mention in *Original Manuscript* or *Authentic Autobiography* of his family having lived in Ayrshire or Orkney. There is no reference, either, to William's brothers and sisters.

This second telling of McGonagall's upbringing was rehashed two years later for his first dated memoirs, *The Autobiography and Poetical Works of William McGonagall, Dundee,* a 40-page booklet published by Charles Mackie & Co. of Peter Street, Dundee in 1887. Most of this pamphlet's content is devoted to poems written to that date. Only 10 pages are culled from the second autobiography and still it does not take his story beyond 1878. Essentially, it is an abridged version of what had been printed by Luke, Mackie & Co., with no attempt at revision or updating.

William McGonagall's next autobiography appeared three years later and applied the necessary modifications to take his narrative into the 1880s. It was titled *Brief Autobiography* and was a preface to his first all-embracing book of poetry, *Poetic Gems,* published by Winter, Duncan & Co., Dundee in 1890. McGonagall devotes nine pages of this book to biographical notes. He retains the long and winding tale of his Balmoral journey, removes some of the fantasist banter from *Authentic Autobiography,* but provides no new information on his formative years. Instead he fast-forwards his life from 1878 to 1887 to disclose details of his adventure in America that year. At the end of *Brief Autobiography* he hints at the illness which befell him in the 1880s and ends: 'Since this Book of Poems perhaps will be my last effort . . .

> I earnestly hope the inhabitants of the beautiful city of
>   Dundee,
> Will appreciate this little volume got up by me,
> And when they read its pages, I hope it will fill their hearts
>   with delight,
> While seated around the fireside on a cold winter's night,
> And some of them, no doubt, will let a silent tear fall
> In dear remembrance of
> William McGonagall.

The Dundee bard survived, however, and was encouraged by sales of *Poetic Gems* to return to his printer the following year and arrange

Poetic Gems (Second Series), containing a completely new selection of verse. This omitted the first edition's *Brief Autobiography*. Rather, McGonagall incorporated a passage discussing his objections to public houses and excessive drinking titled *Biographical Reminiscences*. Although of interest in terms of how McGonagall was received and treated in Dundee, *Biographical Reminiscences* is not regarded as a separate autobiography for the purposes of this work, as it embraces only trenchant views on temperance and disapproval of a citizenry whose idea of enjoyment went no further than getting drunk.

And finally, William McGonagall's most comprehensive account of his life is *The Autobiography of Sir William Topaz McGonagall, Poet and Tragedian, Knight of the White Elephant, Burmah*, written in the last years of his life in Edinburgh, serialised in the *Weekly News* in 1901 and later published as an 18-page sixpenny pamphlet. This comprises a boastful but detailed recollection of his career as a tragedian and poet, yet largely glosses over his early life. He states again that he was born in Edinburgh – the only consistency in the divergent stories. He goes on, 'My parents were born in Ireland, and my father was a handloom weaver, and he learned me the handloom weaving while in Dundee.' There is no mention of Edinburgh, Glasgow, Paisley, Maybole or Orkney, no details of the previously stated period varying from seven to twenty-one years between his parents leaving Ireland and arriving in Dundee. Neither are details of siblings provided. Some severe wielding of the editorial scimitar was thus employed for the final autobiography, which instead concentrates on his adventures and 'achievements' as a poet.

And so William McGonagall offered readers a choice of lives. A quarter of a century passed between the first and the last and they ranged from his scrawled pencil *Summary History* of *c* 1878 to the colourful memoirs offered to the *Weekly News* in lumps of text in 1901, when he was close to 75 years of age. He also provided two dates of birth – 1825 and 1830 – but in true McGonagall style cheerfully corrected himself by noting, 'Like most men I was born at a very early age.' That these accounts are confused and contra-dictory fuels fascination with the man *Punch* called the greatest bad verse writer of his age.

Sadly, the obituaries which marked William McGonagall's death

in September 1902 add little flesh to the bones of his own biographical writings. The *People's Journal*, in a tongue-in-cheek tribute,
noted the death of 'Poor old McGonagall' by reminding readers
that he was born in Edinburgh 'about 80 years ago of Irish parents'.
No details of the half century before his 'discovery' of poetry in 1877
are provided. The passing of what it called 'The Poet Laureate of
the Silvery Tay' was also recorded by *The Courier*. The paper placed
McGonagall's age as between 70 and 80 and repeated that he had
been born in Edinburgh of Irish parentage. The obituary revealed
little of the poet's life before his name became familiar in the 1870s,
though it believed McGonagall had arrived in Dundee 'in early
life'. The *Scotsman* noted his passing in Edinburgh with the melodramatic headline 'Poet McGonagall Dead', though it limited itself
– not for the last time – to plagiarising copy from the Dundee
newspapers.[2]

A century of writers have also followed the poet's confused
reminiscences. The first was John Willocks who, as stated, penned
a controversial 'autobiography' of McGonagall in 1885. McGonagall indignantly halted its publication and drew a humbling apology
from its author, but Willocks published its libels and exaggeration
after his death as *The Book of the Lamentations of the Poet MacGonagall*.
Adopting McGonagall's voice, Willocks comments only that
McGonagall was 'born at a very early period of my existence in
that odoriferous portion of the globe, yclept the Grassmarket of
Edinburgh'. Thereafter he fashions a string of untruths to poke fun at
the life and times of his unfortunate subject. 'My parents were both
poor and bibulous . . .' the nefarious attack begins, McGonagall
reputedly thinking it praised their devotion to the Bible.[3]

There is also more conjecture than consensus about William
McGonagall's birth and upbringing among individuals who claim
to have known or to have encountered him during his lifetime. One
of the earliest sketches of McGonagall was compiled by journalist and
writer Lowden Macartney in *Selected Poems of William McGonagall*,
a sixpenny booklet published in 1934. While usefully providing
an eyewitness account of the poet's character and appearance,
Macartney's short biographical section fails to mention his formative years. This is true also of William Power's brief description of

McGonagall in *My Scotland* (1934) and of Hugh MacDiarmid's unflattering assessment in *Scottish Eccentrics* (1936), although both writers portray the poet in old age.

David Phillips' semi-fictional life of McGonagall, *No Poets' Corner in the Abbey*, published in 1971 and unfairly dismissed as 'totally undocumented', deals rather unsatisfactorily with the poet's early life. Phillips seems to have been swayed by McGonagall's first memoir, *Summary History*. Thus he places him at times in Edinburgh, Glasgow and Orkney and works him into fictitious situations in each location to keep his narrative rolling. Phillips had access to unpublished material relating to the poet's later life and the temptation to focus on these riches at the expense of his early days is perhaps understandable. It is unclear, however, why he felt it necessary to embellish McGonagall's story with fictitious characters and contrived conversations.

Of more recent introductions to McGonagall poetry collections, James L. Smith (1968), Colin Walker (1993), Chris Hunt (2006) and Charles Nasmyth (2007) acknowledge McGonagall's two dates of birth, state 1825 to be likelier than 1830, and claim that it took place in Edinburgh. Smith appears to discount the Orkney years and any time spent in Paisley. Walker asserts that much of McGonagall's childhood was spent on South Ronaldsay until, aged eleven, he moved with the family to Dundee. Hunt accepts that his subject's early life is filled with uncertainty. He highlights the contradictions of the accounts left by the poet, suggests 1825 as a more likely birth date than 1830 and says his trail encompassed Maybole, Edinburgh and Glasgow before he settled in Dundee. Nasmyth's illustrated tribute follows all 'three published "autobiographies"'. These authors offer no documentary evidence to support their claims, relying on the poet's confused memoirs for a précis of his life. Other compilations – including the *Library Omnibus* (1969) and *Collected Poems* (1992) – offer no biographical details whatsoever.[4]

Introductions to William McGonagall's work thus tend to either follow the autobiographical options or to accept that his con-tradictory accounts cannot be reconciled. Most McGonagallian enthusiasts and commentators have traditionally put forward that he was born in Edinburgh, however. These include Grampian

Television's documentary on McGonagall in 1965, Hamish Henderson's scrutiny of his folk heritage (1966 and 1971), William Smith's essays in the 1980s, Dundee Rep's *Made from Girders* play in 1991 and McGonagall's breakthrough entry in the *Collins Encyclopaedia of Scotland* (1994). This view has also been supported by Professor Chris Whatley, Professor David Swinfen and Dr Annette Smith, three of Dundee's most eminent historians.

Yet there is no consensus among them over his upbringing. Diverse and distinct locations are offered for McGonagall's early years. No historian has stated unequivocally which of the mischievous McGonagall's choices is more or less likely. No writer has examined his extravagant claims for truth, perhaps allowing the pauper poet in old age to embroider his early life to give it the interest he may have felt it lacked.

Official documentation, however, can bring a better understanding of William McGonagall's past than conjectural comments within reminiscing articles and poetry publications.

The National Census of 1841 was the first to name individuals in households and list their age, occupation and place of birth. The snapshot of Britain's population that year was also the first to give the numbers, sex and percentage of Irish-born inhabitants in Scotland's parishes. The 1841 census also provides the first mention of William McGonagall in any surviving written record.[5]

The census lists William as a 15-year-old living in Hawkhill, Dundee, with his parents, Charles and Margret, and six younger siblings – Jannet, 13; James, 12; Elizabeth, 9; 'Sally' (later Sarah), 6; Joseph, 4; and nine-month-old Margaret. There is no record in the entry for the older brothers and sisters detailed in *Summary History*. It can be assumed they had left to make their own way in the world – Agnes, Charles junior and Thomas were certainly married by the 1850s.

The entry reveals that the McGonagalls lived in densely populated Hawkhill but does not provide the exact location. It was possibly at No. 199, the address provided by his parents in the 1851 census and near to the water courses that had spawned the town's linen industry and sparked its emergence as a major manufacturing centre. The location of this tenement was close to today's Whitehall Theatre, on the north side of Hawkhill.

Ages entered on census schedules were not always accurate. Enumerators were instructed to round down persons of 15 and over to the nearest five years. Thus, William's father Charles, listed as aged 50, might have been 50 to 54 years old, his mother Margret, given as 40, between 40 and 44. However, as enumerators were instructed to enter the age at last birthday for children between 1 and 15 years it is quite likely that William McGonagall *was* approximately 15 at the census enumeration in June 1841. Detailed information entered on the 1861 census by his father, however, provides William's age distinctly as '34'. This implies an 1827 birth date, probably in March that year, the month McGonagall gave in his first autobiography. As to why he offered 1830 as his birth date in *Original Manuscript* and thereafter, it can be assumed that memory or vanity played a part – McGonagall would not have been the first entertainer to fib about his age.

The 1841 census provides William's occupation as 'HLW', the designated acronym for handloom weaver. It was customary for son to follow father into a naturally inherited trade in which Dundee by mid-century had moved ahead of Hull as Britain's biggest importer of flax and overtaken Leeds to become the nation's leading linen producer.[6] William's 13-year-old sister Jannet is listed as a flax spinner, typical for a period when children as young as 12 entered employment through financial necessity and obligation. James, 12, and Eliza, 9, were probably in some form of schooling, but on the verge of entry to mill work. Along with elementary schools, Dundee had by 1840 five factory schools for children who worked part of the day. Sarah, six, four-year-old Joseph and baby sister Margaret would have lived among the commotion of the congested family home.

Instead of being a wholly reliable record, however, the 1841 census return poses an intriguing question over William McGonagall's birthplace. Research in the 1980s by local history librarian Linda Caston raised doubt over McGonagall's claim to have been born in Edinburgh, an assertion the poet made in all autobiographies and in each census return he provided from 1851 onwards. Caston highlighted the unambiguous presence of the letter 'I' for 'Ireland' in the 'where born' column against the name of every member of the McGonagall family apart from William's infant sister Margaret, who is listed in a separate column as born in Scotland. The entry implied that William, his parents and all the children apart from Margaret were actually migrants from Ireland. Thus international tensions were heightened over the scary possibility that Scotland's most notorious poet was, actually, Irish. Caston's revelation, later highlighted in a *Courier* article, was subsequently reported by media outlets across the globe, including the BBC and the *New York Times*.

Other implications arose. The 1841 census gave 'Irish-born' Joseph's age as four. If this tantalising entry was accurate, the family had spent no more than four years in Scotland and not less than one year, as the final entry in the return is for baby sister Margaret, aged nine months, and born in Scotland. Thus the conundrum is this – either McGonagall's reminiscences of long stays in Edinburgh, Glasgow, Ayrshire, Paisley and Orkney are little more than imaginative waffle, or the McGonagall household entry in the National Census of 1841 is incorrect. Or, if McGonagall's *Summary History* is not a bogus account, and the family spent ten years in Ayrshire, eight in Edinburgh and three more in Orkney before coming to Dundee, the place of birth and thus date of migration of all but one of the McGonagall children must have been incorrectly entered into the census.

Efforts to understand William McGonagall's early life thus depend on how far we can trust the information entered on Page 4 of District 37's return for this official record of Britain's population. The 1841 census in Scotland took place on June 6 under the jurisdiction of the Home Office, assisted by county sheriffs, and was organised mostly along parish lines to allow enumerators to gather information within a single day. It was conceived and organised to be accurate and designed to be carried out over a short timeframe to avoid errors or omissions. Enumeration districts were often given to schoolmasters who were deemed best qualified and most knowledgeable in local affairs. On 5 June, the day before the census, each household received a schedule. On 6 June, a Sunday, the completed schedules were collected by enumerators, and help offered by them to those families where entries were incomplete or literacy skills inadequate. The schedules were then checked and copied into an enumerator's book. These were subsequently despatched to the Registrar General's office in London. The census, therefore, was designed from the outset to be an accurate record of population.

If accurate, and the McGonagalls were Irish incomers to Dundee, why would William have fibbed about his birth in later censuses and contemporary interviews – and manufacture stories of a wandering upbringing for his autobiographies? The implication surely to be extrapolated from the 1841 evidence is that William's 'autobiographies' – penned from the age of 50 onwards – are a sequence of fantastic inventions and falsehoods where his upbringing is concerned. Alternatively, the census entry is wrong – and two speculative slingshots could explain why this might be the case. The first is the possibility of Charles McGonagall's intense pride in his heritage and his desire to give his family an Irish start in life. The second is that the census enumerator made an error in transcribing the information provided by the family.

There were upwards of 5,000 Irish in Dundee when Charles McGonagall provided his family's details for the 1841 census, housed close to the mills and factories that employed them. There was little reason at that time for Charles McGonagall to deny his Irish heritage in the Irish-dominated quarter of Hawkhill, where he eked out a living. His countrymen were the largest single immigrant group in the town. They were not in the habit of burying their background: 'In order to make themselves acceptable, the Irish would have needed to make themselves invisible. But collective assertiveness was more important to the Irish than individual anonymity.'[7] In other words, the Irish shouted their pride in their heritage from the rooftops and would take on all-comers who denied it. Listing his children as Irish – even those born in Scotland – amounted to no more than a sensible placement in a disorderly community where appropriate and familiar family background could guarantee survival.

There was also a practical reason for Charles McGonagall to wrongly list his family as Irish. Immigrants from Ireland were enshrined in Dundee as welcomed workers. More truthfully, they offered a cheap workforce and a handy managerial resource to keep mill wages down. The *Dundee Advertiser* noted with satisfaction: 'Until lately those in the preparing rooms of the mills were all imported from Ireland. Whenever there was a want of hands they informed their friends over the Channel and a new importation occurred. Thus there was always an abundant supply of that class of labour.'[8] Scotland was a tried and tested alternative for the Irish, as it has been in recent times for Eastern Europeans. It was easy to obtain passage and work was waiting, particularly seasonal employment in harvesting, potato-picking and labouring. But Dundee had a specific requirement to feed its worker-hungry textiles trade. In 1791, the town's Catholic chapel had a congregation 'of just eight souls' in a population of around 20,000. By 1861, 15,000 Irish contributed to a total population of 90,000; thus, by then one in six of Dundee's population was Irish-born and located in priest-controlled communities in the town's textile enclaves.

A second possibility is that among Dundee's incendiary incomers the enumerator mistook the McGonagalls for Irish immigrants. Charged with writing up the schedules from dozens of similar working-class families, he might have classified the children as Irish out of habit and in error. Perhaps he was slapdash or simply exhausted after tramping up and down Hawkhill's towering tenements. Accuracy was a census priority. Yet there were ample opportunities for mistakes to be made due to pressure of work or failing memory or, most likely, the receipt of inaccurate or incorrect information. A migrant working family such as the McGonagalls may not have had the necessary literacy skills to complete the census form without third-party assistance. Moreover, the original schedules were destroyed. Scottish – and, indeed, British – records surviving from the 1841 census are the transcribed copies in enumerators' books, not the questionnaires filled in by heads of households. There may have been an error in transcription, just as there was an obvious error made in 1851 when William's first two children were described as 'lodgers', and again in 1861, when his mother's birthplace was stated as Maybole, 'Angus-shire', instead of Ayrshire.

It is also important to stress that William McGonagall consistently and presumably consciously recorded Edinburgh as his birthplace in census entries from 1851 to 1901. He also claimed to have been born in the Scottish capital in interviews given to reporters following his poetic progress. In fact, the one occasion he was labelled Irish in the Press was quickly corrected. This arose when a submitted poem on the Dundee bard used the convenient rhyme 'The Great, the Grand McGonagall/Who came from County Donegal.' The anonymous author explained in a PS to the paper, 'I hope that the illustrious one really belongs to Donegal. I do not know the spot on earth supremely blest with the honour of his birth. He looks an Irishman, and his name is Irish, and I ventured on Donegal because no other word rhymes so naturally with his name.'

This led the paper to consult McGonagall and to set the record straight: 'The "poet" said that these verses contained the finest compliment that was ever paid to him in this world, at the same time he did not belong to County Donegal, but was born in the Grassmarket of Edinburgh.' The Grassmarket was also identified as McGonagall's birthplace in John Willocks' 'autobiography' of 1885 and the expanded edition of *Lamentations* published three years after the poet's death. Willocks obviously knew McGonagall and may have had permission to write the 1885 autobiography, its subject unaware its pages would convey a no-holds-barred condemnation of his life. It seems improbable Willocks would have passed over or avoided calling his subject Irish if this was indeed the case.[9]

And yet it is skating on dangerous historical ice to assume or conclude that an error was made in the 1841 census in relation to the country of birth of five of the six listed McGonagall bairns. While nothing in later life suggests McGonagall could have spent at least 11 and as many as 13 of his 15 years in Ireland, it requires considerable alternative evidence to offset or overturn an official record. Most genealogists are aware that census abnormalities are the exception rather than the rule.

Thus it is the locations presented to readers in his various autobiographies that must be examined to solve the Irish Question. Essentially any evidence indicating a pre-Dundee McGonagall presence in Scotland would vindicate his jottings and confirm a census inaccuracy.

The south Ayrshire village of Maybole has a potentially fascinating link with William McGonagall's family. *Summary History* states that his father settled in Maybole after moving from Ireland. He remained a weaver there until demand for cotton failed about 10 years later. McGonagall also affirms that some of his brothers and sisters were born in the south Ayrshire hamlet.

Minnibolers were proud that handlooming was the first recognised manufactory trade in the district. But gradually weavers from Northern Ireland 'infiltrated and cotton looms were set up and Maybole clacked its way to prosperity and sold its produce to Glasgow merchants who distributed it throughout the country.'[10] One witness from the time Charles McGonagall may have moved there said: 'The Irish in this town belong almost exclusively to the working classes. They are employed principally in weaving, shoe-making and in labourers' work . . . I think about a third of the population of this town is Irish.'[11]

It is possible that, in these early days of expansion, William's parents moved to Maybole for work – a town that had 'risen into considerable importance as a busy outpost of Glasgow cotton manufacturers, and a ready receptacle of the immigrant weavers of Ireland.'[12] It is an intriguing possibility that the first of the family was raised in Ayrshire with William, as he stated, born after a move from there to Edinburgh in the mid-1820s. Such a scenario drew this unsourced comment from the post-war Ayrshire historian James Gray: 'The parents of the famous William McGonagall "the world's worst poet" lived in Maybole for many years and all their family, excepting William, were born there. They moved to Edinburgh and William was born three months after they left Maybole.' Gray, however, provides no evidence for this information.

Maybole looms large in William McGonagall's earliest autobiography. It is also given by his mother late in life as her birthplace in two census entries. It is therefore a challenge to discount the family's presence in the village at some point. Yet no official documentation supports a stay there and today's Maybole Historical Society has found no local link to the Dundee poet. Thus evidence is insufficient to challenge the 1841 census, which indicates they could only have lived there as an incoming Irish family some time around 1836/37, when Joseph was born in Ireland, and 1841 when the census data was provided in Dundee. It is possible that they stayed in Ayrshire prior to moving to Dundee, but there is no surviving record of their children being born in Maybole to the background whirr of its 1,380 weaving looms.[13]

William McGonagall's earliest and most detailed recorded childhood memory concerns South Ronaldsay in Orkney. According to *Summary History* the family stayed on the island for three years and it was there that William's formal schooling took place under a master called James Forbes. McGonagall claims that while at school in South Ronaldsay an extraordinary event took place in which he dropped the teacher's pet tortoise 'which almost killed it' and thereafter 'the Dominie chanc'd to see him at the time through the back window of the Schoolroom, and he rattled on the window with his cane to William, which startled him'. Afterwards he was severely punished by the school tawse 'untill some of the elder Scholars cried out to him to Stop!' In recent times, the owner of the two-roomed schoolhouse rediscovered behind plasterwork the back window that McGonagall apparently recalled in his memoirs. Jammed into its frame were red chalk pencils that Forbes might have once used to correct McGonagall's work. Alas, there was no 'W. McG' among the schoolboy initials the current owner found carved into the slate lintel above a fireplace also uncovered during the renovations.[14]

In the early 1970s the Orcadian historian and broadcaster Ernest Marwick examined McGonagall's claim to have spent his schooldays in Orkney. Marwick left two short typescript articles implying a strong possibility of truth to the poet's story. His investigation confirmed the tradition of a family known as 'the wild McGonagalls' on South Ronaldsay. Marwick discovered that James Forbes had a pet tortoise as well as other exotic pets, including peacocks and an eagle. Piecing the jigsaw of evidence together he concluded that William's memory 'was not at fault'.

James Forbes is recorded in the 1841 census as living at the schoolhouse in St Peter's (North) Parish, just outside the village of St Margaret's Hope, on South Ronaldsay. He was then given the age of 40. A letter in Forbes's hand to Thomas Balfour MP regarding ornithology survives with Orkney Archives. Thus the parochial schoolmaster is not simply a McGonagall myth and suggests an element of knowledge on McGonagall's part of goings-on in Orkney.[15]

How Orkney life might have shaped William McGonagall we cannot know. His family would have been regarded as poor 'Irish' tinkers. But islands being islands, any pedlar had the opportunity of providing goods and services not available locally and Orkney needed 'wood, iron, flax, coal, sugar, spirits, wines, snuff, tobacco, leather, hardware, broad-cloth and printed linens and cottons'. If indeed young William was a pupil at this little school looking down to the village of St Margaret's Hope, he is likely to have been among children of various ages drawn from across South Ronaldsay. And if McGonagall's earliest version of his life is a faithful account, he spent three years with this scattered farming and seafaring community seven miles from the Scottish mainland while his father hawked cottons and linens to its inhabitants.

The problem with William McGonagall's entire Orkney saga, however, is that no documentation linking the family to South Ronaldsay has survived. There are no rentals or stent rolls for the time and the parish poor board records start in 1846, by which time the McGonagalls lived in Dundee. Prior to this it was the church which dealt with the poor and offered them assistance, but the parish records for St Peter's on South Ronaldsay hold no mention of the name McGonagall or anything approximating to it. That no McGonagall appears on Orkney Sheriff Court records for the period suggests creditable unblemished behaviour if they were indeed present on the island, but leaves no family footprint to follow.[16]

One important link to the wider area does survive. The 1861 census finds William's parents fallen on hard times, moved away from Dundee and living close to the Caithness hamlet of Halkirk, intriguingly just a short boat trip from South Ronaldsay. They appear to have quit Dundee in 1858 and are listed in 1861 as 'pauper' and 'pauper's wife', aged 70 and 67, and living on Lower Westerdale farm with their unmarried daughter Margaret, William's 27-year-old sister. The entry for the Halkirk Poor Law Board

list in 1865 confirms Charles McGonagall's plight: 'In wandering
about as a Hawker had a paralytic stroke and had to be put upon
the roll of the poor.'[17] Thus, a fascinating picture can be sketched of
William's father returning to the neighbourhood of Orkney after an
absence of nearly 30 years and attempting again to trade as a
pedlar, selling cottons in car-boot-sale style from a cart as he had
done on South Ronaldsay in his younger days. Romantic conjecture is outweighed by a complete lack of evidence, however.
Most likely William learned of Orkney life from his parents or sister
and wove the island story into his first autobiography for reasons
known only to himself. His father's story also went downhill. He
returned to Dundee in the summer of 1865 and died at a house in
West Port in October that year, aged 74.

Similarly, no evidence has been found to confirm William McGonagall's asserted three years in Paisley, and we are left to wonder again if it
was a story hatched to suit a later purpose. However, perhaps the
family's presence there should not be entirely discounted as a possibility. Paisley, like Maybole, was a centre of textiles production, most
famous for the manufacture of cotton shawls. In 1837, around the time
the McGonagalls might have lived there, over 6,000 handloom
weavers were recorded in the town, many of them Irish. Significantly,
there was a near collapse of the Paisley trade around 1841. The
downturn – which saw the numbers of handloom weavers halve to
3,000 – hints at the peripatetic movement of experienced weavers
between textile towns referred to in McGonagall's autobiographies.
Adding further interest to the Paisley scenario was the presence there
of the mill poet Robert Tannahill (1774–1810). McGonagall later
termed his brother poet 'poor ill-treated Tannahill', suggesting a level
of intimacy, if not a local connection.

Having examined William McGonagall's autobiographical wanderings to determine how the 1841 census return might be wrong,
equally worthy of exploration is why he would have turned his back
on his Irish background to claim, from 1851 onwards, that he was a
native Scot. The probable motive was that he had an imperative
incentive to conceal his family's background – namely to cover the
stigma of being Irish.

The Irish were not a popular colony in Scotland and, as their communities grew, there was prejudice against them for being poor and for allegedly spreading epidemics of typhus and smallpox. They were accused of taking indigenous jobs and tempting manufacturers to impose lower wages. They were also slandered in print for being politically disruptive. James Myles, in *Rambles in Forfarshire* in 1850, summed up Dundee's Irish with blunt brutality: 'The low Irish are not a very improvable race. They cling to their rags, their faith and their filth with all the besottedness of perfect ignorance and stupidity.'[18]

Further, the Poor Law Inquiry of 1834 had highlighted problems with Irish immigrants – not least that many arrived on Scotland's shores on the brink of destitution and in need of immediate employment. Then, under parochial boards established by the Poor Law (Scotland) Act of 1845, qualification for financial relief from a parish was set at five years' continuous residence without recourse to begging in the interval. The Irish were particularly badly treated, however, many having no birth qualification to obtain relief. Viewed today as a stain on Scotland's character, repatriation of Irish paupers became the blunt remedy for dealing with the legacy of a once-important workforce.

By the late 1840s, nearly 6,000 Irish paupers were being sent home annually by Scottish parishes. Authorities 'attacked with renewed vigour the problem of vagrancy in the hope of separating the Irish goats from the native sheep and consigning the former to their own country'.[19] Outbreaks of disease, notably the dreadful cholera epidemic of 1848, heightened fears and led to the repatriation of vagrant immigrants, sometimes with the encouragement of a few pennies in their pockets.

Thus there was a fear among the Irish that in an economic crisis their nationality alone might be sufficient to debar them from relief. Repatriation was an extremely real threat. Those not in work, or unable to support a family, were regarded as beggars and were likely to be excluded from support mechanisms. And Dundee did not take readily to the Irish poor. The authorities in the town refused relief to them wherever possible, 'And when they did it was at rates below those given to the Scots-born population.'[20] One Irish woman, who had been refused financial help by Dundee's inspector of the poor, was said to have lived in the town for four years. This led to the comment: 'The poor creatures came here when trade was brisk; and then they are left to sink or swim when the manufacturers have no use for them.' A local priest at the time claimed that fewer than 50 of his flock of 7,000 parishioners had qualified for relief.[21]

The Irish felt the system was stacked against them and McGonagall would have been well aware of the implications of an Irish background and what it could mean if he fell on hard times. He may well have been Irish, but required the 'insurance' of a Scottish background. He may have chosen Edinburgh as his place of birth for no other reason than that it was a romantically acceptable alternative, with the literary mystique to suit his artistic ambitions. He may have passed through other towns on his journey to Dundee, but it is just as likely that his autobiographical stories were part of a reinvention of himself as a Scot, as much as they formed part of what actually happened during his upbringing.

Any lingering Irishness was excised by the time William McGonagall entered adulthood. By all accounts he did not speak with a trace of an Irish accent and contemporary interviews describe only his powerful voice, with no reference to an Irish dialect. Neither Irish words nor slang emerge in his writing, nor do staple Irish songs, ballads and political recitations appear in his performance repertoire. It is also to be supposed, however, that a Shakespearean actor who could offer himself for 'elocution' instruction by 1879 could well have disposed of any lingering sign of Irishness – or Irish accent – in adult life without difficulty.

In any case, by the time McGonagall wrote his memoirs he had formed an exclusive interest in Scotland's culture. He was best known as a heroic champion of Shakespeare's eponymous Macbeth, but he had reworked Scottish warrior epics and conveyed them spectacularly to audiences. He had praised Burns and versified on Scotland's towns, ports, villages, rivers, mountains and lochs. Almost all work was explicitly Scottish in nature and delivered in 'high' English language. All traces of his Irish background had been deliberately expunged.

To conclude, proof for William McGonagall's autobiographical memorial is lacking. No record survives detailing his activities prior to the census of 1841, with most Irish records of the period destroyed by fire in Dublin in 1922, including the Irish census for 1821 and 1831. The UK census, however, clearly implies that he was born in Ireland and it is an ironic oddity that a man who devoted much of his life to recording deeds and stories showed himself to be such a misty and mysterious figure. That said, no evidence has been found to overturn the census data.

Indeed, late in life, McGonagall appeared to confess that he had strung everyone along about his birthplace. In 1894, on the cusp of leaving Dundee, McGonagall sent a friend on the *Weekly News* a 'farewell' note containing a list of 33 poems in praise of Scotland he had composed. Appended to this catalogue 'in the Poet's beautiful calligraphy' was the enigmatic stanza offering teasing proof by his own hand that McGonagall was not Scottish-born . . .

> Who composed these poems big and small?
> I answer McGonagall.
> Deny it who can,
> And, be it said, an Irishman.[22]

Thus, myriad writers, poets, historians, commentators and enthusiasts who claim McGonagall's birthplace as Edinburgh and their hero as a Scot, may be harnessing the same imaginative powers that the poet employed 140 years ago, embellishing their own stories in the manner he did.

While doubt remains over William McGonagall's Irish lineage, he was almost certainly not Roman Catholic. The acceptance that Victorian Dundee became a Catholic Irish town through a massive influx of millworkers – 'it appears to have attracted only the Catholic Irish' – has been bracketed with his parents' Irish background to leave a suspicion that McGonagall was of that religious persuasion. The entry for McGonagall's marriage to Jean King in 1846 survives in the Dundee burgh register for Presbyterian weddings. An application for poor relief, dated 1865, lists his family as 'Protestant', and a medical certificate for his son Joseph in 1893 clearly records his religion as 'Protestant'. McGonagall's parents were probably from Northern Ireland.[23]

Although unnamed in its records, the McGonagalls probably

attended St Peter's Free Church in Dundee, as their entry in the census falls under the St Peter's registration district. St Peter's survives today between Hawkhill and Perth Road, adjacent to both Paton's Lane and Step Row, where McGonagall lived for 30 years. St Peter's was opened as a Protestant church in 1836. The Disruption in William's teenage years saw ownership pass to the congregation of the Free Church. In 1864 McGonagall was provided with a testimonial by its minister confirming his good standing in the community. He also used Free Church schoolrooms and halls for reading tours and insisted on clergymen to chair his 'entertainments'. Later he appears to have worshipped at the new Gilfillan Memorial Church in Whitehall Crescent. Had McGonagall been Catholic it would be unlikely that he would have forged such a lasting friendship with the Free Church minister George Gilfillan, the subject of his first poem in 1877. Many looked up to the famous preacher, but McGonagall appears to have been spiritually close to the town's greatest public figure. Willocks claimed the poet was to be found at Gilfillan's manse in Paradise Road every Friday evening, 'receiving and imparting stores of poetical lore'. The *Weekly News* put it more evenly: 'George admired McGonagall and McGonagall admired George. They formed a mutual admiration society.'[24]

Although certainty is impossible with William McGonagall's early wanderings – including any time spent in Edinburgh and Glasgow – much is known about *c* 1840 Dundee where the family eventually put down roots. They would have been unaware of it, but history had been made that year when the barque *Selma* unloaded the first cargo of raw Indian jute that underpinned the mighty manufacturing citadel that became Juteopolis. A Castle Street printer, James Chalmers, had just entered a Treasury competition to reform Britain's postal system. It was also unrecognised at the time that he would be regarded one day as the father of the postage stamp. Chalmers in 1842 published his *History of Dundee*. Here he summed up the town by highlighting its principal advantages – its riverside location, fertile hinterland, excellent turnpike roads and 'the industry, sobriety and frugality of its inhabitants'. On the downside, he perfectly captured its idiosyncratic character: 'The lanes and even several streets are uncommonly narrow, and the dwellings of the inhabitants too close upon one another, the greatest parts of the families living by halfdozens.' Thus the town was situated in a grand location but its people lived cheek by jowl under the same roof. Suburbs had been built 'without the least regard to health, elegance or cleanliness' and there was almost a total want of open spaces. After a fleeting visit in 1844, Queen Victoria summed up William McGonagall's adopted home with royal precision: 'The situation of the town is fine, but the town itself is not so.'[25]

Work still awaited William when the power loom was introduced to Dundee towards the end of 1836. Many attempts to adapt cotton power looms for linen had been made, but it was the urgent demand for coarse sailcloth during the Napoleonic Wars that galvanised the weaving of linen or flax by steam power. In this period it was common for factories in domestic weaving suburbs to house power looms in the same sheds as surviving handlooms, and William was probably taught to use both. The generation to which his father belonged had resisted the inevitable advances of an era in which technological development was every bit as pacey as today's computer age. Few Dundee weavers were happy about a situation in which an unskilled lad could weave three and a half pieces of material using a power loom in the time a skilled handweaver wove only one. Handloomers could not compete and faced wage cuts, if they could find work. Peter Carmichael, first manager of Baxter's, recalled handweavers who were 'ever jealous' of opposition and 'were ready to resist whatever seemed to them an encroachment on their proper trade'.[26]

According to *Summary History* William McGonagall's first place of work in Dundee was a mill in Scourinburn owned by Peter Davie. This was South Dudhope Mill in West Henderson's Wynd, sadly long demolished. It was constructed in 1818, one of 30 mills started in the period 1811–35, when flax imports into Dundee had reached a peak. By McGonagall's time it was owned by Davie & Boyack and had been extended to a two-and-a-half-storey mill with power looms on the ground floor and winding and warping rooms above. It could be seen from the McGonagall family home in Hawkhill.

William would have stepped upon the lowest rung of mill work, and it was no ladder to a fun-filled factory floor. Boys were beaten unmercifully by tyrannical foremen and were the objects of humiliating attention, particularly from millgirls and older women. James Myles, who wrote an underrated fictitious autobiography, *Chapters in the Life of a Dundee Factory Boy*, exposed the long hours and deprivation in Victorian Dundee: 'In no establishment does moral poison circulate so rapidly as in a spinning-mill.'[27]

Myles also explained what might have been McGonagall's experience had he been catapulted into the alien environment of mill work. 'The dust, the din, the work, the hissing and roaring of one person to another, the obscene language uttered, even by the youngest, and the imperious commands harshly given by those "dressed in a little brief authority" struck my young country heart with awe and astonishment.' One can imagine young William's shocked senses; rising at five, starting at six, stopping for a brief breakfast at nine, working until two, half-an-hour for dinner and slogging on until six at night – and later if the masters moved the clock hands back. His 'Irishness' would have been ridiculed, another reason for losing it. He would have felt strange and perhaps stupid. He may have been picked on by his peers, worked in an atmosphere of promiscuity and in terror of an overseer seizing on petty faults. He probably suffered from 'mill fever' caused by heat, dust, chemicals and confinement, and at times of exhaustion slept on his feet. And a boy might make just three shillings a week. Later there was better protection in linen factories, but experienced weavers were to be regarded with deferential respect. McGonagall recalled in his writings that it was only after his 'apprenticeship' that 'his Father took him from the Mill, and learn'd him the handloom himself'. Eventually he progressed to working on carpet handloom machines, which required dexterity, concentration and a good eye. But it was also a routine with monotonous repetition, and one which allowed his thoughts to wander to other matters.

Technological change in the town's competitive staple industry caught many manufacturers on the hop and news would have travelled fast when William Boyack suffered terrible losses and was declared bankrupt in 1842.[28] McGonagall relates in *Summary History* how he moved from Davie's Mill 'to Ex-Provost Reid's factory in Scourinburn'. This was a factory owned by Reid bridging Blackness Road and Larch Street which eventually boasted 140 power looms. The 1840s was a healthy decade for linen production and several factories and mills started to cope with expansion, not least the massive Seafield Works in Taylor's Lane. And it was at Seafield Works, owned by Thomson & Shepherd, and run by three en-trepreneurial Thomson brothers, that McGonagall says he spent his final days as a carpet weaver.

Less certain is how William separated from the factory floor and the turmoil of domesticity to meet and marry the young millworker Jean King. They probably encountered each other at work, though there were opportunities in Dundee to meet at wake or wedding, festival or fair, or family gathering. William may have known her brothers as friends or workmates. Courting might have taken place during brief lulls at work, in front of Seafield Works on Magdalen Green, or possibly on the traditional Sunday promenade on Dundee's esplanade. We are left to wonder what she thought of him, or saw in him, for that matter. She may have been impressed with his learning or his limitless ambition. His looks may have won the day.

William and Jean's marriage in the warm Dundee summer of 1846 sets the scene in which they are brought to life for historians. The official record survives, bearing their names, the date of the nuptials and adding, 'Both this parish'. He was around 20, she a year younger. Census data shows that Jean was born in Stirling of Irish parents. She would have come to Dundee for work. And we can suppose that Jean's parents sanctioned her choice of husband and that the families were on good terms. It is possible that they were married by his friend, George Gilfillan. 'No minister in Dundee had so many couples to marry as George Gilfillan. He was a great favourite with the working people, and they liked, when they could, to get "Maister Gulfullan" or "oor George", as they often called him, to tie the knot.' Gilfillan married so many of the poorer classes that he was known as 'Buckle the Beggars'.[29]

It is doubtful whether marriage marked a dramatic change of status for William, though it passed Jean legally from her father to the authority of her husband. And it left the unfettered freedom of her girlhood far behind. Marriage mostly anchored nineteenth-century working women to a household life of obedience. In practical terms, William's betrothal to Jean also meant for her a move from a home filled with family to tenement lodgings where William was head of the household. The bearing and rearing of children soon after enhanced what was a critical transformation in her life from urban daughter to wife and mother. Yet she was marked out for a life less ordinary, and one can wonder how much of an inkling she had of the future that lay before her.

We have no description of Jean and none for her husband at this time. That would come later. One rare sighting – published in 1872 and a survivor from McGonagall's pre-poet days – looked back 25 years to when, at the time of his wedding, he was emerging as an amateur actor. This recalled with cruel candour how William, 'Had such a grim and ghastly look about him' and how, 'he had likewise an air of sorrow and melancholy about him that one could not help thinking there was some cankering care or secret sorrow gnawing away at his peace of mind'.[30] We can only conjure up a characterisation based on what William McGonagall was to become. He was probably quite self-absorbed as a young man, but also capable of sudden enthusiasms. He was a man of strong emotions, a lover of nature and an enthusiastic observer of the world around him. But there is nothing to suggest he presented an odd appearance at this time. The steady flow of stories of eccentric and delusional behaviour was for the years ahead.

Their first child – another William – was on the way before the opening year of their marriage was out. Their son was born at 44 West Port, where the couple set up home after their wedding. They probably rented a single room costing between £2 and £3 yearly and baby William's birth would have prompted extra expense for the services of a local midwife. Towards the end of the 1840s Jean was pregnant again, this time with a daughter, Margaret, named after William's mother. The decade ended with these two bairns bustling around her skirts.

The Dundee of their new home was a busy community where 'merchants, manufacturers, writers and shopkeepers' were building elegant homes to the east and west of the town centre, on the gentle slopes of the Law and on the opposite side of the river. Panmure Street was laid out, Bell Street extended and St Andrew's Cathedral finished, all in 1839 – the end of a decade in which Dundee experienced an extraordinary 40 per cent leap in population. Dundee's Custom House was built in 1842, the harbour outside bustling with the 300 vessels now using it as their home port. Other new churches were hurriedly constructed after the religious schism of 1843. And when Queen Victoria passed under the new Royal Arch on her visit to Dundee in September 1844 she discovered a town with new-found importance and limitless ambition. It possessed 'a buoyant spirit of intelligence, enterprise, assiduous labour and successful speculation'.[31] And still there was not a fibre of jute in sight. It was the linen woven by the McGonagalls and their kin which gave the town its mid-century manufacturing muscle.

Yet where the McGonagalls lived, next to Scouringburn and the Hawkhill, was the greatest concentration of textile mills and with them 'miserable unwholesome dwellings'. The working classes were anchored to their tenements, which offered only spirit-sapping overcrowding and permanent stench and, for respite, there was nothing but the pubs in which Saturday's wages were spent. The town centre was characterised in 1852 as 'a sink of atrocity which no moral flushing seems capable of cleansing'. Diseases such as typhus affected the sickly and undernourished and spread quickly in close confines. All-embracing cholera crossed society's class barriers and left many dead. Smallpox, which terrified everyone, stalked urban Dundee long after it had faded in rural communities. While the population jumped by 30,000 in the 20 years between 1841 and 1861, only 568 new houses were built for manufacturers. Tenemented properties were divided, then let, then sub-let, then filled 10 to a room. Small wonder that a new burial ground was badly needed, 'the present one being fearfully overcrowded'.[32]

That William McGonagall, husband, father and weaver, was to all intents and purposes ill-equipped to deal with industrialising Dundee mattered not. He was on the cusp of discovering an extraordinary way to channel his creative energies.

STAGE DEBUT – HURRAH!

THE McGONAGALLS' migratory peregrination ended at Dundee. The family lived, worked and grew older in the community William was to make his home for half a century. His marriage to Stirling-born Jean King in 1846 had swiftly produced William junior and the infant Margaret, both recorded in print for the first time in the 1851 census, aged four years and 17 months respectively. The family now lived at 44 West Port, close to the Hawkhill, a sunlight-deprived, seething enclave dominated by the town's working people; the women, men and bairns who made the bobbins fly and the mills bustle. Home for the McGonagalls was a cramped room in a long-since-gone tenement divided and sub-divided into lettings. Here, hard by the mills, the poorer classes were piled into overcrowded and unsanitary single rooms by unscrupulous landlords. The best looked out to the street, others to forlorn paved or grassed yards. The top floor was reached by dirty stone stairs with windows covered with net instead of glass, allowing clothes to dry on landings. Grimy stair toilets were shared by dozens of residents. Furniture was limited to bare essentials, beds sometimes a pathetic bundle of rags. Health was deplorable and many occupants lived in a pitiful state.

By 1851 William's lodgings were shared with Jean's mother and 33-year-old brother, described in the census as 'lodgers' and listed as millworkers. They would have followed work to the town but, as housing seldom caught up with mercantile expansion, inevitably faced boarding with nearest kin. Providing shelter to extended family unable to obtain accommodation was typical during accelerating industrialisation. Those least able to afford decent housing had the added burden of the extra mouths of incomers to feed.

The 1851 census gives William's place of birth as Edinburgh, his occupation as weaver and his age as 26, supporting the 1825 birth date offered in *Summary History*. Jean is 25. The enumerator incorrectly lists their children with the surname 'King' and dittoes them as 'lodgers'. The youngsters were certainly the first of William and Jean's brood. William's parents remained at 199 Hawkhill. As textile technology transformed the workplace, his father Charles, given as aged 63 in 1851, would likely have had to give up handloom work and was probably being supported by William's younger siblings, Joseph and Margaret, who still lived with them at Hawkhill. His parents would soon abandon the town in search of a better life in the north of Scotland. From West Port William would have kept in close contact with his teenage sisters Elizabeth and Sarah, both described as unmarried millworkers in 1851. His family was a microcosm of the manner in which Dundee was changing its manufacturing clothes. Its once-dominant linen industry did not disappear overnight, but, as the transfer to jute forged ahead, mill after mill converted for the preparatory and spinning stages of the ascendant new fibre. Rapid mechanisation absorbed traditional skills and left workplace status on a slippery downward slope.

As the century's middle decade began, a trail of families left West Port for the short walk to either mill or factory – and it is possible that William's wife worked at busy times, leaving their children at home with her mother. Jean may have taken on spinning work, sack sewing at home, or winding weavers' pirns, where a female working for three handloom weavers might earn 6d or 9d a day. This would have helped with rent, which cost from two shillings a week for a room, or around £5 annually. William's income from weaving probably averaged 12 shillings weekly. After deducting rent, coal, water and candle he would have been left with about half to clothe and feed his family. Jean's older brother, another William, and also a millworker, would have contributed to the family's outgoings.[1]

Dundee's population in 1851 was 79,000. It nearly doubled to 140,000 over the next 30 years – rising at a rate twice that of Scotland as a whole. This astonishing growth added pressure to the dreary search for accommodation. At the same time, it increased opportunities for abuse by landlords, not least for weary arrivals like the Irish. But what made the town really different was that two thirds of its employed population worked in manufacturing compared with a third in Aberdeen and Edinburgh and a half in Glasgow. Textiles dominated Dundee and no other major British industry – not even the mighty Lancashire cotton trade – was concentrated into such a small area. At its nineteenth-century peak, jute and linen in Dundee employed 40,000 in 125 mills and factories.[2]

McGonagall's Dundee must have been an extraordinary place in which to live.

What is rarely recorded in modern scrutiny, however, is William McGonagall's emergence as a public figure fully two decades before he 'became a poet' in 1877. His appearance in print that year has become the springboard for comments on the famous crop of poems that followed. Yet for over 20 years McGonagall was known not as a purveyor of badly rhyming verse, but as an amateur actor and reciter of historical drama, one capable of amusing audiences of workmates and fellow-townsmen with avant-garde tragedian entertainment. With little scrutiny of the first half-century of his life, this important performance period of McGonagall's pre-poet career has escaped the historian's pen and has been bypassed in biographical notes prefacing collections of his verse.[3]

We have to take McGonagall's word as to how it came to pass that a poor and intermittently educated weaver's son was able to master Shakespeare before he was out of his teens. And we have to swallow his story that enacting Shakespearean tragedy after what was probably rudimentary schooling was a self-taught talent. Looking back on his life in *Brief Autobiography*, first published in 1890, he claims he read numerous books and improved his handwriting in his 'leisure hours at night' after becoming 'an expert' handloom weaver in Dundee.

He liked best Shakespeare's plays, especially 'Macbeth', 'Richard III', 'Hamlet' and 'Othello', 'and I gave myself no rest until I obtained complete mastery over the above four characters. Many a time in my dear father's absence I enacted entire scenes from Macbeth and Richard III, along with some of my shopmates, until they were quite delighted; and many a time they regaled me and the other actors that had entertained them to strong ale, biscuits, and cheese'. And in his final stab at an autobiography, published in September 1901, he recalled: 'My dear readers, I must inform ye that as early as ten years of age I was very fond of reading Shakespeare's Penny Plays (Vicker's edition), and from them I received great knowledge regarding the histrionic art.'

McGonagall's dogged self-improvement was not part of a gimmicky new fad. The trend towards more privatised home life espoused by a motherly new queen was accompanied by popular retellings of the works of Shakespeare adapted for family use, partly for entertainment, partly for the cultivation of minds.[4] Many mid-century periodicals were realigned towards instruction and intellectual stimulation, and this trickled down to a zest for learning among aspirant working classes. McGonagall's contemporary, William Thom, recalled in 1845 how his weaving shopmates at Newtyle drew pleasure and inspiration from classic novels and poetry: 'The Wizard of Waverley had roused the world to wonders, and we wondered, too. Byron was flinging around the terrible and beautiful of a distracted greatness . . . nearer and dearer to hearts like ours was the Ettrick Shepherd, then in his full tide of song and story; but nearer and dearer still than him, or any living songster – to us dearer – was our ill-fated fellow craftsman Tannahill. Poor weaver chiel! What we owe to thee!' In one politicising Paisley cotton mill, 'The *Glasgow Chronicle* came to the shop three times weekly, and all the looms were stopped when it was being read and its leaders discussed.' And in Dundee, not only was Vicker's edition of Shakespeare available at the Free Library along with six copies each of the *Advertiser* and the *Courier*, the 1846 journal of the Dundee Literary and Scientific Institute hammered home to all the importance of 'cultivating a taste for literary pleasure'.[5]

Books did their duty in young McGonagall's grounding in drama, but it was in Dundee's theatre-land that the stimulus is to be found which instilled in him a longing to act. The Yeaman Shore Theatre had opened in 1800 with a performance of 'The Merchant of Venice'. The larger and more sumptuous Theatre Royal was a new building in Castle Street in 1810. The Thistle Hall, known as the Music Hall, opened in the Exchange building at the foot of the same street in 1841, and from 1846 the smaller Royal

Victoria Theatre operated in Meadowside. Scott's Theatre, in South Union Street, officially The Pantheon, must have particularly appealed and provided inspiration to McGonagall. Here was a building 'gorgeously decorated in front, and adorned with full-length figures of Wallace, Burns, Rob Roy and other famous historical and dramatical figures'. There were also 'penny' theatres, known as gaffs, often no more than temporary wooden and canvas platforms where knockabout comedies and one-act wonders were performed. These shows anticipated music hall entertainment – 'cheap, noisy, broad and running several houses nightly'. The most notorious locally was Fizzy Gow's, a booth of a very miserable description in Albert Square which the owner looked upon as second only in importance to the Theatre Royal. There Fizzy Gow assembled 'a few lazy, drunken tailors and hecklers who imagined they, too, had a talent for the stage, and exhibited Shakespeare to the juvenile portion of the community.' McGonagall could spare the halfpenny admittance from his modest income and here he would have learned rudimentary stage skills to enliven memorised passages of Shakespeare.[6]

Alas, all mid-century theatres struggled to remain viable and passed through many changes of ownership and lessees. The Theatre Royal barely operated a handful of years before a portion of it was given over to a collection of wax figures, including a macabre effigy of Nelson lying in state. On other occasions 'Hamlet' was adapted to allow the introduction of the manager's dog, the Fire-Proof Lady went up in flames and actors were accidentally shot or stabbed – even harpooned. Little wonder several seasons were brought to an abrupt end after 'the frequenters had been allowed to degenerate into turbulent audiences'. Besides, the two main theatres in Castle Street were located in a part of town where the intimidating realities of dockside Dundee were seldom distant. The area was home to 'the riff-raff who infested the water front' and the only direct access from the High Street was by two narrow lanes . . . 'both narrow, evil ways'.[7]

From time to time visiting professionals pepped up this troubled scene. McGonagall's prose pamphlet *Shakespeare Reviewed* recalls several theatrical grandees who inspired him during his teenage

years. In making the case for the public to 'understand' how to
appreciate the Stratford bard, McGonagall wrote firstly of the
tragedian Samuel Phelps, one of the greatest actors of the century,
whose visits to Dundee began in 1835. He recalled: 'I once saw him
play "Macbeth" in the Theatre Royal, when he was in the full
zenith of his profession: and with the little judgement I have
pertaining to the histrionic art, I consider he played "Macbeth"
surprisingly well. Owing to the great amount of electricity that
emitted from him, the audience could not refrain from cheering
him.' He then dwells upon the distinguished tragedian Gustavus
Vaughn Brooke, who appeared in Dundee in the early 1840s. In
McGonagall's opinion Brooke was even more commanding than
Phelps: 'I remember seeing Mr Brooke playing 'Macbeth' in the old
Theatre Royal, Dundee. It was a masterpiece from beginning until
the end. I remember the first sentence he spoke, the audience rose
with one general applause, which was deafening to hear. I venture
to say that I shall never look upon such a great piece of acting
again.' McGonagall was also impressed by Edmund Kean, the best-
known English actor of his day. Kean had appeared as a teenage
comedian at Yeaman Shore and McGonagall told an interviewer,
with characteristic modesty: 'The only man I ever knew who could
come up to me in versatility was Edmund Kean; he could tell a
story, he could sing a comic song, and declaim a tragedy.'[8]

Among other professional actors who may have influenced the
stage-struck but still youthful McGonagall was Sir Henry Irving,
whose melodramatic portrayals of historical figures were widely
renowned. Irving, in June 1869, was 'heartily applauded' for his
performance in 'The Weavers' at the Theatre Royal. He returned
to Dundee for 'Hamlet' and 'Charles I' in 1876 and the following
year – the same that McGonagall 'discovered' poetry – he appeared
for three nights playing Hamlet and Richard III. *The Comet*, a short-
lived Dundee newssheet dedicated to promoting theatrical events,
reported excitedly that 'Irving does not act Hamlet, he *is* Hamlet'.[9]
In 1880 McGonagall attempted to bump into Irving at the Adelphi
Theatre in London but failed to persuade a doorman he was a
genuine caller. In 1895, however, he was visited at his flat in
Edinburgh by Sir Henry and the celebrated Victorian actress Ellen

Terry. Perhaps that encounter inspired the Adelphi's production of
Bonnie Dundee in 1900, in which Irving played a part.

Among local influences was Tom Powrie, later to use the *nom de
theatre* T. Power. William and Powrie were roughly the same age,
the latter born in Dundee in 1824. It was in a Tay Street stable,
coincidentally near today's Rep, that Powrie and his pals performed
to admiring audiences of juveniles. McGonagall must have been
aware of this clutch of amateur actors barely half a mile from his
home, not least when Powrie made his debut at the Yeaman Shore
in May 1845. Sucked into their activities, he would have become
one of the amateur thespians who magically materialised during the
season: 'They were a rather numerous body in those days. Every
tailor, weaver, heckler and baker thought himself possessed of the
requisite talents to enable him to become an actor, and kept
continually pestering theatrical managers for an opportunity of
displaying them.'[10]

Within this kaleidoscope of local entertainment McGonagall
appears to have moved from drolly reciting Shakespearean stan-
dards to gustily acting them out with a group of like-minded friends.
His first paying performance was in Mr Giles' theatre, a crude oval
playhouse chiselled out of Lindsay Street quarry. 'The way that I
was allowed to perform was in terms of the following agreement,
which was entered into between Mr Giles and myself – that I had to
give Mr Giles one pound in cash before the performance, which I
considered rather hard, but as there was no help for it, I made
known Mr Giles's terms to my shopmates, who were handloom
weavers in Seafield Works, Taylor's Lane. No sooner than the
terms were made known to them, than they entered heartily into
the arrangement, and in a very short time they made up the pound
by subscription.' McGonagall also recalls the 'rapping of the lays' in
the weaving shed as the deputation of workmates returned with
confirmation of the performance to come, 'which I shall never
forget as long as I live'.

Brief Autobiography continues breathlessly: 'When the great night
arrived my shopmates were in high glee with the hope of getting
a Shakespearian treat from your humble servant. And I can
assure you, without boasting, they were not disappointed in their

anticipations, my shopmates having secured seats before the general public were admitted. It would be impossible for me to describe the scene in Lindsay Street, as it was crowded from head to foot, all being eager to witness my first appearance as an exponent of Shakespeare.'

McGonagall also recalls – with unquenchable enthusiasm – how it almost required a detachment of Bell Street's finest to keep order: 'What a sight it was to see such a mass of people struggling to gain admission! Hundreds failing to do so, and in the struggle numbers were trampled under foot, one man having lost one of his shoes in the scrimmage; others were carried bodily into the theatre along with the Press . . . The house was crowded during each of the three performances on that ever-memorable night, which can never be forgot by me or my shopmates, and even entire strangers included.' He concludes, with equal spoonfuls of pomposity and pride, 'So much then for the true account of my first appearance on any stage.'

And in the final retelling of his life, *The Autobiography of Sir William Topaz McGonagall*, first published in the *Weekly News* in 1901, McGonagall passes over his pre-poet stage career with few words, though confirms the characters he played, the venue of his first performance and, of course, the ringing endorsement received at the end of each show . . .

'The plays or tragedies I studied most were Macbeth, Hamlet, Richard III, and Othello, the Moor of Venice, and these four characters I have impersonated in my time. During my stay in Dundee my first appearance on the stage was in the character of Macbeth in Mr Giles' Penny Theatre, Lindsay Street, Dundee, to an overflowing and crowded audience, and I received unbounded applause.' Abandoning modesty completely he winds up this fleeting flashback by adding nonchalantly, 'I was called before the curtain several times.'

It is not wholly necessary to rely on McGonagall's 'without boasting' soliloquies for proof of his participation in amateur dramatics in the 1840s and 1850s. His early stage appearances were corroborated in 1872 by a contributor to the *People's Journal*. Predating McGonagall's debut as a published poet by five years, thus providing extremely rare and important scrutiny of his pre-poet life, the extensive article by the anonymous 'Old Stager' describes McGonagall's theatrical apprenticeship around the time of his marriage to Jean King.[11]

According to Old Stager one of McGonagall's earliest perfor-mances took place around 1847 at a temporary booth in Meadow-side. He recalled for the paper's claimed 630,000-strong weekly readership that while Shakespeare and other minor dramatists were dished up at this time to gaping crowds of young boys at a modest penny admittance, McGonagall had apparently to serve a hum-bling and self-effacing apprenticeship. 'The "parts" given to this gentleman were certainly not such as would enable him to show the audience what acting was, as he was generally engaged in that necessary and indispensable business of removing the chairs and tables from the stage, and also in keeping the candles throughout the establishment properly "snuffed".'

Introduced to elementary stage management and thespian roles in this deprecating manner, McGonagall was the object of jeers and catcalls from the young audience, yet 'all this he bore with the most calm and stoical indifference'. This imperviousness to insult became in future years a fascinating trait of McGonagall's character and it is interesting to see it identified as early as 1872. In later years his deadpan response to audience ridicule marked out his perfor-mances as extraordinary. Thus to be explored in a following chapter is the central question – whether or not William McGo-nagall's public buffoonery was carefully constructed as a stealth strategy to support his family when mechanisation and de-skilling limited opportunities for work. If so, Dundee's 'daft laddie' knew precisely what he was doing with every wayward poem and each eccentric performance.

Old Stager also recognised the arrogant side to McGonagall's personality which materialised in his poetic heyday. 'At times, if you watched him narrowly, you could observe that when any of the "leading" members of the company got hissed for not playing their parts well, a Mephistophelian gleam of pleasure would flit across his countenance, which would afterwards change into a settled and self-conceited expression, as much as to say, "If I only had the opportunity of playing those parts, *I* would soon show you *how* they should be acted".' McGonagall's self-belief was limitless for the ensuing half century: 'You see, I am much more versatile than Shakespeare', he reminded one interviewer in 1880.

Old Stager's reference date of the late-1840s in his retrospective of McGonagall's early performances ties in with the poet's later testimony that he was working in Thomson & Shepherd's Seafield Works at the time of his stage debut. This vast sandstone complex in Taylor's Lane, off Perth Road, began in the 1840s as a handloom carpet and matting weaving factory. Increased trade in the early 1850s added its decorative low preparing mill and a high spinning mill for powerloomed carpet-backing. The iron-framed weaving shed of William's 12-hour day was 10 metres long by 10 wide and lined with looms below angled, sun-lit roofs. Old Stager confirmed McGonagall's reminiscences that his earliest performances were held there at the behest of his shopmates. 'I found that he was in the habit of going through the principal speeches of some of Shakespeare's greatest characters for the edification of his fellow workers.'

It was when Old Stager himself moved to Seafield Works in the 1850s that he came across McGonagall again. He discovered then that William had developed an embedded belief in his acting abilities, 'only requiring an opportunity of making his appearance on the boards of "Drury Lane" to enable him to electrify the theatrical world with the grand display of his genius'. He related how he had once accompanied his friend to the Theatre Royal to see professional actors in Shakespearean roles. Naturally, McGonagall felt he could do better than the standard shown on stage. He took particular exception to one celebrated tragedian's Richard III, whose conception of the 'crook'd back tyrant' was not up to scratch. When a patron sitting behind the pair mentioned in a stage whisper that the actor was getting £5 a night for the engagement, it was all too much for McGonagall . . . 'He immediately sprung to his feet, and in a voice that I am sure must have been quite audible over at least one half of the house, exclaimed, "What! Give that man £5 for doing that! By heavens, if they saw me do it they would give me ten".'[12]

Some 2,000 hands were eventually employed at Seafield Works.

The potential for McGonagall to fill a theatre from his own neighbourhood was thus considerable. Old Stager summoned up the day when, ignoring any whisper in his ear of the well-known aphorism, 'fools rush in where angels fear to tread', McGonagall called at Giles's Penny Theatre and begged the manager to be allowed to give a performance. A large number of workmates thought he had acting abilities, he said, and if he would only grant him 'one night in which to appear in one of his favourite characters, he would guarantee a crowded house'. The offer was accepted and Old Stager recalled three performances in one evening, each house crammed, many of the audience going to all three, 'while most went in twice'. This observation confirms McGonagall's 1890 memory of a trio of sell-out shows.[13]

Old Stager portrays McGonagall in a pusillanimous and mockingly negative light, however, and without the wily humour conveyed in contemporary reports. His identity is not known. He seems to have had a decent understanding of poetry and drama. He tracked McGonagall's subsequent career and on several occasions appeared under his pseudonym to comment on McGonagall's early poems in the Dundee papers. His 1872 characterisation is crucial in providing evidence of McGonagall's interest and participation in amateur dramatics fully two decades before he introduced himself to the world as a poet. It presciently anticipates character traits to come. It also serves to confirm McGonagall's autobiographical comments on his early life, but reads between the lines of the would-be entertainer's boastful memoirs to portray him as a gullible teenager egged on by workmates to dream of, and then to partially realise, his tragedian debut.

Despite McGonagall's claim to have smitten his audience to the point of 'scrimmage', including 'entire strangers', there were no easy routes out of a Dundee mill. The Theatre Royal in Castle Street struggled at every turn and one miserable season followed another. Even when theatrical stars gave way under new management to exhibiting Aztecs and Chinese jugglers, to illusionists, acrobats, comedians, dancers and fire-eaters, only McGonagall's neighbour Tom Powrie could command decent crowds. It seems the theatre promised much, but delivered little, kept alive 'with flaming bills, helped up with fictitious names and unfulfilled promises'. Little wonder the town's prudish magistrates regarded playhouses as wicked dens of roguish and drunken thespians.[14]

Besides, there were more mouths to feed at home. William junior and Margaret had turned from toddlers to time-consuming adolescents. Third child Joseph was born in 1854, and in May 1857 Jean produced another son, Charles, named after his paternal grandfather. This birth took place at Roseangle, which connects Perth Road to Magdalen Green and overlooks the town's clanking railway yards. McGonagall is hitherto unrecorded as living in Roseangle. If it were so, it helps to explain his poetic devotion to 'the bonnie Magdalen Green' in years ahead. Yet it can only be wondered how arduous it must have been for a weaving husband and a young wife to raise a family at times of sporadic employment and uncertain income. One observer noted in 1850: 'It is quite common to see a pair united not out of their teens, and living in what they seriously term furnished lodgings, which being interpreted means living in one small house of one apartment.' And Irish incomers, he added ruthlessly, 'Wallow in all kinds of wretchedness, and long for nothing which tends to enlighten and improve; and their numerous families are sent out in society, charged with the seeds of moral pollution and wickedness, and we pay no attention to them until they get involved in misdemeanours. Then the law provides punishment.'[15]

Neither were conditions better in McGonagall's workplace. The prosperous early 1850s soon gave way to severe cutbacks in textiles production. The end of the Crimean War in 1856 resulted in a downturn in demand for linen and created 'a panic among holders of flax'. Men, women and children were put out of work or forced on to short time. If one manufacturer reduced wages and got away with it, others followed. In 1858 a crash in American financial institutions caused tremors throughout mercantile Britain. Banks failed, firms went bust and there was a scandal over spurious paper money. In Dundee the prices of goods tumbled . . . 'The distress of the working classes throughout the town was very great.' And it was at this point that once-thriving linen manufacturers, obsessed by falling markets, bit the business bullet and switched to jute – or went under.[16]

Into this gloomy scene, in the winter season of 1858, stepped 'William McGonagall, Tragedian' in his first major public performance. In that year the lease and management of the Theatre Royal were taken up by John Caple, a comedian and budding impresario. Caple immediately revived Shakespearean drama. At first his wife played the male tragedian roles as well as that of Lady Macbeth, in the manner that Mrs Giles had done a decade earlier. Caple then imported the American McKean Buchanan for King Lear and Othello, and the 'Celebrated Mr Powrie' returned to play Rob Roy and Henry IV, but trade by and large remained indifferent.

William McGonagall's debut in a major theatrical performance took place under Caple's invitation and watchful eye at the Theatre Royal on 2 December 1858. The surviving evidence for it is a large theatre handbill bearing his name in bold. Topping the bill and 'positively for this night only' was 'The First Appearance of Mr Alex Davidson and Mr Wm. McGonagall'. Both Davidson and McGonagall had landed significant roles, McGonagall taking on the demanding lead for Acts 4 and 5 of 'Macbeth', the first the famous cavern and cauldron witches' scene, the second the 'Lay on, Macduff' combat finale. Listed in smaller type are a further 12 actors, with the evening to be rounded off with a comic song.[17]

Although unreported at the time, McGonagall's appearance at the Theatre Royal should not be understated. The Castle Street venue had seen lean years since its opening in 1810, but it remained an impressive venue. It comprised an oblong auditorium with a stage at one end and a double gallery on three sides. Back and side galleries were divided by partitions into boxes and seats. The rest of the audience in the pit had to stand, for which they had to pay sixpence. Even the abundantly confident William McGonagall would have flinched at facing its tightly-packed 1,200-strong clientele.

Looking back from 1872, 'Old Stager' confirms his subject played Macbeth at the Theatre Royal. He also relates how the performance descended into farce when McGonagall elected to develop Shakespeare's text in the combat scene: 'Instead of dying when run through the body by the sword of Macduff, he stayed on his feet and swished his sword about the ears of his adversary in such a way that there was a probability of the performance ending in tragedy.' When the actor playing Macduff repeatedly told him to 'go down', McGonagall refused. 'Macduff' became so incensed that he rapped his belligerent rival over the fingers with the flat of his sword. This had the effect of making McGonagall drop the weapon, but he evidently had no intention of dying . . . 'for he kept dodging round and round Macduff, as if he had made up his mind to have a wrestle for it. The representative of that character, however, becoming tired of such tomfoolery, flung his sword to a side, and seizing hold of him, brought the sublime tragedy of Macbeth to a close in a rather undignified way by taking the feet from under the principal character.'[18]

Brief Autobiography proudly confirms Old Stager's account of its author's reluctance to abandon the character part to which he was clinging – though McGonagall conveniently fails to mention the slap from his opponent's sword which released him from it. Rather, the other actors felt 'very jealous owing to me getting the general applause. When it came to the combat scene betwixt me and Macduff, the actor who was playing Macduff against my Macbeth tried to spoil me in the combat by telling me to cut it short, so as the audience, in his opinion, would say it was a poor combat, but I was too cute for him, guessing his motive for it.'

Their hero's enthusiastic performance was inevitably egged on by his workmates. We can imagine as many shouts of 'Keep fighting, Wullie' as there were 'Lie down, yer deid.' It must have been sensational entertainment and the talk of the mills for days. Even Old Stager could not resist rushing into rhyme to mark the occasion . . .

> He seemed to think Shakespeare had erred
> In getting *him* killed by Macduff,
> Though oft his body felt the sword
> Yet he disdained to cry enough.
> He fought on madly, blind with rage,
> When bold Macduff began to frown,
> Then flung his sword upon the stage,
> And with one blow knocked William down.[19]

A more significant conclusion is that William McGonagall's debut at the Theatre Royal indicates that he was an established amateur actor 20 years before his debut poem was bravely put into print in 1877 by the *Weekly News*. He had made the artistic leap from showboating in canvas gaffs to headlining a theatre capable of seating 1,000 paying patrons. He was not the 50-year-old of bad poetry fame. He had barely turned 30, a working-class weaver who had intuitively carved a path in the world of amateur dramatics. Through mastering Shakespeare to his own satisfaction, he had established himself as a popular raconteur, and doubtless few of his colleagues ever shared his extraordinary experience. McGonagall's 1858 performance also implies he was known outside the tightly bound world of the working-class underprivileged – even if only as an eccentric showman and figure of fun.

In spite of his self-absorbed memories, written much later, William McGonagall's run at the Theatre Royal was short-lived. Inspection of handbills and analysis of newspaper reports suggest he never again topped the bill in the theatre, which itself was severely troubled. The *Courier* commented on unprofitable season after unprofitable season as the 1850s moved aside for the 1860s. In fact, within six months of McGonagall's Macbeth the morning daily was mourning: 'In Dundee the drama seems to be dead, and beyond all hope of recovery.' Not even the first attempt at Italian opera in May 1860 prevented the town's leading cultural venue from entering another period of recession.[20]

Instead, McGonagall probably returned to the factory floor, where as near as he ever got to a satisfactory income was possible during unprecedented trading years in the early 1860s. A huge demand for coarse linen and jute grew out of urgent orders for tents and opportunities to replace blockaded cotton manufacturers during the American Civil War. The hasty rearmament in the lead-up to the Franco–Prussian War of 1870–71 also boosted trade. This stimulated prices for Dundee-made goods and created full employment and prosperity. Linen kings Baxter's, for example, claimed in 1864 their highest profit of the nineteenth century – £159,627, equivalent today to around £100 million. In the four years following, a dozen new firms came into existence, increasing the town's textiles workforce by 5,000.[21]

By then the McGonagalls had moved from Roseangle to 24 Mid Wynd, which connected Perth Road to Hawkhill on a north–south axis. The family had grown to seven. Daughter Mary was born there in March 1860, her father attending to the baptismal register with the scratchy black signature familiar in later years. The 1861 census gave William's age as 33, provided his birthplace as Edinburgh and occupation as carpet weaver. Jean was 32. William junior and Margaret were teenagers aged 15 and 13, both millworkers and contributing to the family coffers. Two children had been born in the previous decade, sons Joseph, now 7, and Charles, 4, and the first arrival of the 1860s was Mary. The eighth member of the household, 18-year-old Margaret King, was probably Jean's niece. She is properly entered as 'lodger' and, inevitably, as a millworker.

Some details of William's nuclear family are also known. As already mentioned, by the 1861 census William's parents had left Dundee and were listed as 'pauper' and 'pauper's wife' at Lower Westerdale Farm, near Halkirk, where his father was attempting to make a living as a hawker. They applied for aid in 1865, and the amount of relief they received was given as two shillings weekly, with flannels. Their daughter Margaret, William's younger sister, aged 27 in 1861, was living with them along with her illegitimate daughter Thomasina, aged two and born in Caithness. Several of William's other siblings were still alive. His sister Agnes and brothers Charles and Thomas were married. Thomas was listed as a teacher but his whereabouts were not recorded. Apart from Margaret, others mentioned at this time were younger siblings Jessie (Jannet?) and Joseph, the latter being married in Dundee to a Margaret Galloway, daughter of a coalman, in 1867. Joseph was later described as a seaman.[22]

The birth of fourth son James in February 1863 was recorded to William and Jean at another address hitherto unlisted for the poet – Robertson's Land, Pennycook Lane. This small street was located almost directly across Perth Road from his later well-known addresses in Paton's Lane and Step Row. The move to a new location is a reminder of the peripatetic life of the mill-working community and provides another landmark in the misty history of this study's subject. Frequent changes of accommodation were normal for Dundee's poorer classes. House transfers could be brought about by levels of rent, location, family size, job change or landlord demand. Moves could occur after only a few weeks and be to another property within yards of the previous home. McGonagall barely travelled a mile in half a dozen flittings. Now mostly university buildings, Pennycook Lane housed then a double row of workers' tenements and a school.

Yet if the McGonagalls periodically benefited from good times and regular work as the 1860s progressed, the head of the McGonagall household also found occasional acting work. The *Courier's* theatre critic told how a Miss Annie Manners had opened the Music Hall for summer seasons in the 1860s and how, 'The famous tragedian, Mr William McGonagall, frequently trod the boards here in the highest walks of tragedy.'[23] McGonagall confirmed these appearances in his 1901 memoirs: 'He has also play'd the Characters of Hamlet and Othello, Macbeth, and Richard III, in the Music Hall . . . to delighted and crowded audiences.' One surviving poster from the Castle Street venue, proclaiming a grand, vocal, instrumental, thespian and terpsichorean festival, advertised 'Wm McGonagall, The Royal Poet' second on the bill as part of a programme which included dancers, vocalists, variety artists, balladeers, comedians – and performing dogs and monkeys.

Proof of performances at this time is provided by handwritten references to William McGonagall from influential acquaintances. Firstly in 1864 a trio of Dundee intellectual luminaries granted him a glowing testimonial, which he kept safely until his old age . . .

'We have heard him recite some passages from Shakespeare with great force; and are of the opinion that he is quite competent to read or recite passages from the poets or orators in villages and country towns with pleasure and profit to his audience. We also believe him to be an honourable man.'

This supportive document was signed on 29 March 1864 by the theologian Islay Brown, minister of St Peter's Free Church in Dundee, and his former assistant William Knight, who had just taken up a professorship at St Andrews University from St John's Church in Small's Wynd. It is countersigned by John Banks, headmaster of the 'Propy School' in Dundee, possibly a school for younger children established by 'the proprietors' of the larger manufacturers.

The following year the Rev. George Gilfillan, preacher and orator, author and scholar, and the most respected citizen in the town, provided McGonagall with a flattering and useful reference. This, too, would have been used by the Paton's Lane poet to charm theatrical managers. This document was dated 30 May 1865 . . .

'I certify that William McGonagall has for some time been known to me. I have heard him speak, he has a strong proclivity for the elocutionary department, a strong voice, and great enthusiasm. He has had a great deal of experience, too, having addressed audiences, and acted parts here and elsewhere.'[24]

McGonagall kept these testimonials and passed them to the antiquarian A.C. Lamb late in life. From there they found their way to the McGonagall Collection at Dundee Central Libraries, where they can be seen on the flimsy scraps of paper the poet treasured for over 30 years. His reputation duly enhanced, McGonagall must have approached the 1870s in expectation of supplementing meagre mill wages with paid acting work. The nose-in-the air loftiness adopted by factory weavers over jute-spinning counterparts was by now almost entirely pretence. Life as a handloom operator was only marginally better and, indeed, a protracted and polarised debate in the Dundee papers at this time had many supporters for the view that jute-spinning required more skill than weaving. What risked both roles were the vagaries of the market and erratic wage movements. And in the McGonagall household there were more mouths to feed than ever.

Towards the end of the 1860s the McGonagalls moved from Pennycook Lane to a tenement flat at 41 Step Row, a street directly opposite the lane, which led south from Perth Road to Magdalen Yard Road. His block on the west side, now long demolished, contained over 20 families, most of whom are listed in valuation rolls as weavers or textile workers. It must have been no more than a small single room, as the yearly rent was a lowly £2.10 shillings.[25] With William and Jean remained three working sons – William, aged 20, Joseph, 16 and Charles, 12. William junior and Joseph were entered in the 1871 census as millworkers, but Charles had broken the family's links to textiles and was serving an apprenticeship as a ropemaker. Also at home were daughter Mary, 10, already working in a mill, and a trio of younger sons, James, 8, John, 5 and Thomas, 1. Thomas, born at Step Row in March 1870, did not survive infancy. He died from bronchitis in 1873, aged three, at the new family home at 19 Paton's Lane. The duties of many working-class women involved bearing, rearing and – all too often – burying children, as the tombstones in the Howff testify with harrowing regularity. The dangers of childbirth were far greater then than now, and the death of a child in infancy was often an inseparable part of Victorian parenthood.

Yet if William McGonagall had filled his lungs he would have breathed the fresh air of change in his adopted town. The 1871 Improvement Act had spurred a physical transformation across Dundee. It led to the clearance of slum areas and the creation of new buildings as the town's boundaries were squeezed again. Piped water became available, ending years of inadequate supplies. A municipal library was opened in 1870, a new museum in 1873 and four new schools followed the creation of school boards in 1872. Thoroughfares were widened or lengthened, dozens of new streets planned and public parks gouged out and opened. Mills, factories and cheap tenements for textile workers were hurriedly constructed. In the decade 1871–80 alone, nearly 10,000 working-class houses were jammed close to workplaces as mighty Juteopolis took shape.

McGonagall, too, was on the brink of change and announced his public persona to the *Dundee Advertiser* in May 1872. This amounted to a request to the paper by McGonagall to publish a perspicacious tribute to the actor Charles Dillon, who was appearing at the Theatre Royal with a London company. The *Advertiser* succumbed: 'We gladly comply with the request of William McGonagall, tragedian, to publish the following highly flattering opinion . . .

'Sir – perhaps you will be kind as to allow me a little space in the columns of your paper to express my opinion regarding Mr Charles Dillon . . . I venture to say he can acquire and beget a temperance in the very torrent tempest and whirlwind of his passion. He can give it smoothness on the instant and, in the proper place, and in patchectc [pathetic] passages he can almost melt his audience in to tears.' McGonagall concluded, 'I declare him to be the great Shakespearean Declinator of the present day.'[26]

It was the first time William McGonagall's name had appeared in print by his own hand – and was still five full years before the fateful day the Muse of Poetry visited Paton's Lane. The publication of his opinion appears to have resulted in him assuming the self-awarded authority to comment upon theatrical matters, especially those where the merits of the Stratford bard were discussed or questioned.

He wrote again – this time to the *People's Journal* in January 1876 – to extol the virtues of Shakespeare, but was rebuked with the peremptory comment: 'Shakespeare requires no defence at the hands of "William McGonagall, local tragedian", or anyone else, and if he did, we doubt if Mr McGonagall is exactly the man to do it.' He was thereafter put down by the same paper when he tried to become involved in a public collection to mark George Gilfillan's 40 years as a pastor at School Wynd Church.[27]

But that was nothing to what was around the corner. Such was the flood of contributions from McGonagall's pen as the 1870s progressed that local newspapers by the end of the decade were despairingly begging him to stop.

Sprung on the world as a bawling reciter of Shakespeare, McGonagall confirmed the launch of his poetical career in pseudo-humble third person narrative in his first autobiography, *Summary History*, written barely a year after the muse had muscled into his life . . .

'The desire for writing Poetry came upon him in the Month of June 1877 that he could not resist the desire for writing poetry. The first piece he wrote was An Address to the Rev. George Gilfillan, to the *Weekly News*, only giving the Initials of his name, W.M.G. Dundee, which was received with éclat.'

His Damascus moment was also captured in *Brief Autobiography* in 1890, a version repeated with knobs on in his final autobiography of 1901 . . .

'The most startling incident in my life was the time I discovered myself to be a poet, which was in the year 1877. During the Dundee holiday week, in the bright and balmy month of June, when trees and flowers were in full bloom, while lonely and sad in my room, I sat thinking about the thousands of people who were away by rail and steamboat, perhaps to the land of Burns, or poor ill-treated Tannahill, or to gaze upon the Trossachs in Rob Roy's country, or elsewhere wherever their minds led them. Well, while pondering so, I seemed to feel as it were a strange kind of feeling stealing over me, and remained so for about five minutes.

'A flame, as Lord Byron has said, seemed to kindle up my entire frame, along with a strong desire to write poetry; and I felt so happy, so happy, that I was inclined to dance, then I began to pace backwards and forwards in the room, trying to shake off all thought of writing poetry; but the more I tried, the more strong the sensation became. It was so strong, I imagined that a pen was in my right hand, and a voice crying, "Write! Write!"'

And that was that. One blinding vision safely transmitted and received, McGonagall was then struck with the notion to write about 'my best friend', the Reverend George Gilfillan. The minister was one of Dundee's most eminent figures – a striking personality, polymath and a man with many devoted followers. A performance preacher, Gilfillan seldom shied from supporting the McGonagalls of the world during his 42 years in Dundee. During the factory reform campaign of 1873, for example, he poked the town's unscrupulous child employers in the eye by telling a meeting of mill operatives, 'Brutality enjoys its greatest triumph when children are made slaves.'[28] In McGonagall's opinion he 'could not have chosen a better subject, therefore I immediately found paper, pen, and ink, and set myself down to immortalize the great preacher, poet, and orator'.

McGonagall then made the short walk from Paton's Lane to the *Weekly News* office in North Lindsay Street, delivered his lines on Gilfillan and waited in impatient anticipation for the following Saturday to see if the penny paper had opted to publish his verse in its well-stocked amateur poetry column. It had, along with the mischievous comment . . .

W.M.G. Dundee, who modestly seeks to hide his light under a bushel, has surreptitiously dropped into our letter-box an

'Address to the Rev. George Gilfillan'. Here is a sample of this worthy's powers of versification . . .

> Rev. George Gilfillan, of Dundee,
> There is none can you excel,
> You have boldly rejected the Confession of Faith,
> And defended your cause right well.
> The first time I heard him speak,
> 'Twas in the Kinnaird Hall,
> Lecturing on the Garibaldi movement,
> As loud as he could bawl.
> He is a literal gentleman,
> To the poor while in distress;
> And for his kindness unto them,
> The lord will surely bless.
> My blessing on his noble form,
> And on his lofty head;
> May all good angels guard him while living,
> And hereafter when he's dead.[29]

This debut version of the Gilfillan address, published in the *Weekly News* of 7 July 1877 alongside a recipe for stuffing small birds, differs from those included in most anthologies of McGonagall's work. The *Weekly News* stanzas give a nod towards 'normal' poor poetry and are not typical of the grammatically disobedient McGonagallisms treasured today. The lines are short, sharp, with passable scansion. Second and fourth rhyme at leisure with surprising smoothness. Yet later published versions include dysfunctional grammar, hopeful couplets, laboured last lines and the usual McGonagall struggle to perform the mechanics of verse-making. One begins . . .

> All hail to the Rev George Gilfillan, of Dundee,
> He is the greatest preacher I did ever hear or see,
> He preaches in a plain, straightforward way,
> The people flock to hear him night and day,
> And hundreds from his church doors are often turned away,
> Because he is the greatest preacher of the present day.

Another appears on a surviving manuscript version. This begins . . .

> All hail to the Rev George Gilfillan of Dundee,
> He is the greatest preacher I did ever hear or see,
> He is a man of genius bright,
> And in him his congregation doth delight,
> Because they find him to be honest and plain,
> Affable in temper, and seldom known to complain.

So it was not uncommon for McGonagall to tweak poems in this manner as the years passed, perhaps, indeed, to live up to his reputation for wayward verse. Early examples were particularly prone to rewriting. But why the Dundee weekly opted to publish McGonagall's amateur verse in the summer of 1877 is impossible to know, as it regularly dismissed contributions which did not meet its quality threshold. Countless hopefuls were dumped derisively in its waste bin. But any gentle satire intended by its editorial quip was utterly lost on William McGonagall, who took the printed appearance of his first poem as the godly green light to dip his quill in its ink pot and engage the gears of full production. Not only that, he believed his 'gift of poetry' had been received with 'éclat' – praise enough, he thought, to instantly raise him on a pretend plinth alongside Tannahill and Tennyson.

Just over a month later, on 11 August, the *Weekly News* featured William McGonagall's second contribution, 'The Railway Bridge of The Silvery Tay'. This was preceded by the explanation: 'W. McG., having immortalised the Rev. George Gilfillan and the other subjects on which his muse has alighted, now constitutes himself as the Poet Laureate of the Tay Bridge, of which he sings in the following sublime strain.' It published verses one, three and four of the poem McGonagall later claimed made him famous. The 'most beautiful to be seen' aphorism, introduced in the first stanza, has passed into McGonagallian folklore . . .

> Beautiful Railway Bridge of the Silvery Tay!
> With your numerous arches, pillars in so grand array,
> And your central girders, which seem to the eye
> To be almost towering to the sky.

The greatest wonder of the day,
And a great beautification to the River Tay,
Most beautiful to be seen,
Near by Dundee and the Magdalen Green.

Beautiful Railway Bridge of the Silvery Tay!
The longest of the present day
That has ever crossed o'er a tidal river stream,
Most gigantic to be seen,
Near by Dundee and the Magdalen Green.

Beautiful Railway Bridge of the Silvery Tay!
Which will cause great rejoicing on the opening day,
And hundreds of people will come from far way,
Also the Queen, most gorgeous to be seen,
Near by Dundee and the Magdalen Green.

The *Weekly News* adjudged McGonagall had achieved his exceptional standard again and appended a mocking postscript to its assessment: 'If the "Queen most gorgeous to be seen" does not "on the opening day" bind the laurel crown upon the poetic brow of W. McG., some people will think, at all events, that the poet who can sing in this fashion, deserves to be bound in the same manner.' The queen, forewarned, stayed well away from the opening ceremony.[30]

The Tay Bridge took six years to build and one day to fall down and became synonymous with McGonagall. He fearlessly recalled that it made him 'famous universally'. Living by then in Paton's Lane, which ran between Perth Road and Magdalen Green, now with a modern square named in his memory where his tenement dwelling once stood, McGonagall was intimately familiar with the ill-starred crossing. Its fateful curve over the estuary began barely yards from his door and the cacophony of construction sounds would have disturbed even a weaver used to the clatter of countless shuttles.

Lacking McGonagall's foresight – or perhaps editorial judgement – the paper did not publish the infamous sixth verse which foretold the collapse of the bridge two years later. Thus its huge readership was oblivious then of the link often made today between McGonagall's hunch and the 1879 tragedy. Indeed, in an unpublished letter dated

1 September 1877, McGonagall pointed out that although the poem had been 'highly appreciated' by the *Weekly News* editor, 'he had only published one half of the Tay Bridge Address'. It was not because it lacked quality, he maintained, just that 'space would not permit any more'.[31] Its sixth verse, however, did appear to foretell its fall, enlisting the protection of God to prevent any accident befalling passengers crossing the bridge . . . 'for that would be most awful to be seen'.

This earned for its author a reputation as a mystic which he was only too happy to own, and in later years he claimed 'to have had a premonition a few days before the bridge fell'. He also asserted that Glasgow poets laid the blame for the calamity on his shoulders.[32] Had he possessed mystical powers, however, he might have quit poetry while the going was good. By the end of 1877 the *Weekly News* was in effect telling him to put a sock in it.

For now, though, the next drop-off to Lindsay Street was 'An Address to Shakespeare', an eight-verse tribute which drew this comment from the paper in September 1877: 'Wm McGonagall, Dundee, having successfully sung the praises of the Tay Bridge has at length, like so many of the poetical fellowship, laid the homage of his verse at the feet of Shakespeare. It is appropriate that a tragedian who is also a poet should venture upon an "Address to Shakespeare", and we think it will be admitted by a perusal of the following verses that Mr McGonagall's efforts as a poet are worthy of his talent as an actor.'[33]

This sarcastic reminder of McGonagall's nuisance-making theatrical career jogged the memory of a familiar antagonist – 'Old Stager'. In the paper's next issue, the anonymous onlooker responded with a 10-verse exposition of McGonagall's greatness as an actor, but questioned his motives in turning to poetry . . .

> What was't that woke the dormant lyre,
> And with the muse did thee inspire?
> Did the bright grandeur of theme
> Steal o'er thy spirit like a dream?
> Or, now that you have left the stage
> Where oft you shone in mimic rage
> Did'st think to gain a brighter name
> Aspiring to poetic fame?[34]

A 'brighter name' is exactly what McGonagall craved and, undaunted by public mimicry, he established a routine of daily writing. One of his next actions was uncharacteristically astute. In September 1877 he sat down and composed 'A Requisition to the Queen', a short letter which comprised an appeal for royal patronage and a new poem of four numbered verses . . .

1. Most August! Empress of India, and of Great Britain the Queen,
   I most humbly beg your pardon, hoping you will not think it mean
   That a poor poet that lives in Dundee,
   Would be so presumptuous to write unto thee.

2. Most lovely Empress of India, and England's generous Queen,
   I send you an Address, I have written on Scotland's Bard,
   Hoping that you will accept it, and not be with me too hard,
   Nor fly into a rage, but be as Kind and Condescending
   As to give me your Patronage.

3. Beautiful Empress of India, and England's Gracious Queen,
   I send you a Shakespearean Address written by me.
   And I think if your Majesty reads it, right pleased you will be.
   And my heart it will leap with joy, if it is patronised by Thee.

4. Most Mighty Empress of India, and England's beloved Queen,
   Most Handsome to be Seen,
   I wish you every Success.
   And that heaven may you bless.
   For your Kindness to the poor while they are in distress.
   I hope the Lord will protect you while living
   And hereafter when your Majesty is . . . dead.
   I hope the Lord above will place an eternal Crown! upon your
      Head.
   I am your Gracious Majesty ever faithful to Thee,
   William Macgonagall, The Poor Poet,
   That lives in Dundee.

This poignant – at times pathetic – appeal was accompanied by fresh poems dedicated to Shakespeare and Burns. It was, in effect,

William McGonagall's first 'collection' of the now-familiar stramash of couplets and nonsensical metre, but it was nevertheless a gentle request for acknowledgement and he had the good sense to send a copy to London for the queen's perusal on 6 September 1877, in the hope, as he hinted heavily in his ode, of winning royal approval. This was in spite of willing away her life in his last verse in the pessimistic manner that he had killed off Gilfillan in his first poem. The response from Buckingham Palace six weeks later was far from the letter of endorsement he had hoped for, however. One of the queen's administrators simply returned his verses, adding in polite terms that she was not able to receive them personally. Dated 16 October 1877, the reply read:

'General Sir Thomas Biddulph is commanded to thank Mr McGonagall for sending the enclosed lines which, however, the Queen regrets must be returned, as it is not usual for Her Majesty to receive manuscript poetry.'

Such a return would be viewed as an out-and-out dismissal by most folk. Not McGonagall. He regarded the Buckingham Palace letter as an endorsement of his work. He took the black wax seal of the Royal Privy on the reverse of the envelope and Sir Thomas Biddulph's signature as proof of its royal authenticity and his appointment as poet under the protection of Queen Victoria herself, almost as if it had been ordained by an Act of Parliament. And he was immensely proud of the royal 'blessing' for the rest of his days, a point lost on the twentieth-century writer and broadcaster Magnus Magnusson, who believed the royal letter – still extant – to be a hoax.[35]

The following Saturday's paper contained yet another of the enthused poet's effusions. This was an intriguing composition called 'The Testing Day of the Bridge of the Tay'. Sadly, the paper decided not to print the submission, explaining its reluctance to do so: 'The piece, it need hardly be said, is worthy of his previous efforts, but as it might be possible to surfeit our readers with a feast of the sweet things supplied by Mr McGonagall, and as there is a danger of some of us falling victims to Tay Bridge on the brain, we have thought it advisable to sacrifice this latest fruit of the Tay Bridge Poet Laureate's poetic brain.'[36]

It was literature's loss that McGonagall's effort was subsumed among scores of verses spawned overnight by 'Tay Bridge on the brain'. Famed today for his Tay Bridge trilogy – his 'Railway Bridge of the Silvery Tay' (1877), 'The Tay Bridge Disaster' (1880) and the 'Address to the New Tay Bridge' (1887), it is evident that McGonagall celebrated the Tay crossing with a fourth poem, one that would have described in verse the 30,000 citizens who watched the contractors' 'donkey' engine Mongrel make the first pass over the newly-laid rails in September 1877, and the grand fireworks display which lit up his beloved Magdalen Green thereafter.

Undeterred by the prospect of *Weekly News* censorship, McGonagall laid his pen to paper at the slightest provocation. He next submitted his address to Robert Burns, which extolled Scotland's national bard over a handful of generous verses. The paper chirped gleefully: 'We give the following in order that our national poet may not be behind Shakespeare in receiving the praises of one who can do the thing so neatly and impartially.' There followed extracts starting with the now-familiar couplet, 'Immortal Robert Burns of Ayr/There's but few poets can with you compare'. It was dated by McGonagall 27 September 1877.[37]

Another composition landed on the correspondence editor's desk the following Saturday. He told readers: 'William McGonagall, Dundee, has forwarded us a "Summary History of Sir William Wallace" which we are requested to publish, because it will be long before he sends any more. On that distinct understanding, we subjoin the production, which, it must be confessed, is as original a summary of the life of Scotland's patriot as we have seen for a long time.' All 64 lines of McGonagall's debut at historical storytelling were placed before the public, the entire poem. The editorial aim was to see off the Paton's Lane poet and when it failed to do so the paper tersely suggested McGonagall had been in the column's spotlight long enough. The following week it noted: 'William McGonagall's address on "Bruce at Bannockburn" is declined with thanks.' It can never be known if it subsequently received complaints over McGonagall's sidelining, but an editorial addressed to 'poetical correspondents' that month rowed backwards by explaining: 'We have to inform our obliging poetical contributors generally that they must not think themselves neglected if their pieces are not immediately noticed, as we find this class of correspondence is accumulating in our hands.'[38]

It was a fair defence. Most Saturdays the *Weekly News* correspondence column was given over to submitted poetry or to reasons why submitted verse was too bad to publish. Its rules ensured that only poems verified by their senders' full names and addresses were eligible. Thus verses ascribed to William McGonagall were truly his, and were usually signed and dated on despatch to the paper. He would have set the record straight with an indignant letter had anyone had the temerity to impersonate him – as modern writers are prone to allege for poems undoubtedly his own. Indeed, he did so in years ahead – rushing into print on one occasion to publicly disown the author of a counterfeit as a 'coward'. The column's editors considered themselves expert in evaluating contributions. They were quick to separate the poetic wheat from the chaff and the new bard of Paton's Lane was not alone in bearing the brunt of their pen.

In the space of a month, contributor 'MAB' of Dundee was brusquely advised, 'We give one specimen: the others we must consign to the waste basket.' 'PG' of Montrose was bluntly informed, 'spelling all right, grammar very imperfect' and that he could 'hardly be described as proficient in English composition'. 'CN' of Newburgh was curtly counselled, 'We cannot consciously recommend you to endeavour to develop your "poetical powers" as you are pleased to call the faculty to which you ascribe such nonsense.' And 'Ramor' of Perth was told, 'Your writing is so execrable that we could not afford the necessary time to decypher it.' Across town the *People's Journal* was equally dismissive of time-wasters and amateur versifiers. On a single Saturday in 1877 it told consecutive contributors . . .

'The "Ode to Autumn" is a piece of nonsense.'

"'Life" – good, but we cannot afford space for it.'

'G. Speed's verses, we are sorry to say, will not pass the ordeal of criticism.'[39]

Somehow, however, by the end of 1877 the Saturday *Weekly News* had established William McGonagall as a poet of considerable local celebrity and provided a showcase for his poetry for close on a million readers from the north of England to Shetland. His 'powers of versification' had produced his tribute to his 'best friend' George Gilfillan, the first of the Tay Bridge trilogy and its lost companion piece, 'Ode to the Queen', 'The Bonnie Lass o' Dundee', 'A Summary History of Sir William Wallace', 'On the Silvery Tay', 'The Battle of Bannockburn' and several others, including tributes to Burns and Shakespeare. These poems progressively laid down the pattern of verse to come, functional couplets on the day's events rushing headlong to meet each other in rhyme, last lines shortened or prolonged as necessary, with hardly a nod to metre and scansion.

And thus the heavens opened up as William McGonagall's extraordinary doggerel increasingly became the butt of ridicule to some and the bottomless well of wit to others.

THREE

'POET AND TRAGEDIAN'

WILLIAM McGONAGALL'S transformation from carpet weaver to 'royal poet' rapidly made him a figure of ridicule. In his own mind he had added verse to his quiver of talents and his business cards now reflected this lofty promotion by reading 'Poet and Tragedian'. Others saw him differently, the reviewer of his first published pamphlet of verse cheekily calling for the beheading of the Poet Laureate to offer the position to the Dundee bard. The satirical penny did not drop, however, and McGonagall's pen became mightier than the sword he wielded so passionately as Macbeth.

But for all William McGonagall's memory of the blinding vision on that summer's day in June 1877, his decision to abandon work to promote self-penned poetry was probably a consequence of a chain of events as much as the munificent muse wafting through a Paton's Lane window and tapping him on the shoulder.

Dundee's manufacturing sector plunged into recession as the 1870s progressed. In December 1874 millworkers began a bitter dispute over a proposed wage cut as demand for products collapsed after the Franco–Prussian War. After a vociferous and violent campaign, the wages stood. In June 1875, however, manufacturers announced wages would be reduced by 10 per cent, attributing their actions to depressed markets. Within a week 12,000 strikers were locked out of 29 different works. Reports of stone-throwing and noisy intimidation led Peter Carmichael of Baxter Brothers to note in his diary: 'From the temper of the crowds I passed through on my way to the train this afternoon I fear mischief tonight.'[1]

In 1876 – the eve of William McGonagall's 'discovery' of poetry – 22 jute works employing 5,000 hands stood idle in the town as manufacturers struggled for orders. Carmichael recorded sombrely:

'Dundee trade is very bad, linen now as bad as jute or worse. We know not from day to day if we can keep on and find employment for our people.' And in McGonagall's fateful year of 1877 Carmichael picked up his quill again: 'The state of trade in Dundee is giving us much anxiety – prices at zero, stocks accumulating and wages as high as ever.' It should be no surprise that William McGonagall's first published poem that year was dedicated to a man who had championed Dundee's low-waged working class and who had openly criticised the profiteering jute barons for the town's social inequalities.[2]

Neither was it a good time to be a weaver. Long gone was their one-time superiority over mill hands through apprenticed skills, aristocratic habits and persuasive abilities to command higher wages. The conversion to power looms, unstoppable mechanisation and the expansion of jute eroded piecework and reduced income. The poet William Thom recalled how, at the changeover of the eighteenth and nineteenth centuries, 'four days did the weaver work – for then four days was a week, as far as working went – and such a week to a skilled workman brought forty shillings'. Come the 1830s, Thom found wages as low as six shillings weekly and grumbled: 'The weaver of forty shillings had money instead of wit, the weaver of six shillings wit instead of money.'[3] At the time of William McGonagall's conversion to poetry Dundee weavers were earning between eight and 13 shillings a week for a single loom and 12 to 17 shillings for the double looms given to the fastest workers as shopfloor promotion. Such wages were barely half that of bakers, blacksmiths and bricklayers and barely a third of what engineers and sailors earned. In other words, weavers had dropped in both spending power and status. McGonagall related in June 1878 how he could not pay his grocery bill through 'the scarcity of work', and stated how, during the 1870s' downturn, 'Some weeks I might earn 7s, or 10s, or 15s, but it's not very regular.'[4]

James Myles recorded how such intermittent employment had a debilitating effect on mid-Victorian Dundee men: 'Does the reader know what it is like to be out of employment? Has he ever wandered about the streets looking for work, and unable to find it? If he has, he must know, as he meets a rebuff here and another there, that his heart sometimes fails him, and he gives way to despair.' Such men became the town's infamous 'kettle boilers', the 'loafers' left at home to mind the bairns as employers encouraged women like Jean McGonagall to work for lower wages. Unemployed husbands often felt worthless and humiliated and lounged about the house or stood sullenly at street corners waiting for the pubs to open. This unique swapping of economic roles gave Dundee a dynamic shared with no other city.[5]

In McGonagall's case, descending into debt and reinventing his way of life was probably no coincidence. Unemployment could demolish financial stability. Day-to-day survival was difficult and distressing. While linen's golden age had once provided the sailcloth for British shipping, tenting for Europe's armies and clothing for Afro-Caribbean slaves, coarser jute was becoming the preferred option for wrapping, sacking and bagging. There was no stopping the linen-to-jute revolution. The erosion of income through de-skilling and sporadic interruptions to employment were probably reasons enough for William McGonagall to consider how to feed his brood as the 1870s drew to a close, and may have been the spur to order his thoughts around poetry production.

Less likely, the McGonagall family income could have improved at times of plenty to the extent that the head of the household was able at last to fulfil his urge to write, recite and perform. At least five of William's children were working. William junior and Joseph were mill hands, with Joseph later finding a better job in Dundee's dockyards as a ship's painter. Charles worked as a hackle maker in the linen industry. The teenagers Mary and James had followed their elder brothers and found employment in the mills. Thus several modest wages were entering Paton's Lane. Had William, then aged around 50, found himself out of work, he inevitably would have considered alternative options. He had always harboured ambitions to act. He was actively scanning local newspapers by 1877 and probably writing intermittently for leisure. Rhyming verse was a Victorian passion and would have presented an obvious challenge.

McGonagall was also familiar with the work of local writers and perhaps felt his own creative efforts were worthy of publication.

Poems in local papers covered a spectrum of subjects – and quality – and could have been his motivation to compose his own. The *Weekly News* published half a dozen amateur efforts weekly. The *People's Journal* filled its own correspondence column with verse and staged prize poetry competitions every Christmas-time, attracting hundreds of entries. McGonagall's name was not among published winners, but he may have entered – not least since George Gilfillan was often the celebrity judge. This, too, could have contributed to his poetical awakening.

One obvious influence among local mill poets was the so-called 'Factory Girl', Ellen Johnson. Ages with McGonagall, Johnson's father was also a Dundee handloom weaver. He had moved to Glasgow, married, and Ellen had grown up there, becoming a mill girl at 11. Like McGonagall, she was largely self-taught in reading and writing and claimed later she had received only nine months of formal schooling. Mirroring McGonagall's reading of Shakespeare and his guile for discreet self-improvement, she had finished Walter Scott's novels by the age of 13. In 1854 she had a poem published by the *Glasgow Examiner*. She moved to Dundee in 1861 after her mother's death and lived with her father's sister, finding work at Verdant Works and Chapelshade Mill. *Poems and Songs of Ellen Johnson, The Factory Girl*, was published in Glasgow in 1867. It contained a preambulatory note from finger-in-every-pie Gilfillan: 'I hope she will be encouraged by this to cultivate her mind, to read and correct the faults in her style – arising from her limited opportunities – and in doing so, she cannot fail to secure still increased respect and warmer patronage.' The words could have been addressed to his acquaintance in Paton's Lane.[6]

Other influential weaver poets included William Thom of Inverurie, who published *Rhymes and Recollections of A Hand-Loom Weaver* in 1845. Thom and McGonagall shared many tribulations, including poverty and hunger, the former losing his baby daughter to exposure as his family slept rough near Dundee. Thom recalled an experience, shared by McGonagall in 1877, when a composer of poems at his weaving factory in Aberdeen decided one verse was good enough to grace the pages of the local newspaper. Thus, as McGonagall contemplated the delivery of 'Gilfillan' to the

Weekly News, this writer wended his way to the printing office of the *Aberdeen Journal* accompanied by a friend. Thom described the agonising wait to see if the contribution had been published: 'Early on the morning of publication the anxious pair stood watchfully in a court that led to the printing-office. Did his verses exist in print? Woe on me! Why didn't they buy a paper?' Patience fading fast, the pair resorted to kidnapping a sulky little lad who had bought a *Journal*. They dragged him up a close 'and while he kicked and roared, we groped for the Poor Man's Corner in the *Journal*, and were blest – the song was there!'[7]

McGonagall's need to write poetry to relieve poverty was familiar territory to Thom . . . 'After some consideration another mode of exercising my talents for support occurred to me. I had, ever since I remember, an irrepressible tendency to make verses, and many of these had won applause from my friends and fellow-workmen.' McGonagall probably knew of Thom and, indeed, may have read these very words in *Rhymes and Recollections* prior to testing his own verse on unsuspecting shopmates.[8]

If there was a single catalyst for William McGonagall's debut poem in the *Weekly News* on the 7th day of the 7th month of 1877 it can be found in the paper nearly three months earlier. On 26 May the short poem 'To A Local Star' was set before its readers. It was signed 'P. Stewart' and began . . .

> There may have been mightier minds, my friend, than thine,
> And there be many, meantime, mightier far,
> Yet art thou not illustrious, no dim star,
> Art thou: and then, thy light, O, how divine.

A curious letter arrived at the *Weekly News* the following week. The correspondence column's editor noted: 'G. Fairplay' Dundee, is very much exercised in soul about a piece of poetry in last week's issue addressed "To A Local Star", and thinks it would only have been true manliness had the author named the individual to whom he referred.' The paper then provided 'G. Fairplay's' letter *verbatim et literatim* . . .

'Sir – I noted a piece of poetry in the *Weekly News* of last week to a

Local Star in Dundee and the Author has written the poetry in such an obscure way that I am at a loss to comprehend his meaning or what Local Star he alludes to in his poetical effusion . . . Sir – I would wish to know from him or any of the *Weekly News* readers what Local Star he alludes to – and that would be true manliness.'

The *Weekly News* assumed 'G. Fairplay' was the praise-hungry William McG. and responded: 'We think "G. Fairplay" may console himself with the reflection that he is not the star in question.'[9] This did not the end the matter. The following week another odd letter arrived at the paper's Lindsay Street offices. Excerpts were placed before readers with the authorial interjection . . .

" 'To A Local Star" – A piece with the above heading and signed "W. Shakespeare" was dropped mysteriously into our letter box this week. The effusion is in celebration of a local tragedian, whose talents are celebrated in the following lofty strain: "All ye who are disciples of Shakespeare, I hope you'll pay attention unto a few incidents regarding Mr McGonagall, which is worth of been made mention – he is a gentleman of great abilities and few can him excel o', I wonder how Mr McFarland doesn't make him an engagement, with him he could do well o" '.'[10]

Here was William McGonagall's unveiling in rhyme – 'few can excel o'/with him he could do well o". Yet what must have appeared humorous false modesty to readers was to him a despairing plea for recognition. This extraordinary self-promotional appeal to the Theatre Royal's manager was also McGonagall's last throw of the acting dice. He had nowhere else to go in terms of artistic outlet. It was at this point that poetry became to him a possibility for personal expression and promotion.

McGonagall was about 50 in 1877 and beyond middle age. It was not a typical time for a career change. Yet over the next 25 years this unstoppable versifier would compose 270 poems, sell thousands of broadsides, publish several books and be acclaimed by 'housefull' audiences across Scotland. Through extraordinary self-belief and determined dedication he would court the muse that called at Paton's Lane and emerge from the nineteenth century a household name.

By the end of 1877 William McGonagall was already known as a composer of bizarre verse through regular appearances in W. & D.C. Thomson's *Weekly News*. As 1878 began, the paper continued now and then to publish his effusions and seldom flinched from criticising his dubious abilities. In January 1878, for instance, its readers were shown 14 lines of 'Bonnie Dundee in 1878' and informed with inflated frankness: 'William McGonagall does not improve with practice if Bonnie Dundee can be taken as a specimen. We give the following extract, which we can scarcely persuade ourselves is even amusing. Perhaps Mr McGonagall will say that is because it was never intended to be amusing.'[11]

'Bonnie Dundee in 1878' expresses McGonagall's pride in the town's built environment and is mostly celebrated for a memorable couplet . . . 'And for stately buildings there's none can excel/The beautiful Albert Institute or the Queen's Hotel'.

But the waspish editorial drew McGonagall's wrath the following Saturday – accompanied by a flicker of the humour he disguised so extraordinarily later in life. The paper published his complaint in full . . .

'My dear sir, I do not feel satisfied with your criticism regarding my poem titled Bonnie Dundee in 1878. If I cannot persuade you and others into the belief that the beauties of Dundee that I have referred to cannot be surpassed in any other town I know of, that is no reason for you to give against publishing it.' As to the amusement qualities of his craft, McGonagall added defensively: 'My dear sir, I consider all sensible poetry to be amusing, and worth perusing. I consider your criticism to be a very unfair one. I consider that every poet is justified in writing about any subject he chooses.'

Then, in a delicious riposte which invalidates modern claims that McGonagall was humourless, he added, 'But perhaps you are angry because I forgot to introduce the *Courier* and *Argus* office as a stately building. If so, I beg pardon for being so neglectful for the many kindnesses you have done me.'[12] This was McGonagall at his indignant best – which was always when his poetry was under fire. A friend recalled, 'If anyone dared to laugh at his work his flow of language was almost Shakespearean in its grandeur.'

It is difficult to say whose ego was more bruised – McGonagall's or the newspaper's. But during the reflective stand-off that followed, 'Old Stager' returned to the fray with a six-stanza effort lamenting the poet's purdah and revealing again his intimacy with his hero . . .

> I heard folk say the other day,
> McGonagall was dead:
> If this be true, what shall we do?
> Who can we get instead
> To sing sweet lays on Balgay's braes,
> And such themes and turns,
> As Wallace wight – that hero bright –
> Shakespeare and Robert Burns?
> I knew him well; my heart doth swell
> With rapture at the thought;
> Yet oft again it bleeds with pain
> To think how he had fought
> In many ways with Shakespeare's plays
> To gain undying fame;
> And now he's gone, the world must own
> It's very much to blame.[13]

Thankfully, Old Stager – and McGonagall – were spared a trip to the Western Cemetery. Very much alive and kicking, McGonagall submitted a new poem in March 1878 which he titled 'Genius'. The paper responded sulkily, 'Our old friend, Mr McGonagall has once more favoured us with an effusion; in which he has poured out the thoughts of his soul on the nature and rewards of genius, a subject we leave our readers, by the following specimen, to determine whether he has any right to speak.'

We must be thankful for a 'specimen' published however petulantly, as it is all that remains of this contemplative poem. In print here for the first time in 132 years is William McGonagall's 'Genius' . . .

> What is genius?
> 'Tis a thing seldom rewarded;
> If you are in poverty
> 'Tis sure to be disregarded.

But if you are a rich man
Your company is courted
By the high and low,
Throughout all the world wherever you go.
Whereas the poor man
By his fellow-workmen is spurn'd;
They look upon him with a jealous eye,
And their noses upturn'd,
And they say to themselves,
You are no greater than we;
If you are, show it,
And we'll all worship thee.
And rally around you,
And applaud you to the skies;
And none of us all
Will ever you despise,
Because you can help yourself,
You are a very great man,
And every one of us
Will do all that we can,
You for to please,
And never will tease,
Nor try to offend you,
By any misbehaviour;
And to court your favour
We will always endeavour.
That is the way genius
Is rewarded;
But if you are in poverty
'Tis sure to be disregarded.[14]

McGonagall expresses the vulnerability of the educated working classes. Even the intelligent poor are 'sure to be disregarded' in recognition and reward. Worse, fellow workers disparage those hopeful of progress through education and self-improvement. Their altruistic intentions are looked upon with a 'jealous eye'. 'Genius' demonstrates McGonagall's frustration at being creatively disadvantaged by poverty. The better-off would never be rejected in such a situation. Thus he appeals for consideration of 'poor' genius – and, thereby, himself. 'Genius' is a landmark in McGonagall's self-belief as a poet. In it he feels sufficiently important to teach and preach through verse.

Naturally, the notion of genius was one happily assigned by others to McGonagall. In the following Saturday's paper 'Old Stager' probably spoke for many among the far-flung *Weekly News* flock in welcoming the fun derived from the determined Dundee bard's offerings, and chastised the newspaper for sidelining his work . . .

> This puir but highly gifted bard,
> Tae please them he's been working hard,
> Will they his efforts still discard,
> An' gi'e him nae aid,
> Or will they gi'e him his reward,
> An' see it paid?

Such support inspired William McGonagall to his next poetic adventure, the publication in early 1878 of his first 'collection' of verse. This was a quartet of poems on a flimsy four-page pamphlet titled *Poems and Song by William McGonagall*. He also felt able to append *Poet to Her Majesty* with the justification in smaller type on the front page: 'Mr McGonagall holds in his possession an Acknowledgement from the Empress of India, dated Buckingham Palace, sixteenth day of October, anno domini, 1877, and signed by Sir Thomas Biddulph.' It amounted to no royal reference, of course, but it served his purpose.

Phillips (1971) and others since – including the Dundee Library catalogue of McGonagall's work – suggest that no copy of this early printed pamphlet has survived. At least two fragile copies are known, however.[15] McGonagall's first collection comprised the 'Address to George Gilfillan', 'The Railway Bridge of the Silvery Tay', 'The Inauguration of the Hill o' Balgay' and the song, 'The Bonnie [Broon Hair'd] Lass o' Dundee'. *Poems and Song* was reviewed by the *Evening Telegraph* in May 1878 under the heading

'Job's Reflection on the Great McGonagall'. Job, a pseudonym for a journalist who wrote a topical column, quickly set the tone of the mocking review to follow: 'Money may make a city beautiful, the almighty dollar may make a village great, but no amount of wealth can produce a poet.' He reminded readers how Dundee had been raised to the seventh heaven of poetical fame by the bursting forth of a 'bright particular star of the first magnitude', adding, 'while the Editor of this paper neglects his duty by dealing with unimportant matters, such as the annexation of Bessarabia [in the Romanian war of independence], cotton strikes, the town's finances, and British interests . . .'

Thus it was both the reviewer's 'privilege' and 'pleasure' to introduce the debut publication of the mighty Poet of Juteopolis in the same issue of the *Evening Telegraph* that carried reviews of the high-status *Blackwood's*, *Cornhill* and *Gentleman's* magazines. Firstly he calculated that at tuppence for four pages McGonagall's *Poems and Song* worked out at exactly a halfpenny a page, noting, 'But every purchaser will have the worth of his money in the title-page alone, so the other three pages go to making up a capital bargain.' The title page is quite elegant, in fact, with a decorative Celtic frame enclosing its wording. Thereafter Job swished the editorial sabre to decapitate two of the pamphlet's verses. " 'The Railway Bridge of the Silvery Tay" ', he said, trying to keep a straight face, 'will arouse a feeling of satisfaction in all interested that though Royalty cannot find leisure to grace the opening ceremony, Royalty has had an opportunity of reading so vivid a description of the great under-taking.' At least he was also having a dig at the conspicuously absent monarch. Next he turned to 'The Inauguration of the Hill o' Balgay' which, he suggested, showed McGonagall was alive to the benefits of an unsullied atmosphere – innocently inviting a comparison with the claustrophobic, light-deprived world that was the poet's lot in the roll of the domestic dice. If anything, McGona-gall's poems dwelled on the beauties of the world around him long before they reported natural and man-made disasters.[16]

For all its puns and innuendoes, Job's review delighted McGona-gall to the extent that he dipped his pen into ink and faithfully copied it into his second manuscript autobiography. What probably tickled him most was the improbable comparison it made between Alfred Tennyson, the distinguished Poet Laureate, and himself. Job commented that while Tennyson lived it would be invidious to promote McGonagall to take his place. He warned readers: 'Time will change all that, however, and now when McGonagall is definitely fixed upon as the successor to Tennyson, McGonagall can afford to wait.' From then until Tennyson's death in 1892 McGonagall as Poet Laureate-in-Waiting was a recurrent theme. And with the double-edged comment, 'I have no hesitation in declaring that Shakespeare never wrote poetry like Mr McGona-gall's', the *Evening Telegraph* correspondent also placed in McGona-gall's mind the notion that he was the reawakened Shakespeare. Thereafter, he was filled with the idea that he was at least the equal of the Stratford bard. This did not go unnoticed in the rival *Weekly News*, whose readers were also invited to be gobsmacked at the presence of an appendage to the cover of *Poems and Song* which read, 'Gentlemen waited upon at their own Residences and Readings given from the British poets'. McGonagall was back in business as a public performer.

Reviews of the 1878 compilation show there was no honeymoon in how William McGonagall's early poetry and eccentric lifestyle were reported. For the quarter century between his Gilfillan address in 1877 to his death in 1902, McGonagall was portrayed as a figure of fun and his poems universally mocked. He was the Daft Laddie of Dundee in a town itself a fostering centre of quick humour and one so full of eccentrics it spawned not one but two books titled *Dundee Worthies*. The *Weekly News*, for instance, followed up its ridiculing assessment of his first pamphlet by announcing in May 1878, 'We are afraid our readers are beginning to think they have had enough of Mr McGonagall.' At the same time, though, the poet enveloped himself in a self-promotional aura based on the deluded belief that his poetry was without equal.[17]

It cannot be said for certain whether printing costs for the 1878 pamphlet or a downturn in the town's staple trade made money scarcer than usual, but McGonagall fell foul of cash-flow problems shortly after his landmark publishing debut. Within a month of 'Job's Reflection on the Great McGonagall', the *Evening Telegraph* made more space in its tightly-packed dreels of type to dwell upon 'The Great McGonagall in Financial Difficulties'. Below appeared the humiliating washing of the poet's dirty financial linen in the public domain . . .

'On Tuesday, in the Dundee Sheriff Small Debt Court, before Sheriff Cheyne, William McGonagall, Paton's Lane, Dundee, who styles himself "Poet to Her Majesty", was sued by David Stewart, Grocer, Perth Road, Dundee, for the sum of £6 3s 6d, as an account for grocery goods supplied to the poet's family during the last six or eight months. From the state of the passbook, it appeared that the poet had been gradually falling into arrears with the grocer.'

When the case was called McGonagall appeared in the witness box, cleared his throat and with a magnificent tragic air, addressed the sheriff:

'Well, sir, I am a handloom weaver, and the charge against me is debt, and poverty is the cause of my being unable to pay. I am willing to pay if I am allowed time to do so.'

The Sheriff: 'Why have you been getting all these goods since the New Year and not paying for them?'

The Poet: 'The cause is scarcity of work, my Lord.'

Mr Paul (fiscal): 'I believe, my Lord, he has given more of his time to other things – poetry and drama – than to weaving.' (Laughter) 'I believe that has something to do with his difficulties.'

The Poet: 'I would pay willingly if time were given me.'

The Sheriff: 'What are your wages?'

The Poet: 'My Lord, I have no wages. Some weeks I might earn 7s, or 10s, or 15s, but it's not very regular.'

Mr Paul: 'How much can you give a week?'

The Poet: 'In my present circumstances I could not give more than 1s a week.'

The Sheriff: 'That would take 120 weeks to pay off this debt.' (Laughter.) 'You will have to pay 3s a week.'

The Poet then left the court.[18]

If William McGonagall returned to Paton's Lane with the notion of reapplying himself to a 12-hour day of carpet weaving to meet his penury punishment, it was not a thought that lingered. Perhaps the ignominy of being criminalised in a debtors' court triggered the remarkable reaction that followed. The same month, June 1878, McGonagall embarked on an extraordinary attempt to gain an audience with Queen Victoria. This was not the relatively simple task of jumping on a train to the desired destination, as his friend George Gilfillan was prone to do to meet lecture appointments. For a penniless poet it meant a walk of 60 miles to Balmoral Castle.

McGonagall's autobiographies dwell on the ill-starred excursion, 'truly as it happened' as he asserts. As to why he wanted to walk to Queen Victoria's highland home, it is possible that he felt frustrated by the financial constraints preventing him accompanying the estimated 12,000 Dundonians who left town by train and boat at the start of holiday week – and was too egotistically embarrassed to remain at home while others had a purpose to their annual break. More likely, he regarded it a commercial necessity. Space remained on his business card for 'By Royal Appointment'.

McGonagall's memoirs chart his journey and reveal with stark honesty the uncompromising rebuttal he received on demanding entry to Balmoral, where the queen was staying. Leaving Dundee his heart was 'light and gay'. But when he arrived in Alyth, some 15 miles distant, 'I felt weary, foot-sore, and longed for rest and lodgings for the night. I made enquiry for a good lodging-house, and found one very easily, and for the lodging I paid fourpence to the landlady.' McGonagall's lack of disposable income is evident on this and expeditions to come. There is seldom any lavish purchase. Jean despatches him on a limited budget and her husband is acutely aware of the paucity of shillings in his pocket. At Alyth, for example: 'I felt very hungry, not having tasted food of any kind by the way during my travel, which caused me to have a ravenous appetite.' No couplets of admiration are penned for this town, beautiful to be seen or not.

Blistered feet washed and rested, McGonagall trudged north as the summer weather deteriorated. 'A dreadful thunder-storm came on, and the vivid flashes of the forked lightning were fearful to behold, and the rain poured down in torrents until I was drenched to the skin, and longed to be under cover from the pitiless rain. Still God gave me courage to proceed.' McGonagall's memory pin-points his journey's second day to the end of the trades holiday – Thursday, 27 June – when severe thunderstorms affected many parts of Scotland. The Dundee bard, however, possessed a steely determination to fulfil his mission: 'I remembered saying to my friends in Dundee I would pass through fire and water rather than turn tail, and make my purpose good, as I had resolved to see Her Majesty at Balmoral.' Cold and hungry, wet to the skin, desperate for shelter and undoubtedly miserable, McGonagall reached the Spittal of Glenshee, around 13 miles from Alyth. There he sought lodgings at a shepherd's bothy, the householder eyeing him warily, 'perhaps taking me for a burglar, or a sheep-stealer, who had come to steal his sheep. But when I showed him Her Most Gracious Majesty's royal letter, with the royal black seal, that I had received from her for my poetic abilities, he immediately took me by the hand and bade me come in'.

He took to the road again next day, 'travelling on courageously'. Surviving on his breakfast of 'porridge and good Highland milk, enough to make a hungry soul to sing with joy', he covered the 12 remaining miles to the gates of Balmoral in three hours and crossed the little bridge spanning the River Dee leading to the porter's lodge. Confronted by the duty policeman, he produced the letter from Sir Thomas Biddulph and asked to see the queen. McGona-gall's autobiography conveys the impending disappointment: 'He returned with an answer as follows: "Well, I've been up at the Castle with your letter, and the answer I got for you is they cannot be bothered with you", said with great vehemence.'

After further questioning, McGonagall produced his slim pamphlet of poems. He claimed in *Brief Autobiography* in 1890 to have shown 'the second edition, of which I had several copies'. In his final memoirs in 1901 he mentions it was the twopenny copy with 'Poet to Her Majesty' on its cover. Unless there is an unrecorded second edition, he probably took with him the *Poems and Song* reviewed by the *Evening Telegraph* in May 1878, just a month before his Balmoral adventure.

The 1901 autobiography adds arms and legs to the incident in an obvious watering-down of his inhospitable reception. In this version McGonagall has a premonition that he would not gain access to the queen which is not present in his earlier writings. 'I saw a carriage and four horses, and seemingly two drivers, and also a lady in the carriage, who I thought would be the Queen. Then the carriage vanished all of a sudden, and I thought I had arrived at Balmoral Castle, and in front of the Castle I saw a big Newfoundland dog, and he kept barking loudly and angry at me, but I wasn't the least afraid of him, and as I advanced towards the front door of the Castle he sprang at me, and seized my right hand, and bit it severely, until it bled profusely. I seemed to feel it painful, and when I awoke, my dear readers, I was shaking with fear, and considered it to be a warning or a bad omen to me on my journey to Balmoral.' McGonagall's right hand was his writing hand and this curious dream sequence, omitted from earlier memoirs, appears an awkward device written by that hand to explain away his frosty reception in the Highlands.

Looking back from 1901, he also adds or invents that he faced arrest by 'a big burly-looking man' and an accusation that his royal letter was a forgery. Putting his life into print for the last time, there is a reputation to defend and enhance. When the Spittal of Glenshee shepherd heard that his guest was a poet, for instance, 'He asked me my name, and I told him I was McGonagall, the poet. He seemed o'erjoyed when he heard me say so, and told me I was welcome as a lodger for the night, and to make myself at home, and that he had heard often about me.'

McGonagall disappointedly retraced his steps to Blairgowrie, Alyth and, via Birkhill, towards his home town. 'I was on the road again for Dundee . . . which I accomplished in three days . . . footsore and weary, but not the least discouraged.' On his return journey he managed to sell six copies of *Poems and Song* at Blairgowrie – 'with a great struggle' – which earned him a shilling. 'I was very thankful, because it would tide me over until I would arrive in Dundee.'

So ended William McGonagall's journey to Balmoral. Settled with Jean at home, he set out his memories in the tribute poem,

'The Spittal o' Glenshee', the first verse setting the scene, the second conjuring up a rival for the silv'ry Tay, the third conveying forgiveness for being dismissed so forcibly. McGonagall must have been well satisfied with his latest work. A copy was quickly despatched to the *Weekly News* . . .

The Spittal of Glenshee,
Which is the most dismal to see –
With its bleak, rocky mountains,
And clear, crystal fountains,
With their misty foam;
And thousands of sheep there together do roam,
Browsing on the barren pasture, blasted-like to see,
Stunted in heather, and scarcely a tree;
And black-looking cairns of stones, as monuments to show,
Where people have been found that were lost in the snow –
Which is cheerless to behold –
And as the traveller gazes thereon it makes his blood run cold,
And almost makes him weep,
For a human voice is seldom heard there,
Save the shepherd crying to his sheep.

The chain of mountains there is most frightful to see,
Along each side of the Spittal o' Glenshee;
But the Castleton o' Braemar is most beautiful to see,
With its handsome whitewashed houses, and romantic scenery,
And bleak-looking mountains, capped with snow,
Where the deer and the roe do ramble to and fro,
Near by the dark river Dee,
Which is most beautiful to see.

And Balmoral Castle is magnificent to be seen,
Highland home of the Empress of India, Great Britain's Queen,
With its beautiful pine forests, near by the river Dee,
Where the rabbits and hares do sport in mirthful glee,
And the deer and the roe together do play
All the live long summer day,

In sweet harmony together,
While munching the blooming heather,
With their hearts full of glee,
In the green woods of Balmoral, near by the river Dee.

William McGonagall's mind could not have been exclusively occupied by ending three lines of an eight-line stanza with the word 'see' – just because it conveniently rhymed with 'Glenshee', 'scenery' and 'river Dee'. Thoughts must have turned to the life at home from which he had engineered a temporary escape. Perhaps his wanderings provided freedom from domestic disharmony. A boisterous household it must have been, as some years into the future the McGonagall family's disruptive behaviour would be presented as evidence in court for its eviction from Step Row. And in another court case to come, McGonagall explained away his millworker daughter Mary's breach of the peace conviction by saying, 'She is a well-disposed daughter, only her mother gives her drink at times.'[9] There is no certainty that Jean was over-fond of alcohol, and it is mentioned here only as a possible justification for his jaunts, but he may have enjoyed being out from under her feet. Did he mentally manufacture rhymes while he tramped the countryside, thinking of subjects and the couplets that would give them life via the lamp-black ink he used? Did his thoughts return to acting, his enduring obsession? Inevitably some Shakespearean scene would have kept him bellowing as he walked. Perhaps he ran up and down the list of chums to be consulted in due course for financial help, or the great and good to be applied to for patronage. McGonagall never abandoned those supporters who encouraged his artistic outpourings and chipped in with the odd shilling which allowed printers' costs to be met. He had, for example, dashed off a copy of *Poems and Song* to George Gilfillan. McGonagall's kindness brought a gentle, if tactful, reply from Stonehaven, where the minister was convalescing, in the spidery hand of one in the twilight of his life. Dated 16 July 1878, it read: 'Dear Sir, I thank you for your poems, especially the kind lines addressed to myself. I have read of your famous journey to Balmoral, for which I hope you are none the worse. I am here on holiday, but return in a few days. Believe me, yours truly, George Gilfillan.'

Whether McGonagall or Dundee's publishers were bewitched by Gilfillan – perhaps both – the *Courier* and the *Weekly News* vied to print the preacher's reply to the poet in full. It was one of Gilfillan's last letters – 'Oor George' was dead within the month.[20]

The winter spanning 1878–79 brought a flood of works from McGonagall's pen – so much so that the *Weekly News* raised an editorial eyebrow one week when none of his effusions arrived. Two of his early poems merit wider consideration. He had written 'The Bonnie [Broon-Hair'd] Lass o' Dundee' in October 1877. He described this as a song and it concerned his love for a lass who was 'the joy o' my heart and the flower o' Dundee'. Early in 1878 he composed 'Little Jamie' for 'the best little laddie that ever I did see'.

A century of McGonagall watchers have expressed surprise that the world's worst poet never composed poems in honour of his wife and family. These examples suggest this view is mistaken. 'The Bonnie Broon-Hair'd Lass o' Dundee' and 'Little Jamie' were self-described 'companion' pieces about his children. The former displays a father's devotion to his daughter. There is none like her. She is loved dearly – the joy of his heart. Its first and last verses provide a flavour of the tenderness carried by the composer to the lines on his paper . . .

O' a' the toons that I've been in,
I dearly love Dundee,
It's there the bonnie lassie lives,
The lass I love to see.
Her face is fair, broon is her hair,
And dark blue is her e'e,
And aboon a' the lasses e'er I saw,
There's nane like her to me –
The bonnie broon-hair'd lassie o' Bonnie Dundee.

The lassie is as handsome
As the lily on the lea,
And her mou' it is as red
As a cherry on the tree;
And she's a' the world to me,
The bonnie broon-hair'd lassie

Wi' the bonnie blue e'e,
She's the joy o' my heart
And the flower o' Dundee.

This is a poignant tribute to McGonagall's second daughter, Mary. She was 16 in 1877 and on the cusp of an adult life not blessed with happiness – though she alone among her siblings would move to Edinburgh to look after her infirm parents. Her brother James was three years younger and 'Little Jamie' is a devoted dad's memory of time spent with this, his fourth son. The six-stanza poem's opening lines convey a father's love and pride. Through the presence of such a child domestic difficulties are balanced . . .

Ither laddies may ha'e finer claes, and may be better fed,
But nane o' them a' has sic a bonnie curly heid,
O sic a blithe blink in their e'e,
As my ain curly fair-hair'd laddie, Little Jamie.

When he rises in the mornin' an' gets oot o' bed,
He says, mither, mind ye'll need tae toast my faither's bread.
For he aye gie's me a bawbee;
He's the best little laddie that ever I did see,
My ain curly fair-hair'd laddie, Little Jamie.

Moreover, 'Little Jamie' and 'The Bonnie Lass' are very rare examples of McGonagall's use of the Scots dialect. William Smith, once chairman of Winter's the printer in Dundee and a champion of McGonagall for over 60 years, held the view that McGonagall 'did not write dialect'. It was hardly a surprising comment. These poems stand almost isolated in the poet's cannon of 270. With these tributes, though, McGonagall's style chimes with the currency of working-class attitudes by embodying mainstream popular speech and sentiment for high emotional effect. It is correct, however, that McGonagall prided himself on the superiority of his English. He regarded himself an authority on 'proper' language and noticeably his output ignores the fashion for the Scots' tongue captured in so much Victorian verse. Bambrick noted: 'McGonagall identifies his own mastery of "high" English (as opposed to "vulgar" Scots) as a source of personal power . . . Scots had come to be stigmatized as a sign of both one's lack of education, manners and class.'[21] However, McGonagall's precious tributes to his children are proudly Scottish in style and sentiment. There is a suggestion, too, that Mary and James were their father's darlings.

McGonagall also dedicated a temperance poem to his parents, describing them as 'poor but honest, sober and God-fearing', but it is true that no tribute to his wife Jean is known, though he notes in memoirs his pleasure at returning home to give her money from entertainments. It appears he was diligent in providing her with 'housekeeping' funds whenever possible. In a letter to his patron and friend Alex Lamb from lodgings in Glasgow, enclosing two of his poems, he says, 'You need not send me anything for the copies enclosed but if you wish you can do so, to Mrs McGonagall Step Row.' He signs off with aplomb, 'Give my best wishes to all my admirers in Dundee.'[22]

October 1878 brought one of William McGonagall's most enduring and popular songs, 'The Rattling Boy from Dublin'. The *Weekly News* offered it to readers in all its brilliance, observing that it was a 'new Irish song' with 'all rights reserved' and which the poet had earnestly asked them to publish. It reported magnanimously: 'We are not so hard hearted to deprive our readers of such a treat.' Here was an author thinking so highly of his creativity that copyright was nailed down from the outset – as if anyone were likely in any case to risk a reputation by plagiarising McGonagall's work.

'Rattling Boy' was a song with a foot-stamping 'Whack-fal-de-da, fal-de-darelido' chorus and, along with 'Bruce at Bannockburn', became one of the staple McGonagall performance pieces. It told of the wooing of Dublin girl Biddy Brown, but was really a moralising crusade against drink and womanising. Lustily sung while flourishing props of hat and cane, 'Rattling Boy' appeared on 26 October. On 2 November 1878 McGonagall's 'Lines on a Dog or Something in the Shape of One', was 'respectfully declined as unsuitable' by the correspondence editor. It thus never saw the light of day and one can scarcely imagine the canine couplets conjured up for it.

The same can be said of a new poem sent from Paton's Lane on 16 November. This was titled 'Song Dedicated to Mr Barry Sullivan, Tragedian, without Permission', which survives only as a fragment. The *Weekly News* offered the following sample . . .

> He is an actor of great fame
> He play'd King Richard in Drury Lane,
> He fill'd the house from ceiling to floor,
> For upwards of three months or more.

Sullivan, an Irish tragedian of whom it was once said, 'his deeply pock-marked face did not lend itself to make-up', was booked for a six-night stint at the Theatre Royal in Castle Street. McGonagall was up to his sycophantic tricks again, advancing Sullivan's story to reveal how he heroically overcame near tragedy . . .

> While performing in Drury Lane,
> A theatre of wide world fame,
> Mr Sullivan in combat cut his eye,
> But it didn't make him cry.[23]

Come 1879, William McGonagall's output called for a second collection. This was a card-wrapped A5-sized pamphlet stapled into 16 pages. It was titled *The Complete Poetical Works of William McGonagall, Dundee, With Copy of Letter from the Queen to the Poet*. It was priced twopence and dated 'Dundee 1879'. It comprised 17 poems, including the quartet from his four-page *Poems and Song* of the previous year. 'Address to Shakespeare' featured, as did the Glenshee tribute and the historical epic 'William Wallace'. Local poems included 'The City of Perth', 'Bonnie Dundee in 1878' and 'Mary, the Maid o' the Tay'. Its publication in February 1879 acts as evidence of how McGonagall had accelerated his output, perhaps with an eye on potential profits from an enlarged and more significant body of his work.

One item from *Complete Poetical Works* caught the eye of the *People's Journal*, a weekly which seldom sympathised with the town's bard: 'Mr William McGonagall warbles a lay in praise of the

Newport Railway. The following is the first and funniest half of his
unique production . . .

> Success to the Newport Railway,
> Along the braise of the Silvry Tay,
> And to Dundee straightway
> Accross the Railway Bridge of the Silvry Tay,
> Which was open'd on the 12th of May
> In the year of our Lord 1879
> Which will clear all expenses in a very short time,
> Because the thrifty houswives of Newport
> To Dundee very often will resort
> Which will be to them profit and sport,
> By buying some cheap Tea, Bread and Jam,
> And also, some of Lipton's Cheap Ham:
> Which will make their hearts feel light and gay,
> And cause them for to bless the opening day
> Of the Newport Railway.'

This unedifying, uncorrected and pre-edited version of what is now
one of McGonagall's most familiar poems brought a good-humoured
but teasing response in the following Saturday's *Journal* . . .

> Ye Scottish bardies, ane an' a'
> Our famous poet's praises blaw;
> His verses are withoot a flaw –
> McGonagall;
> They are the best I ever saw,
> In the Journal.[24]

It was not long before the urge to entertain in public renewed its
hold on the Paton's Lane poet. In June 1879, once again during the
annual trades' holiday, McGonagall set off on his second adventure
– a tour of the towns north of Dundee. Curiously, this trek took
place during a period of heightened excitement over a fleeting visit
by Queen Victoria to view the new Tay Bridge. With the bells of
the Old Steeple clanging away, the royal train drew into Dundee

station at 6pm on Friday, June 20. At the station the queen met the bridge designer Thomas Bouch and various dignitaries. The train then rumbled over the bridge with the boys of the Mars Training Ship saluting with oars as it passed high above them. There is no evidence, however, that McGonagall attended the event or commemorated the historic scene with a poem. The humiliation at Balmoral possibly remained too sore a memory for him. Instead, it seems he remained at home and abandoned Dundee for Strathmore as soon as the royal train puffed southwards. One report suggested he had taken a stubborn wee huff . . .

'We were informed by this neglected son of genius he modestly remained in obscurity all the while the royal train stopped at the station, lest it should be reported that he wished to thrust himself a second time under the notice of royalty. Of course, Mr McGonagall added, had Her Majesty sent a deputation asking an interview, as a willing and obedient subject, he would have felt bound to comply. But alas! The royal summons did not come, and Mr McGonagall, wearied hoping against hope, resolved to set out in quest of fresh fields and pastures new.'[25]

McGonagall fails to mention the 1879 expedition in his autobiographies. He did, however, provide a contemporary interview in which his trek was described as a 'holiday tour'. With a nod to the recent court case, the report noted: 'Times of late have been hard and money scarce with the "Weaver Poet" and that he had hence resolved to give a series of entertainments, consisting of readings of his own works, varied with selections from the other great poets.' As to the choice of destination, it was possibly fresh in the weaver poet's mind that the Theatre Royal's touring company had made profitable visits to Blairgowrie and Coupar Angus over the previous two years.[26]

McGonagall's journey was again fruitless. He arrived at Coupar Angus late on a Saturday, drenched by a downpour and with hardly a penny in his pocket. His attempt to secure a venue from which his 'entertainment' could be placed before unwitting villagers proved a failure. So he trudged on through rain and mud until he came to Burrelton, arriving too late in the day to arrange a performance. However, in the midst of his perplexity, 'a simple, kind-hearted country woman, who had admired the poet's effusions in the *Weekly News*, took pity on the forlorn stranger and entertained him most hospitably until Monday morning.'

In Burrelton he secured Robbie Fenwick's smiddy for the first performance of the Perthshire tour. Here, on the Monday evening, 'a goodly number of the rustics' assembled to hear him, but most were village youths bent on having a good time. When a window was smashed the owner appeared and evicted the would-be performer. To quote McGonagall: 'The people just came to make fun of me, and they gave me nothing.'

With a heavy heart and a lighter purse McGonagall took to the road again the next morning. Reaching Perth, he ran into some Dundee acquaintances who gave him money which enabled his return to Dundee, probably by train. He told them: 'Here I am without a farthing in the world, and I know not what to do. I was indebted for my breakfast this morning to a gentleman who had seen me play Othello in the Dundee Music Hall. It is time, I think, that I should be recognised; and indeed, it cannot come too soon, considering my own condition and the circumstances of my family.' But, he added in a more hopeful vein, 'My time will come yet; I will never despair.'[27]

So ended another painful offering of his work to the rural public. Given his reception in country areas, McGonagall was probably wise not to neglect his adopted town, even if he suspected Dundee was not the most hospitable location in which to unleash his genius. For most of his poetic period, in fact, Dundee provided both the inspiration and the meagre profits from sales required to stave off starvation.

William McGonagall's Dundee debut as a performance poet took place in the Cutlers' Hall, Murraygate one week after his holiday tour. Unusually, the event was announced on the front page of the *Advertiser*, squeezed between adverts for a waxworks and an offer to buy shares from Milne's Solicitors of Reform Street. It read: 'Poet McGonagall will give an Entertainment in the Cutlers' Hall, on Friday Evening, July the 4th, consisting of readings from his own Productions; also Shakespeare, Campbell and Mrs Hemans. Doors open at Seven o'clock to Commence at Eight. Admission – Front Seats 6d, Back Seats 3d each.'

Apparently McGonagall stood at the door and welcomed each customer with a shake of the hand. A bumper house was duly obtained, reported the journalist despatched by the *Weekly News* to the event. Inside, 'he produced from his coat pocket a written programme, which he handed to the chairman'. The only surviving hand-written programme from a McGonagall entertainment – now part of the McGonagall Collection – is probably this one held by McGonagall in the Cutlers' Hall in July 1879. Though undated, the nine items listed on this surviving manuscript were in McGonagall's repertoire that night, and none of his own works on the document post-date 1879 in composition. Thus he gave his audience a selection which included 'The Rattling Boy', Hamlet's soliloquy on death, 'Lord Ullin's Daughter', a scene from Macbeth and 'The Bonnie Broon Hair'd Lass o' Dundee'.

The Dundee audience was more than happy to join in, interrupting McGonagall with loud questioning and a running commentary. McGonagall treated all these untimely diversions with silent contempt and with the gravity of a philosopher. When he brought from his wallet a manuscript copy of Tay Bridge, his reading of it was met with 'tremendous cheering, waving of hats and repeated calls to give it over again'. This debut Dundee performance ended with the audience crowding the platform in its enthusiasm. But the poet, in all modesty, shut himself up in his dressing room.[28]

As he became better known, it was inevitable that William McGonagall would be baited wherever he attempted to purvey this peculiar brand of entertainment. On the other hand, his eccentricity and rising public profile invariably led to heavily-subscribed performances. It was a Catch-22 – if he raised his head above the parapet, his kids could eat. An evening show in the 'village' of Lochee in late 1879 provides an agonising account of a typical day at McGonagall's 'office' . . .

The Weavers Hall in the Irish-controlled enclave was filled by a large and noisy audience, mostly lads out for a laugh. Many had come from Dundee, reported the journalist covering the event. McGonagall appeared on an improvised stage and, amidst the cheers and laughter of the audience, made his bow to them. The first item on the programme was 'The Rattling Boy from Dublin'. McGonagall explained that it should be executed in character, and thus wore his hat and carried a large umbrella. At the end of each verse the audience joined in the chorus and kept time by tramping with their feet. Several readings and recitations were then delivered from the poet's own works, all received in the usual uproarious manner . . .

'Every now and then, and particularly when the performer was uttering some choice bit and giving it the "sweetness long drawn out" the audience would burst out with the chorus of "John Brown's Body" in a manner that completely "shut up" the gifted artiste. Notwithstanding all this "irreverence" on the part of the audience, the bard remained perfectly calm, and seemingly not in the least disturbed by the riotous proceedings around him. And whenever the noise ceased he resumed where he left off with the greatest nonchalance.'[29]

Thus, McGonagall's insensitivity to implicit insult is pinpointed early in his poetic career. He is deaf to the ridicule flying his way and oblivious to what others would view as a public put-down. Spence recalled an occasion when McGonagall 'performed his "Battle of Tel-el-Kebir" at a smoking-concert to the accompaniment of outbursts of ribald laughter, which seemed to pass him as idle as the wind.' That he appeared insensible to abuse and had an extraordinary ability to turn the other cheek was a fascinating character trait that developed in the years ahead as the lampoonings, hoaxes and public peltings became commonplace.

Matters in Lochee soon got out of hand. McGonagall had not got far with 'Hamlet' when a number of the audience invaded the platform to offer to play Shakespeare's famed ghost. Without warning, the men forcibly seized the poet and notwithstanding his frantic struggles carried him shoulder high to the street. Survival instinct outweighed the poet's usual indignance. McGonagall took shelter in a shop front until the mob melted away. Yet not for the first time, the audience, if not the evening's star performer, felt the proceedings had gone well. 'The general impression seemed to be that they never in their lives were so thoroughly entertained as they were by the celebrated McGonagall.'[30]

It will be assessed later why a weaver poet would willingly confront ridicule and risk. What is evident is that barely two years after his first poem to George Gilfillan, McGonagall had a dyed-in-the-wool following – the fun-seeking Dundonians who had walked up the brae to Lochee for this performance, for instance. He also had audience participation of a kind most performers could only dream of. But a feeling was growing that the rhymester they laughed at was perhaps beginning to have the last laugh.

And so the 1870s drew to a close. William McGonagall's life had been transformed by his self-proclaimed awakening as a poet, the challenge of making a living from his new 'trade' and his relentless determination to make a go of it with the courage and tenacity he would require in abundance as the new decade beckoned.

There is a remarkable facet to this period. Prior to 1877 there is just one written record of McGonagall's inner thoughts in his first half-century of life – a backslapping letter to the *Dundee Advertiser* praising a comrade tragedian. After that date, there is no end to them.

Almost overnight, we have William McGonagall's words to test against what he told us of his life.

FOUR

POET LAUREATE OF PATON'S LANE

WILLIAM MCGONAGALL grew alarmingly in self-image after his decision in 1877 to compose poetry. Within a year he had despatched verses to Buckingham Palace, published his first twopenny pamphlet and passed word around that the Victorian equivalent of a CBE was expected any day at Paton's Lane. He had hoped by then to be on speaking terms with the queen herself. Alas, his adventure to Balmoral had not had the desired outcome. But his princely address to the new Tay Bridge had been generally welcomed – though it had not generated the thunderous acclaim recorded in boastful autobiographies. Like most of McGonagall's output, it had been met with a nod and a wink by some, indulgent smiles by others – and legitimate alarm by brother poets.

Come 1879 the long-coated, priest-hatted McGonagall was a familiar fixture on Dundee's streets. He shuffled up and down the Perth Road with the first of his poetry pamphlets and, despite a disappointing trek to the Strathmore towns, he was able to publish that year his second collection of verse, *The Complete Poetical Works of William McGonagall, Dundee* containing 17 poems over 16 pages, probably his entire yield to that point.

As Dundee went about its business William McGonagall had transformed into a performance poet, and probably neither he nor anyone else could say whether it was through literary ambition or to avoid the poorhouse. By 1879, his poetry had won admirers and found buyers. But it was read and bought because of its limitations, not its quality. It was his developing notoriety for dysfunctional rhyme and dreadful scansion that put him on Dundee's desired reading list that year.

Yet scrutiny of William McGonagall's early output highlights abilities that cast doubt on the absence of schooling claimed in his memoirs and the put-downs by critical commentators in the century since. While the modern world clasps McGonagall to its bosom as the greatest bad verse writer of his or any age, it is not difficult to discover surprisingly convincing evidence that he was not the writing novice so often portrayed. Forgive the plagiarised rhyme, but there was more to his vocabulary than 'most beautiful to be seen' and 'near by Dundee and the Magdalen Green'.

Despite the chaotic composition, McGonagall hardly ever spoke or wrote prose in the manner of an educationally disadvantaged peripatetic weaver. His contributions to newspapers, petitions to parliament and begging letters seldom display word poverty. He held his own in conversation and debate. He could chastise the *Weekly News* for refusing to print his work, and order and express thoughts in a rational if modest manner in correspondence with acquaintances. Lewis Spence recalled how the poet could discuss the merits of writers, how he talked like a gentleman and knew entire Shakespeare plays by heart. Spence added ruefully: 'Whenever he left me after a long and interesting conversation, I could always rely on finding myself half a crown the poorer.' McGonagall published a short but fluent treatise on Shakespeare and quoted Byron in a letter to his grocer. He advertised to visit the homes of Dundee's middle-class 'gentlemen' to deliver private recitations on the great poets. He also added boldly at the end of another pamphlet: 'Parties desirous of being taught Elocution may be waited on at their own residences. Wm McGonagall. Fees moderate.' And it hardly exhibits a lack of literary confidence to be able to instruct his readers, 'Every gentleman's library is considered to be incomplete if it does not contain a volume of Shakespeare.'

These are not the words, intentions or ambitions of a man unable to write a rhyming couplet without taking a new page for its second line. They instead counter claims that McGonagall was poorly educated, provincial and capable of only primitive writing. He was much more than a writer 'so bad that he was good' and, actually, must have been looked upon as an intellectual by workplace and domestic peers. In short, McGonagall possessed perfectly adequate language skills in a time of limited literacy, remembering that even on his death certificate in 1902 his name was incorrectly spelled and his wife of 56 years could only 'sign' it with a cross.

Yet, in accepting that he possessed reasonable language skills we face the complex and literarily-dangerous question of whether William McGonagall purposefully opened himself to ridicule after his poetical awakening to cash in on his notoriety. This will be an important focus of a later chapter.

The puzzle is that contributions despatched from Paton's Lane to the *Weekly News* between 1877 and 1879 were often carelessly written, badly punctuated and grammatically wayward. The paper frequently made fun of McGonagall's curious way with words, often preceding them with replies, rejoinders and comments such as 'preserving as usual his ornate spelling and grammar' and 'violating all the rules of syntax'. When he unintentionally headed one letter '1878' instead of '1879', the paper ripped into him again . . .

'We have received a contribution from Mr McGonagall entitled "Song: The Flower Called Forget-me-not", accompanying which is a letter dated March 5, 1878, which, from some unaccountable delay, somewhere has required a whole year to reach our hands.' The paper revisited the subject the following week, causing McGonagall in a further letter to angrily promise he would never date anything again. The *Weekly News* had no hesitation in embarrassing its contributor, emphasising its bullying bent by offering readers the opening lines of the new poem exactly as received . . .

> A gallant knight and his betroth'd bride,
> Was walking one day by river-side:
> The talked of love and the talked of war
> And how very follish lovers are.[1]

By the time 'Forget-Me-Not' appeared in *Poetic Gems* in 1890, 'was' had become 'were', 'the' was 'they', the couple walked 'by a river side' and 'follish' was no longer foolishly spelt. Such spelling aberrations and compositional rule-breaking detracted from McGonagall's genuine accomplishments: a self-taught knowledge of literature and drama; an extraordinary ability to perform with self-belief; the marshalling of facts and the ability to commentate on and communicate to the world around him. In fact, William McGonagall's qualities have been routinely obscured by the impression that all he did was write bad poetry.

But when the Paton's Lane larder was emptier longer than usual, a darker side to McGonagall's character materialised through his poetic calling. His attempted coercion of the *Weekly News* to highlight his own accomplishments in 'To A Local Star' had come to nothing in 1877. He schemed a similar underhand ruse with the *People's Journal* early in 1879. The paper received a letter from 'An Admirer of True Genius' stating: 'With regard to the opening of the Tay Bridge, has our friend the Poet Laureate William McGonagall been invited? If not the sooner the better so that he can be prepared for the occasion, and not be receiving an invitation when it is too late. He has written a "Poetic Address to Prince Leopold" which he intends to publish on that occasion, and which excels any of his previous efforts. He is to deliver it as well as the "Tay Bridge" poem in Highland costume. Unless the "Poet" is invited it will be considered by his admirers to be discourteous and ungrateful.' The paper was not taken in and McGonagall was not invited.

McGonagall's devious side was also on display when he wrote upfront to the *Weekly News* in the spring of 1879: 'At the request of several of my admirers I have been requested to get this new song published in the *Weekly News* of Saturday the 15th of March 1878 [1879], because they intend to buy a copy of the *Weekly News* if it is published.' The correspondence editor was not so easily intimidated and responded to the poet's clumsy attempt at self-promotion with a defensible dollop of sarcasm: 'We regret very much to have to disappoint our Paton's Lane poet and his admirers, and we mourn over the fillip which our circulation might have received on the date named.'[2]

McGonagall persisted, sending the editor his 'Convict's Return to Scotland' in April 1879, of which three verses saw the light of day. His work was also supported in the paper's columns by various amateur rhymesters. One contribution, in July 1879, proclaimed his genius over no fewer than 60 lines, this extract typical of its softly sardonic approach . . .

McGonegal! McGonegal!
Illustrious royal poet!
To your footstool I humbly crawl,
In hopes to get below it,
To see your Muse's fancy shawl,
When o'er your head she'll throw it.
McGonegal! McGonegal!
Great honours lie before you;
Display your powers and raise a squall,
That Scotland may adore you;
Our Sovereign then may you install,
And waive her laurels o'er you.

Another 'tribute' that month sang of his 'wondrous works' while gently reminding McGonagall it was his contrary style that made his verse uniquely popular. But other submissions suggested the poet had been exposed too often in the paper's spotlight. One epistle from an anonymous 'friend' who had known McGonagall in pre-poet days offered some frank advice: 'Your estimation of your worth has made your brain go giddy.'[3]

Pro and anti public outpourings earned McGonagall celebrity status – but he was convinced his poetry deserved a wider audience. In the autumn of 1879 he embarked on a reading tour of Fife. We know of this journey from a more authoritative source than his hazy memories many years distant. On his return, McGonagall described his adventure for the *People's Journal*. Given the immediacy of the report, there is no reason to delve into the veracity of the poet's story on this occasion.[4]

The tour of Fife was recounted by McGonagall himself in an unconvincing, self-effacing third-person narrative. He described how he left Dundee by steamer on Monday, 20 September and landed at Newburgh. He could find no accommodation there as the lodging houses were filled with men from a travelling menagerie, so he crossed the border into Perthshire and paid fivepence for bed and breakfast at Abernethy. There is no comment on the physical hardship of these miles of walking. Perhaps he enjoyed better weather this time. When he inquired if a hall might be available for him to stage his 'matchless entertainment', his landlady told him bluntly it would be 'very foolish for the poet to try to give an entertainment there'. The propensity for public disorder had been firmly pinned to his reputation.

So McGonagall left Abernethy and walked across another county border to Kinross-shire, where he obtained lodgings for his second night away from Jean. He had better luck securing a venue in Kinross, booking the Templars' Hall for a shilling. The rest of McGonagall's day was spent promoting the entertainment planned for Wednesday, for which the townsfolk would be invited to pay twopence for adults and a penny for children. The show was to begin at 8 o'clock and was to be announced by the town's bellman, 'for which he would charge the poet 1/- for doing so'.

Come Wednesday the bard discovered the bellman double-booked and departed for another job in neighbouring Milnathort. McGonagall admitted he was 'discontented' with the situation and offered *Journal* readers the comment: 'Therefore the poet's entertainment proved abortive all through the bellman of Kinross.' His time in the town was not entirely ill spent, however. He had strolled to the shores of Loch Leven, where the views towards Queen Mary's castle inspired one of the earliest 'Beautiful' poems. Verses one and two . . .

Beautiful Loch Leven, near by Kinross,
For a good day's fishing the angler is seldom at a loss,
For the loch it abounds with pike and trout,
Which can be had for the catching without any doubt;
And the scenery around it is most beautiful to be seen,
Especially the Castle, wherein was imprisoned Scotland's
    ill-starred Queen.

Then there's the lofty Lomond Hills on the eastern side,
And the loch is long, very deep, and wide;
Then on the southern side there's Benarty's rugged hills,
And from the tops can be seen the village of Kinross with its
    spinning mills.

On day four of his journey, the Thursday, McGonagall walked the eight miles from Kinross to Cowdenbeath and arrived there, 'with one shilling in his pocket and a little dispirited, owing to the failure of his entertainment in the village of Kinross.' His thoughts were absorbed again with finding a hall suitable for a recital. He sounded out and befriended Charles Baxter, known as 'the poet of Cowdenbeath.' He was given a decent dinner, but was disillusioned once more to hear the only available hall was priced beyond his pocket at ten shillings and sixpence. Next stop, on the Saturday, was Lochgelly. He reached the mining community with high hopes – Saturday being pay day – and sought out the Chief Templar, a Mr McConnell, thinking he would help him get a venue. McGonagall was apparently a member of the Independent Order of Good Templars, a temperance organisation introduced to Britain from America a decade earlier. The order had a presence of abstaining members in Dundee from 1870 and 12 lodges established in the town by 1876. After he told McConnell he was Poet McGonagall from Dundee, and how he was a 'good' templar, McGonagall secured the Co-operative Hall and was soon publicising the evening's entertainment, which was to be reduced in admission price to one penny.

Readers, then and now, will be expecting another failure – and so it turned out. The audience comprised only two boys. McGonagall noted disconsolately: 'So William returned the boys their pence again and locked the hall rather downhearted, owing to the second failure he had met with. Then when Mr McConnell heard of the failure William had met with he gave him a sixpence, also Alexander Skene and David Anderson, also James Greenhill, which helped to keep poor William McGonagall living until Monday.'

McGonagall's tour of Fife was not entirely a disaster. At Crossford, just outside Dunfermline, he succeeded in hiring a blacksmith's smiddy for a recital. Although the audience was small, mostly comprising boys again, he instructed the proprietor to take the money at the door 'while he was delighting his little audience with his matchless entertainment'. His takings amounted to two shillings and 10 pence and 'he returned his most sincere thanks to God and his little audience for their kind support, for which McGonagall received a hearty vote of thanks'.

With the deafening plaudits of Crossford fading behind him, he returned to spend the night at lodgings in Dunfermline before applying himself the next day to the familiar routine of finding the evening's venue. When there was no luck at Limekilns he applied to the Worthy Chief Templar at Dunfermline, 'who received him in a very unchristian manner by telling him he could not assist him, and besides telling William his poetry was very bad; so William told him it was so very bad that Her Majesty had thanked him for what he had condemned, and left him, telling him at the same time he was an enemy and he would report him.' McGonagall did not take kindly to criticism of his poetry.

On Thursday, 2 October, McGonagall walked wearily north-wards, his tour of the Kingdom over. It had not after all provided his pathway to fame and fortune and he must have been desperately disappointed to return to Jean without the hoped-for stories of sold-out success and accumulating profits.

By mid-October, however, he was sufficiently revived to appear at Blair's Hall in the Overgate in a programme the *Courier* warned would contain songs, readings and recitations from his own and other works. From his stance atop a wooden table, 'which stood against the wall as an apology for a platform', McGonagall deliv-ered a new poem dedicated to the Reverend David Macrae, who had taken over from George Gilfillan as Dundee's champion of religious liberty. Gilfillan had nominated Macrae as his successor in 1879, and it was Macrae, along with 600 parishioners, who built on Gilfillan's memory and legacy to found the Gilfillan Memorial Church in Whitehall Crescent that year, where McGonagall even-tually worshipped. With Macrae devoting many sermons to the drunkenness and crime he witnessed in the slum city centre, he found a ready listener in arch-abstainer McGonagall.[5]

'A Tribute to the Rev Mr Macrae' – first and last verses below – has remained unpublished since October 1879 . . .

All hail to the Rev Mr Macrae,
He is an elegant preacher, I venture to say,
And his religious views I appreciate right well,
Because he does not believe in the eternal punishment of hell.

Rev Mr Macrae, I must conclude my lay,
And tell the world fearlessly, without the least dismay,
That you are the Second Gilfillan of the present day,
And in conclusion I must say, Dundonians, remember,
He will preach his Induction Sermon on the First Sabbath
  of November,
In the year of our Lord 1879,
Which will be remembered for a very long time.

At Blair's Hall our hero coped expertly with audience mockery and read on without paying the least attention to interruptions until his voice was drowned out by a lusty chorus of 'tra-la-la'. Such disturbances usually abated long enough for McGonagall to recite an item or two from his repertoire and on this occasion he reminded the Overgaters that the Macrae poem was available as a penny broadside. And so the programme progressed with both performer and audience well aware of the evening's formula and separate role-playing.[6]

Thus, by the autumn of 1879 McGonagall was printing his poems in the form of penny sheets – the Macrae verse the earliest of the printed tracts known to survive. These were inscribed rather daringly with the 'VR' royal cipher and proudly proclaimed him 'Poet and Tragedian to the Queen'. The first broadsides, or broadsheets, were printed on A5-width paper. Later they were produced on larger, better-quality sheets. Almost all broadsides are printed in black ink and on rare occasions coloured paper was used. The broadsides normally contained one poem or, from 1894, occasionally two. McGonagall provided his address on them – Paton's Lane, Step Row or, latterly, various lodgings in Edinburgh. None show printer's details, though David Winter & Son of Dundee certainly printed many of them. The early poems are bordered with flowers or other decorative devices. Later verses are enclosed by plain black rules, sympathetically widened for funereal tributes. From the mid-1880s most display quotations from replies to sample poems sent to VIPs. Apart from early examples, broadsides usually list a date of composition – and these are just as often incorrect. For example, 'Jottings of London' is said on a penny tract to have been composed in 1886, six years after it was written. On the other hand, his tribute to the Kessock ferry sinking in March 1894 was dated the month before the tragedy occurred. Occasionally McGonagall notes 'special' printings, such as 'Published by Particular Desire', or endorsements such as 'By Special Permission' and 'Dedicated to . . .' Once throwaway items, these ephemeral poetry sheets are today rare and desirable.

Mass production, the poet presumed, was the means to earn income from his efforts as opposed to submitting unpaid work to newspapers. Broadsides gradually became vital to his family's survival to the extent that his poetry was composed with sales in mind. For example, the little-known poem 'The Horse Parade: or Demonstration in Respect of the Royal Wedding', a verse written to commemorate celebrations for the marriage of the Duke of York and Princess Mary in 1893, unashamedly courted customers. Mr Smail's premises in Reform Street are praised in the fourth verse, the flags of James Spence's City Wares in the fifth, the Bank of Scotland in the seventh, A.C. Lamb's hotel in the eighth, Melville's shop in the High Street in the ninth and Messrs Philip, drapers, and Mr Hynd, clothier, in the twelfth. The royal newlyweds hardly get a mention – but the foundation for sales across the city is established. Another unpublished poem, 'The Royal Visit of the Princess Louise and the Marquis of Lorne' (1892), performs a similar promotional function . . .

> Mr Hurrie's buildings were ablaze with flags and draperies,
> Which did the sight-seers greatly please.
> And on the opposite side, and facing Whitehall Street,
> Mr Melville's establishment was very neat.

He increasingly peddled such publications, folded over his arm, and made a shilling here and there. Lowden Macartney, who knew McGonagall in Dundee, noted: 'He moved about the streets, from shop to shop, from office to office and from house to house in the residential parts of the town, vending his broadsides.' Isabella Carrie, best known for her suffragette activities during the 'Winston Churchill' by-election in Dundee in 1908, recalled seeing him walking through the town, 'selling his poetry to anyone who was interested'. Looking back for an interview in 1980, shortly before her hundred and second birthday, she remembered Princes Street was one of the poet's regular sales pitches and that 'everybody knew who he was'.[7]

Most of William McGonagall's printed poems were priced at one penny. Later, when he lived in Edinburgh, he was advised to double the price if the sheet carried his autograph. Cottoning on to a good thing, the cover price soon became twopence. Selling broadsides on the streets – or perhaps it was his persistent sales technique – occasionally became dangerous to life and limb. Such was the case on a visit to Laskie's grocery at 35 Commercial Street, Dundee. What happened next is conveyed in an unpublished letter from Paton's Lane . . .

Mr Laskie, my dear Friend . . . I must tell you so far you have always treated me in a friendly way – but I am sorry to inform you that I received rather foul treatment in your office in Commercial Street yesterday afternoon when I called to sell my latest effusion, which is enclosed. Well, sir, my poem was severely criticised by the eldest of the two young men that were there. He condemned it in the reading of the first two lines, then the youngest one called me an Ass and said my poem was very ungrammatical and mocked me about going to see the Queen and so forth, until I felt very aggravated.

Then the boy asked me for my licence, and I told the eldest lad that resides in the Lane near me, that VR was my authority for selling my work and that he couldn't hinder me. Then he threatened me with the police and I told him to call them, but he refused to do so, then he told me to walk outside, then I told him to come outside and I would speak to him, and he did so. So I asked him if he was a man, but my dear sir I received no answer, but according to Lord Byron, he knows no law of charity that throws a barb to wound another – this is the truth my dear friend, that I to you have penned, on my soul and conscience, and my dear sir, let me tell you here I shall never enter your office until the same two men apologises to me for what they have done, believe me yours, William McGonagall, poet.[8]

We can only wonder if this invitation to 'step outside' ever took place beyond Mr McGonagall's imagination. Doubtless he had many refusals for his penny tracts, though there is no indication that he employed strong-arm selling tactics. He seldom lacked in courage when facing larger audiences, however, and this personal account of an altercation with baiting young men is all too believable.

Confronting physical danger was often the price of his poetry. McGonagall records in two autobiographies being assaulted after a performance in an Angus village. In one he locates the incident in Liff, in the other Fowlis, neighbouring villages about eight miles north of Dundee. McGonagall did not provide a date for the adventure. He was active in the area at the end of 1879, however, seeking venues for his 'entertainment'. On 12 December 1879 Auchterhouse School Board, which administered the Sidlaw village school about three miles from Liff, received an application from McGonagall for the use of the school for a public performance. The minutes of the board show that his application was refused, with no reason given.[9]

In *Reminiscences* in 1891 McGonagall states that he organised a performance in the Liff blacksmith's shop, advertised around the village by foot and mouth – admission adults twopence, children a penny – and drew 'a very respectable' audience. The rural patrons gave him 'a very hearty welcome', and he recalled his share of the proceeds came to four shillings and ninepence, 'which I was very thankful for'. Afterwards, as he drew near to Liff school, he heard:

. . . the pattering of men's feet behind me, and an undefinable fear seized me. Having my umbrella with me I grasped it firmly, and waited patiently until three men came up to me near Liff school-room, and there they stood glaring at me as the serpent does before it leaps upon its prey. Then the man in the centre of the three whispered to his companions, and, as he

did so, he threw out both his hands, with the intention, no
doubt, of knocking me down, and, with the assistance of the
other two, robbing me of the money I had realised from my
entertainment. But when he threw out his arms to catch hold
of me, as quick as lightning I struck him a blow across the legs
with my umbrella, which made him leap backwards, and
immediately they then went away round to the front of the
school-master's house, close by the road side, and planted
themselves there. And when I saw they were waiting for me to
come that way as they expected, I resolved to make my escape
from them the best way I could . . . The night being dark, the
idea struck me if I could manage to get away from their sight
they would give up the chase and go home to Lochee without
satisfying their evil intentions!

McGonagall avoided 'being robbed, or perhaps murdered' by
returning to Dundee via Birkhill village and Camperdown woods:
'So, my dear readers, I arrived safe home, and thanked God for
delivering me from the hands of evil-doers, as He has done on all
occasions.'

The same drama in his 1901 autobiography takes place in the
neighbouring village of Fowlis. It follows a different pathway,
introducing a village policeman as an acquaintance and enhancing
the bravery of the intended victim as he makes his way home via
what is now Camperdown Country Park. Moreover, in this version
he diplomatically avoids besmirching the name of Lochee by not
mentioning where his would-be assailants live. He revamps the
story, substituting Fowlis for Liff, and this time bravely swats the
ringleader with a walking stick . . . 'my good oaken cudgel came
across his body with full force' . . . and sends the trio packing.

In this version McGonagall reaches Paton's Lane just before
midnight and relates the events to his family. 'They said that I
should thank God that had saved me from being murdered.
However, the four shillings and ninepence I fetched home with
me – that I had gained from my entertainment – I gave all to my
wife, and she was very thankful to get it, because the wolf was at the
door, and it had come very opportune.'

On his return from Fife on 2 October 1879 McGonagall had crossed the Tay Bridge for the first and last time by rail, reaching landfall at the foot of Paton's Lane, where the aproned Jean waited for news of his rambles. As he passed over the world's longest bridge he must have reflected upon the poem which had contributed so much to his celebrity . . .

> Beautiful Railway Bridge of the Silvery Tay!
> With your numerous arches and pillars in so grand array,
> And your central girders, which seem to the eye
> To be almost towering to the sky.
> The greatest wonder of the day,
> And a great beautification to the River Tay,
> Most beautiful to be seen,
> Near by Dundee and the Magdalen Green.

Two months later the bridge fell down in a howling gale. The *Evening Telegraph* gloomily captured the event so deeply felt in Dundee and beyond – 'Appalling Tragedy in Dundee; Tay Bridge Wrecked; Train Thrown into River; Many Passengers Drowned; Intense Excitement in Dundee.'[10] If the headlines offered a brilliant lesson in tight copy for journalists, it also conveyed the shock and magnitude of the collapse of a structure that was the pride of Dundee. As the town wakened to the terrible tragedy, many thoughts must have returned to McGonagall's eerie sixth stanza and its foretelling of doom and disaster . . .

> Beautiful Railway Bridge of the Silvery Tay!
> I hope that God will protect all passengers
> By night and by day,
> And that no accident will befall them while crossing
> The Bridge of the Silvery Tay,
> For that would be most awful to be seen
> Near by Dundee and the Magdalen Green.

McGonagall was thus wedded to the new bridge and its destiny through his poem. But while his 1877 address hinted at events to come, his epic 'Tay Bridge Disaster' of January 1880, which ranks among his most enduring and popular poems today, is said not to have been an eye-witness account. Verse eight . . .

> It must have been an awful sight,
> To witness in the dusky moonlight,
> While the Storm Fiend did laugh, and angry did bray,
> Along the Railway Bridge of the Silv'ry Tay,
> Oh! ill-fated Bridge of the Silv'ry Tay . . .

Using this stanza as evidence, Phillips (1971) expressed surprise that McGonagall did not provide an on-the-spot report of the tragedy. 'Surely, having written so much about catastrophes of the past, he would have been drawn to the dreadful one at the foot of the street as soon as he learned of it.' Phillips claimed it was a 'tremendous opportunity' which the poet 'did not care to, or perhaps could not, take'.[11]

On the contrary, McGonagall must have composed his tribute very soon after the extent of the tragedy was made known to the public, as it appeared in a newspaper just 10 days after the event. Meanwhile, the time-lagged offerings of rivals continued to flood local papers for several weeks and drew this callous comment from the *People's Journal*: 'We continue to receive swathes of verses on the Tay Bridge catastrophe. We could not make use of the tenth part of it . . . but truth constrains us to say that the most of it is sheer rubbish.'[12] By 1879, in any case, McGonagall had not developed his poetic passion for catastrophes. His early effusions comprised aesthetic comment on locations around Dundee, toadying tributes to prominent individuals or historical narratives. The dozen poems on disasters and the dozen on shipwrecks remained on the horizon.

Instead, the magnitude of the disaster must have impacted on McGonagall's sensibilities and probably prevented him from dwelling on the bloody horrors of the tragedy in his eight-stanza tribute. He lived within yards of where bodies were being washed up, and the harrowing aftermath of the collapse must have been all too visible to his family and neighbours. Proud as he was to be dubbed Poet Laureate of the Tay Bridge, McGonagall was probably swamped by the outpouring of emotion that swept the city and loitered among the thousands of sombre witnesses along the estuary questioning aspects of the bridge's construction and filled with self-doubt over Victorian progressivism. He was a compassionate man and the sudden death of so many innocents must have caused him to pause momentarily before taking his pen and writing his unwieldy tribute to the stricken bridge. Indeed, McGonagall gathered his thoughts on the catastrophe from the vantage point of the Law, sitting in silence, looking down on the awful gap in the crossing where the bridge had been . . .

> Beautiful Railway Bridge of the Silv'ry Tay!
> Alas! I am very sorry to say
> That ninety lives have been taken away
> On the last Sabbath day of 1879,
> Which will be remember'd for a very long time.

> 'Twas about seven o'clock at night,
> And the wind it blew with all its might,
> And the rain came pouring down,
> And the dark clouds seem'd to frown,
> And the Demon of the air seem'd to say –
> 'I'll blow down the Bridge of Tay.'

McGonagall also had the courage to record his thoughts on why the bridge toppled – a question that exercised great minds over the subsequent century. The problem, he disclosed in the dramatic final stanza of 'The Tay Bridge Disaster', was the fragility of its central pillars . . .

> Oh! ill-fated Bridge of the Silv'ry Tay,
> I must now conclude my lay
> By telling the world fearlessly and without the least dismay,
> That your central girders would not have given way,
> Had they been supported on each side with buttresses,
> For the stronger we our houses do build,
> The less chance we have of being killed.

McGonagall's editorial pen swept over this controversial verse later in life. After the fourth line of the poem's appearance in *Poetic Gems* (1890) he added, 'At least many sensible men do say', and after the sixth, 'At least many sensible men confesses'. Thus, mindful of consequences, he eventually weakened the 'fearless' viewpoint expressed in January 1880 by implying a decade later that he was repeating only what the majority were saying about the bridge collapse at the time. He was neither the first writer, nor the last, to douse the passion of a first draft, though it is disappointing that only his diluted version appears in print today.

A misadventurous tour then tragedy so close to home might have inhibited or deterred a lesser man. Not McGonagall. Undaunted by his experiences in Fife and Angus, McGonagall struck out westwards to Perthshire in March 1880 in order, as the local newspaper put it, 'to instil into the dull brains of clowns and clodhoppers in the rural districts around Dundee a due appreciation of his genius'. He performed twice in a back room of a Perth pub, apparently without mishap, and was rewarded with four shillings for his trouble – close to half a weaver's weekly wage. In Perth he penned the eulogistic 'City of Perth', later telling a reporter that it was composed on the North Inch during a thunderstorm, inspiration perhaps flowing from the proximity of the park to his beloved silvery Tay. It opens . . .

> Beautiful and ancient city of Perth,
> One of the grandest upon the earth,
> With your stately mansions and streets so clean,
> And situated betwixt two Inches green,
> Which are most magnificent to be seen.

Sadly, McGonagall's Perthshire tour coincided with a local election – 'every schoolhouse, aye, and even the "smiddies" were closed against poor McGonagall.' He trekked westwards, reaching Stirling, where the last of his money was spent on food and lodgings. Next day he pestered the quartermaster at Stirling Castle to secure a reading room for an evening performance. He was given food and drink and was able to spend the day soaking up the sights of the historic city – his 'Stirling Castle' poem, published in broadsheet in 1892, was probably composed at this time. In the evening he entertained 20 soldiers in the castle barracks. He must have smiled contentedly as he turned for home next morning – a few pennies in his pocket and an army breakfast for ballast.

We know something of William McGonagall's inner thoughts at this time from an interview he gave four months after the Tay Bridge disaster. In April 1880, he took the ferry from Dundee to Newport for what was incorrectly described as the 'first professional visit of the Queen's Poet to Fife'. He had toured the Kingdom the previous year. As usual, his programme was to consist of his own compositions, some Shakespearean drama and a selection of other poets' works. The venue was the Free Church schoolroom in Newport and McGonagall was met by an audience of around 70. So far so good.

Prior to his appearance he was asked by a reporter if his poetry made money, as it was often said that poets were always poor and generally died in a garret. To this McGonagall answered with an ominous shake of his head, 'Ah, yes, like Burns I too have been often craved' – a term used for the knock of a factor looking for rent. Did he ever think of writing a tragedy with himself as the hero? 'No,' he answered, 'but I have all the tragic feelings within me.' What of those who expressed a preference for his own works, rather than Shakespeare's? 'Oh, yes,' was the reply, 'I always find that those who come to hear me do that.' With no outward hint of arrogance he added, 'You see I am much more versatile than Shakespeare.' Did it take someone with the gift of poetry long to compose an epic such as 'The Bridge of the Silvery Tay'? He was unable to say how long this great work had taken him, but, like the bridge itself, it had taken 'a long time'. He was developing skills for dealing diplomatically with a prying Press. He was already a master at keeping a straight face.[13]

McGonagall began the Newport entertainment with the tent scene from 'Richard III'. As usual, his tragedian recital was drowned out by the 'whistles and the tumult of the enraptured voices'. He reappeared with his shillelagh to give his fans 'The Rattling Boy' and then 'Bannockburn'. These became McGonagall's favourite rants and his printed handbills usually mentioned 'Bannockburn' in their come-all-ye appeal to dithering patrons. A Dundee Music Hall poster surviving from 1880, for instance, announced: 'For This Night Only, Wm McGonagall (The Royal Poet) will recite his Original Poem, Bruce of Bannockburn.' Another, detailing a programme at the Comedy Theatre, Seagate, proclaimed: '. . . Mr McGonagall, Dundee's Favourite Poet, who will recite Bannockburn in Full Highland Costume'. The irony is that both the *Journal* and the *Weekly News* rejected 'Bannockburn' in 1877, the former stating, 'The lines on Bannockburn are scarcely worthy of the theme', while the latter had replied to the author, 'Bruce at Bannockburn is declined with thanks.'[14]

McGonagall's Bannockburn at Newport was amply described by the journalist eye-witness: 'Slowly he emerged from the wing and in a thoughtful mood stepped on the platform. Immediately his left leg flew forward in advance of all other limbs, as if it smelt the battle afar, and was eager for the fray. Then suddenly his right hand was raised in the attitude of a pump handle, his mouth was formed into a circle as round as a cannon's mouth, and with the ardour of a warrior who fights for glory, he plunged into a description of that terrible day in June when Bannockburn was lost and won.'

Newport was a landmark performance, but probably not in the way McGonagall intended. The advertising literature distributed prior to his performance had invited the 'nobility, clergy and gentry of Newport' to his evening appearance. Thus, for the first time, the poet attempted to attract the town's elite as his audience, when previously working men anticipating laughs at his expense and ridiculing youngsters had bought tickets for his shows.

McGonagall's determination not so much to climb the social ladder as to reach out to those at the top emerges repeatedly as his wonderful career unfolds. Sycophantic odes and addresses glorify local manufacturers, clergymen, self-sacrificing philanthropists and the ruling classes of royalty, generals and powerful politicians. It was to these well-to-do and influential citizens that his ballads of tribute were despatched in the vain hope of an extolling return epistle. Lowden Macartney, who sold McGonagall's penny sheets from the Poet's Box in the Overgate, recalled: 'No common person, no mere friend or acquaintance, could hope to receive his aid to immortality. Princes and Potentates, great Generals, members of the nobility, and eminent Divines – these and only these would he condescend to sing of when they died.'[15] McGonagall unswervingly regarded VIP flattery as a means of gaining endorsement or, in today's terms, a useful reference, that could lead through recognition to remuneration.

Cosseted within this hero worship was McGonagall's desire, of Dickensian proportions, to enlighten with culture the very social class to which he belonged. His emerging moralising ranged from the roiling habit of telling working folk what was good for them, to a reforming zeal to counter the satanic excesses of industrialisation. His most instructive moralising, though, was reserved for excessive drinkers and invariably couched in godly words. Typical are these lines from 'A Christmas Carol' . . .

> Therefore, good people, be warned in time,
> And on Christmas morn don't get drunk with wine,
> But praise God above on Christmas morn,
> Who sent His son to save us from hell and scorn.

And in 'The Demon Drink', written later in life, he was happy to round on anyone who succumbed to this destroyer of society. Alcohol excess, he warned readers, caused the mother to neglect her child, led to wife-beating, wages spent foolishly, the sinking of families into crime and, perish the thought, aspirations for Scottish independence. And so, he warned of the urgent need for its abolition . . .

> Therefore, brothers and sisters, pause and think,
> And try to abolish the foul fiend, Drink.
> Let such doctrine be taught in church and school,
> That the abolition of strong drink is the only Home Rule.

The Newport performance in April 1880 also brought the first printed description of McGonagall. It was as unflattering as the scrutiny of his poetry: 'We were somewhat disappointed with the personal appearance of the Poet. There was no evidence of a face "sicklied o'er with the pale cast of thought", no sad expressive eyes, and no dome'd forehead. His "crowning glory" consists of jet black hair, with two locks projecting slightly in front of his ears, and the remainder thrown behind, and terminating at the back of his head like the curls of a drake's tail.' This account is consistent with the first newspaper illustrations and cabinet photographs of the poet in the early 1890s.

Around five feet eight inches tall, and worryingly slim, McGonagall wore his dark hair long and swept back. He had a pale complexion and piercing dark eyes. Neither his nose nor his mouth was prominent, but his high and pronounced cheekbones gave him an angular look. Illustrations and photographs show him with thin and downward turned lips. The whole expression had a melancholic air of resignation. It is difficult to say for certain what Jean found attractive in him. The Newport portrayal describes McGonagall aged around 53. Other accounts sketch him in his 'OAP' years. Lowden Macartney, who knew McGonagall in the early 1890s, recalled: 'The present writer, in his boyhood, often met the "poet" and to this day retains a vivid impression of him . . . He had a solemn, sallow face, with heavy features and eyes of the sort termed fish-like (I don't know why). Slow of movement, with a slight stoop, acquired at the hand-loom formerly, but latterly at the desk, when he left off weaving cloth to take up the more congenial task of weaving dreams, leaning as he walked on a stout stick . . .' Later in life, 'He was a strange, weird, drab figure, and suggested more than anything else a broken-down actor. He wore his hair long and sheltered it with a wide-brimmed hat. His clothes were always shabby, and even in summer he refused to discard his overcoat.' Another description – a contemporary's distant memory – 'He was a little man, clean-shaven, with a typical Irish face. He wore a faded frock coat of a sort, baggy trousers and round hat like that worn by a priest.'[16]

McGonagall's looks, like his poetry, were open to ridicule and he was not best pleased when this occurred. He once explained: 'There is one thing in particular that they cry which I do not like, and, mind you, there are married men who cry it as well as boys. You know what it is? – "Get your hair cut." My, I don't like that. But I gave one fellow a sharp reply today – it is not often that I take notice of such remarks.' Playful jibes about his hair eventually became part of McGonagall's act, the chairman at one performance telling the audience that they had gathered " 'to protest against the persecution of the Poet by boys and others, who, when he was seen on the street, advised him to get his hair cut." (Cries of "Shame.") "Yes, I say shame," repeated the Chairman. "Whoever heard tell of a poet with his hair cut? I ask you, gentlemen, did you ever hear of any poet with his hair cut?" (Voices—"Never", and applause.)'[17]

On another occasion McGonagall took grave exception to a rival poet's criticism of his hair. McGonagall's riposte rejected the 'scurrilous' remarks and harnessed the highest possible moral ground in doing so . . .

> And, in conclusion, I'd have him to beware,
> And never again to interfere with a poet's hair,
> Because Christ the Saviour wore long hair,
> And many more good men, I do declare.

Several descriptions also survive of the way McGonagall dressed for public performances. Typical was this, from an appearance at the Nethergate Circus in Dundee: 'McGonagall stalked into the ring with a lordly air. He was arrayed in a kilt, plaid and sporran, and wore a bonnet in which was fastened a feather which would have done credit to the wing of a first-class eagle. The kilt was a trifle short, but the "poet" wore "tights" which, however, seemed to be rather wide for his limbs.'[18] He also wore Highland dress to private functions. At one meeting in the Gilfillan Hall, in which he was invited to meet three 'poets' from Edinburgh, he turned up in kilt, sporran, Kilmarnock bonnet with feather, wooden sword and round targe.

McGonagall also wore spectacles for his readings, and this left him vulnerable to mockery. At one entertainment, 'he began operations by gravely adjusting a pair of "specs" on his poetical nose. A kilted chieftain, armed with broadsword and dirk, and glittering with shining buckles, looked rather droll in a pair of "specs", but though the audience laughed, McGonagall rattled on with his ditty."[19] A similar interruption occurred at Blair's Hall, Dundee, when he lost his place during a recitation and reached for his spectacles. 'The idea of a poet in spectacles tickled the risible faculties of the gods, and the first line of Mrs Goose was drowned in a roar of laughter, which was taken up and re-echoed by a crowd of youngsters outside. Some of the audience declared that the Poet was reading the paper upside down, and one protested loudly that he had missed a verse.' Spectacles were forbidden in many Dundee factories, the masters supposing them evidence of slacking rather than signs of natural and inevitable change. Remarkably, wearing spectacles was often given as the excuse to cut wages. 'The result of this practice was the hundreds of hands who struggled on, perhaps for years, doing their work imperfectly.'[20]

Some audiences behaved – but not many. Such a miracle occurred at the Argyll Hall, Dundee, in June 1880. Not only was McGonagall permitted to go about his business, there was no disruptive jeering, missile launching or disparaging report by a falsely praising Press. The audience, 'though composed of the sterner sex, was very select, intelligent and appreciative' – and a hat was passed around at the interval for a silver collection for the poet. It had been whispered in civic circles that the provost, magistrates and town council might honour McGonagall with their presence, but it was not to be. When they failed to appear the *Weekly News* commented tartly: 'Doubtless those civic functionaries would be more at home in deciding on the respective merits of concrete and paving blocks than on the poetry of McGonagall and Shakespeare.'[21]

Behaving tolerably did not, however, mean neglecting opportunities to lampoon the town's bard. At the Argyll Hall McGonagall appeared plaided and plumed in Rob Roy tartan with a bulging broadsword by his side and solemnly bowed his acknowledgment to lusty cheers. The evening's chairman, after praising the star to the rooftops, reminded his audience that they had gathered to decide an important question – whether Dundee's William McGonagall was a superior genius to William Shakespeare. The audience were to hear recitations from the Bard of Avon and the Bard of the

Silv'ry Tay, and then would be invited to vote. Doubtless our hero
knew he had to win over the patrons, and put so much effort into
his recitation that when he came to his Bannockburn narrative, 'he
drew his long broadsword and cut and slashed the empty air with
the flashing blade like a thrasher on a barn floor, which made the
Chairman and the platform audience quickly evacuate the place of
honour'. At the end, a show of hands was required, but it was a
formality. Not an arm was raised in defence of Shakespeare.
McGonagall thanked his audience for the great compliment before
retiring 'amidst roars of laughter and derisive cheers'.

Contempt was more common. Before June 1880 was out,
McGonagall endured the blackest moment in his career when
he became the victim of a tasteless and much-criticised hoax which
led him for the first time to consider turning his back on his adopted
town. The incident began on 9 June, when the postman delivered
a letter to Paton's Lane headed 'Theatre Royal, Dundee' and
endorsed 'Dion Boucicault', the name of one of the great Victorian
dramatic actors. The envelope contained a note from Boucicault
referring to the Argyll Hall performance and inviting McGonagall
to meet him that day for lunch at Straton's Restaurant in Reform
Street. It can be imagined that the poet hugged Jean and danced a
jig of joy, firstly at the prospect of a free lunch, but afterwards at the
widening possibilities from such an opportunity, including a long-
cherished return to the stage.

McGonagall punctually attended and was led into the presence of
a middle-aged man with a flowing black beard streaked with silver.
The formalities of introductions over, he was requested to take a seat
and 'Boucicault' told him that if he and the poet could make
arrangements for a theatre tour through the provinces it would 'tend
to their mutual benefit'. The 'arrangements' were the first sticking
point, according to the newspaper which covered the meeting . . .[22]

' "What are your terms?" promptly inquired "Dion".

'The Poet thought for a minute. It would not do to sell his talents
for an old song. A guinea a night was a moderate salary to begin
with, but travelling was expensive. Taking all things into consideration the Poet finally came to the conclusion that £2 a night was a
moderate salary to begin with.

" 'Oh, you are very reasonable," replied the famous Irish dramatist.'

If McGonagall did not smell a rat by then, he should have done when one of the hangers-on spoke up to suggest 'Boucicault' should just agree to pay him £20 a week, pay the first week's salary in advance, and give him £5 towards the cost of a new stage costume. To this arrangement the bearded actor readily agreed. The poet was still none the wiser, and the situation deteriorated steadily. McGonagall's suggestion of a contract was evaded and talk flatteringly switched to the versatility of his talent. It was suggested he demonstrated some of his works to his new patron, if 'Boucicault' would condescend to hear him. He was encouraged to perform Bannockburn without his usual props. The small audience, of course, applauded to the echo and 'Boucicault' gushed that if he performed it in London 'it would bring down the house'. After the delivery of 'Address to the Moon' and 'Forget-Me-Not', half a sandwich and a glass of beer was provided for McGonagall's refreshment – hardly the meal expected – before the Boucicault impersonator exited stage left without further acknowledgment, followed one by one by his companions.

Only then did a faint suspicion dawn in the poet's mind that the meeting was a set-up. It was, in fact, the cruellest hoax. McGonagall was gullible and this made him vulnerable. The sham at Straton's Restaurant served the sole purpose of humiliating him for cheap laughs. It duly drew the ire of the Press, which described the poet's treatment as shabby and called upon the perpetrators to stand McGonagall a decent dinner to compensate for his disappointment.

McGonagall refers to the forged letter in his final autobiography in 1901. He remains faithful to the 1880 version in the *Weekly News* until the sandwich denouement, where the customary face-saving comment is inserted . . .

'I stared the impostor Boucicault in the face, and he felt rather uneasy, like he guessed I knew he wasn't the original Boucicault, so he arose from his seat and made a quick retreat, and before leaving he bade me good-bye, telling me he would see me again. Then I kept silent, and I stared the rest of my pretended friends out of countenance until they couldn't endure the penetrating glance of my poetic eye, so they arose and left me alone in my glory. Then I partook of the grand penny luncheon I had received for my recital of "Bannockburn", and with indignation my heart did burn.'

Later the same day McGonagall showed the forged letter to the Theatre Royal's manager, who confirmed it was spurious. Dion Boucicault was not in Dundee at the time and was not due to appear at the theatre. The manager, Mr Hodges, realising the poet's deep disappointment, reacted sympathetically by offering to copy the fraudulent letter to Boucicault in London, adding discreetly that he would explain its intended victim's financial situation. McGonagall, in 1901, takes up the story:

He had no doubt but Mr Boucicault would do something for me by way of solatium for my wounded feelings and for using his name in vain. He told me to come down to the theatre inside of three days, and he would have a letter from Boucicault by that time, he expected, so I thanked him for his kindness, and came away with my spirits light and gay.

Well, I waited patiently till the three days were expired, then called at the Theatre Royal and saw J. M. Hodges, the acting manager, and he received me very kindly, telling me he had received a letter from Mr Boucicault with a £5 cheque in it on the Bank of Scotland, so he handed me five sovereigns in gold along with Boucicault's letter. I thanked him and came away, and in the letter Boucicault felt for me very much, saying practical jokers were practical fools, which in my opinion is really true.

The hoax had raised the notion of a stage appearance and put £5 in William McGonagall's pocket. On the spur of the moment he resolved to use the money to pursue his dream to be an actor like the great Dionysius Boucicault – not in Dundee, though.

He was determined to seek fame and fortune in London.

FIVE

FROM TAY TO THAMES . . . AND BACK

'WEEP AND HOWL ye men of Juteopolis. McGonagall, who has so long gone about unrecognised amongst you, has turned his back on your "bonnie" town.'

And so it came to pass, William McGonagall bade farewell to Dundee and embarked on his most Quixotic adventure – to seek fame and fortune in London. And his determination to abandon Dundee, however temporary a leave-taking, caused playful navel-gazing among the literati of Dundee; those who had rejected his rhymes, poked fun at his appearance, refused use of venues – and offered him a sandwich instead of a dinner.

McGonagall's admirer in the *Weekly News* was in no doubt the Boucicault hoax was the straw that broke the camel's back. The unthinking men who had planned and carried out the 'vile sandwich business' were deemed personally responsible for his impending waygoing. However, the paper pointed out cheerfully that good often comes out of evil and described how, as news of the deception spread, a subscription had been arranged to pay for the poet's passage to London. It diplomatically neglected to say whether the speed with which the fare was collected represented sympathy for McGonagall, or a desire to see the back of him.[1]

Good showman that he was, McGonagall agreed to a performance at the Argyll Hall on 22 June 1880 to milk his hurt feelings and promote his imminent sailing for London. Word had got around of his decision and the townsfolk rallied to hear the last words of departing greatness: 'Long before the advertised time the body of the hall was completely filled, but so great was the influx of visitors, that in the course of the evening the gallery doors had to be thrown open, when the "gods" rushed in like a torrent and filled the spheres above.'[2]

Dion Boucicault's letter was then read out by J.M. Hodges of the Theatre Royal and confirmed the Irish actor's indignation at the fraud practised in his name. In his reply to Hodges, Boucicault spilled noble and generous words: 'The hoax was a very cruel one. It was a heartless affair. I should be glad to give the Poet proof that actors are incapable of such unkindness. Tell him that all poets feel for one another, and that practical jokers are practical fools.' The letter was met with rapturous applause which reached a resounding crescendo when Hodges mentioned the five pounds sent for the slighted Dundee bard.

McGonagall then appeared attired head to foot in tartan. He was met with thunderous acclaim, waving of hats, stamping and whistling, to which he graciously bowed his plumed head and 'smiled complacently'. And so to 'Bruce of Bannockburn', which was fearlessly rendered with formidable lung power and enacted with broadsword drawn and imaginary Englishmen falling bloodied at his feet. The event's chairman fled the platform in terror and the audience near the stage shut their eyes in panic as the glittering blade swept purposefully over their heads. McGonagall was at the top of his game.

The reporter made an off-the-cuff comment on this occasion which modern interpreters of McGonagall might consider. 'All we can say is that McGonagall must be seen and heard before he can be fully appreciated.' Though often impersonated, nobody has ever read McGonagall like William McGonagall read McGonagall. He surpassed himself in volume and emotion when reciting his own works, drawing meaning and feeling from every end-rhyme. He was a tragedian to trade, a dramatic performer who could recite 'Macbeth' by the age of 20 – and Macbeth dominates his play, speaking a third of its lines. McGonagall's powerful voice, facial expressions and theatrical poses were the baggage he brought to poetryhood. It was music hall, burlesque, balladry and Vaudeville rolled into a potent package by a larger than life performer. Quietly read, his verse takes barely a handful of lines to show poetic conventions have been cast aside. His irregular style is viewed as pretend poetry in the form of prose, with violations of syntax and slovenly deficiencies in grammar. But lengths of lines did not trouble McGonagall and his couplets met in rhyme when they were good and ready. Read McGonagall's 'Battle of Waterloo', all 27 stanzas of it, at full voice to a participating audience, and cannons roar, bullets fly and blood flows. McGonagall was a performer of verse and his performance was accepted by audiences as extraordinary. Tame, lame and deformed as his words appear in type, to see and hear William McGonagall was an education in sensational theatricals – and one which required precautionary measures for the safety of those seated close to the point of delivery.[3]

But at the close of the Argyll Hall entertainment in June 1880 McGonagall surprised patrons with a specially composed address which explained how his recently acquired fiver would be spent . . .

> Fellow Citizens of Dundee,
> I now must bid farewell to ye,
> For I am going to London far away,
> But when I will return again I cannot say.
> Farewell! Farewell! to the bonnie banks o' the Silvery Tay.
> Also the beautiful Hill o' Balgay,
> And the ill fated bridge o' the Silvery Tay,
> Which I will remember when I am far away.
> Farewell! to my friends and patrons all,
> That rallied around me in the Music Hall,
> And those that has rallied around me to night,
> I shall not forget when out of sight.

This pathetic farewell was eked out to half a dozen verses and had the desired effect of drawing spontaneous emotional feedback. Every line was applauded until, with a bold stamp of his foot and a majestic wave of his arm, McGonagall held the 'farewell' manuscript close to his flimsy spectacles and cried . . .

> And if ever I return to Dundee again,
> I hope it will be with the laurels of fame.

As he lapsed into exhausted silence, the audience rose to its feet and cheered to a man. Dozens rushed forward to shake his hand and

nearly overturned the spent poet in their determination to honour
him with a triumphal march home.

McGonagall departed Dundee by steamer the following week,
paying £1 for a steerage passage return ticket. He was cheered on
his way, he bragged in his 1901 autobiography, by a loyal group of
friends who thronged the dockyard. Once beyond the estuary bar, a
gullible passenger asked McGonagall to give a recital. 'I gave them
the "Battle of Tel-el-Kebir", which was well received, and I got an
encore, and I gave them the "Rattling Boy from Dublin Town",
and for which I received a small donation, and that finished the
entertainment for the night.' By 1901 he had forgotten that, in 1880,
Tel-el-Kebir was still two years distant.[4] No matter. The journey
south went smoothly enough and the steamer landed its passengers
on the Thames embankment. McGonagall's first steps in the capital
were taken near Billingsgate. It was late June. He was probably still
attired in his signature long coat and pudding hat, carried his spare
clothes and props in a leather bag, and presumably felt the sticky
London heat as he walked through the fish market towards the City.
He recalls in his final autobiography how he found the babbling of
fishmongers 'disagreeable to hear' and that he felt threatened by
men hanging around the market. No doubt his pace quickened as
he made his way to his lodgings in the White Horse Inn, Fetter
Lane, just off the Strand.

William McGonagall's experiences in London mirror his other
peripatetic ventures. He left with his pocket light, but his head
buzzing with possibilities. The object was to secure pay-at-the-door
engagements where he could impart his literary and dramatic skills
to appreciative new audiences. He appears to have landed in
London with about eight shillings and, after paying four shillings
in advance for a week's accommodation, had just under four
shillings on which to live until he could profit from a performance.
Before leaving, he had written a stanza to Dion Boucicault which
thanked him for the consolation money sent after the sandwich
hoax. He warned he would visit the actor to thank him personally
during his visit to London. He also wrote a note of introduction to
Henry Irving, threatening a meeting in the capital.

The next day was spent viewing London's sights. 'I went out and wended my way towards London Bridge, and, oh! such a busy throng of cabs and 'buses rapidly whirling along. After viewing it, I returned to my lodging quite delighted with the sights I had seen.' The following morning he turned to the serious business of touring theatres and music halls in the hope of securing a booking. Where he went in London is not recorded. The response can be imagined, however. McGonagall did not, it seems, possess even a smidgen of an Irish accent and his elocution-tweaked Scots twang was never likely to be welcomed in the capital. According to testimony imparted to the Press on his return, he met with nothing but coldness from Londoners generally, and was insulted and snubbed by the acting profession in particular. In fact, he found no venue willing to allow him a solitary 'entertainment' – hardly a surprise without an up-front payment. The only offer of work came from another lodger at the White Horse. 'This amiable young man proposed he and the "Poet" should enter into partnership with a view to their mutual advantage; in short, that they would take to the streets; he would whistle and the "Poet" would sing. We need not inform our readers that the "Poet" rejected the offer with scorn.'[5]

Not given to busking, and with unexpected leisure time, McGonagall walked along the Strand to the Adelphi Theatre and inquired if Dionysius Boucicault was available. The stage door porter took McGonagall's card to the actor's private secretary and, after a few minutes, according to the *Weekly News*, the secretary returned, tore up the card in front of the poet and informed him Boucicault was busy and could not speak to anybody. Wearied by the unanticipated snub, McGonagall's thoughts turned towards Henry Irving, to whom he had also written a note. He trudged to the Lyceum and asked if Irving was in. 'The porter, scanning the "Poet" from head to heel, saucily informed him that "Mister Henry Irving would not speak to a person like him." The "Poet" retorted that he was as good a man as Henry Irving, but it was of no use. Henry was invisible, and the "Poet" failed to get an interview.'

McGonagall's autobiographies devote few words to the memory of trying to find work in London, other than this, again looking back from 1901: "Unfortunately, I didn't succeed. Owing to the disappointments I met with, I resolved to return home to Dundee as soon as possible. . . . When Saturday came I left my lodgings in Fetter Lane, longing, of course, for to get hame, and embarked on board, with my heart light, and longing to see the Silvery Tay. So the stout steamer from the Thames sailed away, and arrived on Wednesday in the Silvery Tay, and the passengers' hearts were full of glee when they were landed safely in Dundee once again. I was glad to see it, especially my family." His inability to avoid rhyme is ever-present in his prose, even in his last jottings for the *Weekly News* in 1901 just a year before his death . . . sailed away to the silvery Tay, full of glee to be back in Dundee to see his famileee. He had been scarcely absent a week from his home town. He returned with his tail firmly between his legs, wiser if not wealthier, his dreams scattered to the four winds, his gas at a peep.[6]

McGonagall's souvenir from his most adventurous expedition is the 11-verse 'Jottings of London', which reflects on the exceptional opportunity for a working-class Dundonian to spend a leisured week in the capital. Many major tourist sites are captured in rhyme and offered the equivalent of holiday postcards to Jean and his children. Sample stanzas . . .

> As I stood upon London Bridge,
> And viewed the mighty throng
> Of thousands of people in cabs and 'buses
> Rapidly whirling along,
> And driving to and fro,
> Up one street and down another
> As quick as they could go.
>
> And as for the River Thames –
> It is a most wonderful sight;
> To see the steamers and barges
> Sailing up and down upon it
> From early morn till night.
>
> And as for the Tower of London –
> It is most gloomy to behold,

And within it lies the Crown of England
Begemmed with precious stones and gold.

St. Paul's Cathedral is the finest building
That ever I did see;
There's nothing can surpass it
In the town of Dundee,
For it is most magnificent to behold
With its beautiful dome and lofty spire glittering like gold.

And as for Nelson's Monument
That stands in Trafalgar Square –
It is a most stately statue
I most solemnly declare,
And towering very high,
Which arrests strangers' attention
When they are passing by.
And there's two beautiful water fountains
Spouting up very high,
Where the weary travellers can have a drink
When they feel dry.

McGonagall was aware he had a 'devoted' following in Dundee anxious to know how he had got on. On his return an evening's entertainment was arranged by a few friends for the long-demolished Marine Hall in the long-gone Marina Place in the much-changed Hawkhill. They had learned that McGonagall 'was sadly dejected, and sunk in purse and spirits after his luckless tour', and had banded together to organise a fund-raiser to console the poor poet.[7]

The hall filled quickly with a respectable and appreciative audience. The chairman introduced McGonagall and provided a graphic account of his London experiences to much sympathetic 'ooohhhing' and 'aaahhhing'. He reassured the audience that the poet, after undergoing a series of hardships and miseries enough to crush the life out of any ordinary mortal, was still 'alive and kicking'. To this there was prolonged applause. McGonagall was probably quite exhausted, but offered a programme of songs and readings from his own works and some Shakespeare. His new poem on London was read for the first time. If reported correctly by the *People's Journal* in 1880, it differs from the example in later published works by adding a discordant last verse conveying the frustrations he felt in the capital . . .

Oh! mighty city of London! you are wonderful to behold,
But your treatment towards Strangers, I think tis rather cold.
But you are very kind to them,
While they have plenty of Gold.

***

For all his praise of the powerful, McGonagall was unrestrained in relating how difficult it was to make ends meet as a weaver poet, as his surviving 'begging' letters demonstrate. In one plea for funds to the hotelier Alex Lamb, for example, he writes candidly, 'My dear friend, it is with the greatest sorrow, anxiety of mind, I write to you again to let you know that I am in great difficulties with my rent which, I am sorry to say, is beyond my control to meet the demands of the factor.' Another anxious letter to Lamb reads: 'My Dear Friend, I am sorry to inform you that I am in very poor circumstances at present beyond my own control, So far indeed to be unable to put my New poem that I have recently composed to press, because I am in arrears with my printer at present, and if you will be so kind as to help me by lending me £1 you will greatly oblige me in my present difficulty.' As the *Weekly News* painfully pointed out in 1880, 'McGonagall the poet is still alive and struggling on in his endeavour to win fame and fortune. He has succeeded in gaining a wide notoriety, but the goal of his ambition financially is about as far distant as ever.'[8]

So McGonagall was back on familiar ground in his adopted town. It is probably a safe assumption that the normally easy-going Jean booted him towards the nearest mill foreman to find work. He did keep contacts there. By the time he was ready to face the Dundee public again, in late 1880, handbills advertising the performance were distributed to mills and factories as well as to the usual public billboards. Workplace income was still required to pay rent, fuel and food. At the census of 1881 his three eldest sons, William junior, 27, Joseph, 22 and Charles, 20, remained unmarried in a crowded family home. Elder son William was in the mills. Joseph had broken with family tradition by training as a ship's painter, and later went to sea before – forgive the rhyme – returning to Dundee. Charles was employed making the iron combs, or hackles, used to separate flax fibres in the linen trade. Mary, 19, another millworker, was unmarried. Seventeen-year-old James, unmarried, was also listed as a millworker. John, 14, was an unemployed ropemaker. McGonagall's second eldest child, Margaret, had, in 1873, given birth to an illegitimate child, Andrew. He was recorded in the McGonagall household at 19 Paton's Lane in 1881, aged seven, and already a 'scholar'. Margaret, however, was not present at the census and presumably had set up home elsewhere.

Any sympathy lingering after the Boucicault hoax and McGonagall's misfiring trip to London soon evaporated. Two other barefaced frauds were quickly played upon him. Firstly he received a document one night which purported to be a command from the queen to confer a knighthood upon him, accompanied by a cheque for £7. Of course the document turned out to be a forgery and the cheque a sham. Close on the heels of that came another letter enclosing a cheque drawn on the City of Glasgow Bank for £20 to pay for the construction of a wooden theatre in which McGonagall could showcase his talents. The cheque was signed Dick Turpin & Company, a failed financial institution, while the Glasgow bank had gone under, too. The *Weekly News* had readers reaching for hankies as it reported, 'Deceived and hoaxed by pretended friends, the Poet turned aside sick and heartsore.'9

And when McGonagall returned to the Thistle Hall in October 1880 he discovered an unforgiving audience determined to have a night of fun at his expense. Blue, green and yellow handbills had been widely circulated announcing that the 'vocalist, poet, and tragedian' was to be supported by 'his son' and a cast of local professionals, male and female. McGonagall's son John, who later tried to follow in his thespian footsteps, was only 13 in 1880 and presumably the 'son' mentioned here is McGonagall's eldest, William, who also appeared in later performances.

The hall having been duly hired, McGonagall must have been disappointed when the entire audience scarcely numbered a hundred. His sympathiser on the *Weekly News* takes up the commentary: 'Half-a-dozen youths, who had invested 2d each in tin trumpets, took possession of the gallery, and began to act as a volunteer orchestra. While the audience were mustering, the trumpeters blew with might and main. The effect was deafening. It was nearly half-an-hour past the time when the audience were informed that the local talent would not go on, unless the lessee, Mr McGonagall, "stumped up first", and as poor Mac had no money, and the doorkeeper had taken nothing to speak of, the professionals had to be dismissed.'[10]

Deprived of his support acts, McGonagall launched into 'The Rattling Boy' accompanied by a roaring chorus and trumpet blasts. His 'Bannockburn' was fought amidst vociferous cheering, so loud and long that he was effectually drowned out. Next he made his appearance as Macbeth in a new costume glittering with silvery buckles, which brought a louder blast on the trumpets. But before McGonagall could continue, the stage was rushed and the tragedian sought sanctuary in his dressing room. When the crowd burst in, McGonagall lost his temper and his son threatened to fight all and sundry. At this point the manager turned out the lights and shouted that the show was over. The audience dispersed, leaving poet and son to gather up props and trudge back to Paton's Lane.

October 1880 brought another thudding blow to McGonagall's reputation when he was unceremoniously refused a place on the platform at the unveiling of a statue to Robert Burns. The £1,000 statue had been the talk of the town for many months and the positioning of the large bronze sculpture in Meadowside, close to the Albert Institute, was eagerly awaited and drew a huge crowd on the day. McGonagall intended to appear at the ceremony to deliver a public recitation of his tribute to the statue. The authorities imagined public disorder would result, perhaps ruining the ceremony and making the town a laughing stock. McGonagall was therefore refused a place in the procession to the unveiling on the basis that he was not a member of a representative body. When he attempted to take a position on the stage he was forcibly moved on by police. The poet's anger was later conveyed in a letter to a friend . . .

'I will ever remember the day I walked in the Burns' procession in Highland costume with the manuscript of the Burns Statue poem in my hand, which I willingly would have read had I been permitted, but no! when I made the attempt for the third time, to get onto the platform, I was told by police to go away, just the same as if I had been a dog.'[11]

A fragment of the poem survives. Its first three verses were included in *Last Poetic Gems* in 1968. A further verse was rediscovered in 2009 . . .

> This statue, I must confess, is magnificent to see,
> And I hope will long be appreciated by the people of Dundee;
> It has been beautifully made by Sir John Steell,
> And I hope the pangs of hunger he will never feel.
>
> This statue is most elegant in its design,
> And I hope will defy all weathers for a very long time;
> And I hope strangers from afar with admiration will stare
> On this beautiful statue of thee, Immortal Bard of Ayr.
>
> Fellow-citizens, this Statue seems most beautiful to the eye,
> Which would cause Kings and Queens for such a one to sigh,
> And make them feel envious while passing by
> In fear of not getting such a beautiful Statue after they die.
>
> See where he sits on the stump of that tree
> His eyes turned to heaven his Mary to see,
> A scroll at his feet, a pen in his hand,
> Writing to his Mary in the Better Land.

After this sequence of disasters, the Dundee newspapers felt McGonagall's career had run its course. 'Really we would seriously advise him to abandon "poetry and the drama", and turn his attention to some more lucrative occupation, as it is pretty evident that the present generation are not prepared to appreciate his "talents". Whether he will get justice at the hands of generations yet unborn is a question we leave time to answer.' It is a question time has so far left unanswered.[12]

A few lines in the Public Notices columns of the *Courier* or *Evening Telegraph* cost a few pence and the large, literate readership of these papers would have been drawn to the following advert which appeared in November 1880 for McGonagall's next show . . .

Macgonagall in Excelsis, Trades' Hall, King's Road, Friday, the 26th, at 8.30pm.

PROSE and Poetical Extracts from the Foreign Press.— '*No other poet in the universe can extract laughter from the solemn pageantry of a funeral.' – Madagascar Murderer.*

'*But he stood like a modest tobacconist's sign, with his tartan curtain around him.' – Delhi Thug.*

Come early and bring Sixpence.[13]

McGonagall deserves credit for raising his head above the parapet barely a month after his fighting retreat from the Thistle Hall. He was obviously keen to avoid the shambles and financial loss of the previous event, and once a healthy paying crowd of 200 had entered the Trades Hall, representing handsome takings of £5 at sixpence a head, the hall's management barricaded the door to keep out youths bent on having a share of the fun for nothing. As always, McGonagall rose at the call of the evening's chairman and began to read from a sheet of foolscap his new poem on George Gilfillan's funeral. This reported the scene of the burial of his friend reasonably, if repetitiously, well . . .

On the Gilfillan burial day,
In the Hill o' Balgay,
It was a most solemn sight to see,
Not fewer than thirty thousand people assembled in Dundee,
All watching the funeral procession of Gilfillan that day,
That death had suddenly taken away,
And was going to be buried in the Hill o' Balgay.

'The Burial of the Rev George Gilfillan' is a wonderful early example of McGonagall's preoccupation with figures. 'Thirty thousand people' assembled for the funeral, 'three thousand' in the procession alone and 'fifty carriages', he reveals. McGonagall shapes the scene using numbers. He did so many times, a notable example celebrating the arrival in Dundee of the Tay Whale. This specimen, he impressed upon readers, was 40 feet long, with a tail which measured 17 feet 4 inches, and was sold for 'two hundred and twenty-six pound'. The year and date of battles was given, the total enemy put to flight, the numbers drowned, burned or destroyed by demon drink. Then there was the Dundee gale in which 'no less than 250 trees and 37 tombstones were blown down at Balgay'. McGonagall loved numbers. They captured the newsworthiness of events he celebrated in verse. In his epic 'Battle of the Nile', for example . . .

> The French force consisted of thirteen ships of the line,
> As fine as ever sailed on the salt sea brine;
> Besides four Frigates carrying 1,196 gun in all,
> Also 11,230 men as good as ever fired a cannon ball.
> The number of the English ships was thirteen in all,
> And carrying 1012 guns, including great and small,
> And the number of the men were 8,068,
> All jolly British tars and eager for to fight.

The problem was that McGonagall often used numbers to import information better left unsaid, such as the children who had died in a theatre stampede in Sunderland who were 'buried seven or eight layers deep', or the loss of the steamer *Victoria*, which 'sank in fifteen minutes after she was rammed/In eighty fathoms of water, which was smoothly calmed', and not least after 'The Horrors of Majuba', when . . .

> They then went about two hundred yards down the Hill,
> And collected fourteen more bodies, which made their
>   blood run chill;
> And, into one grave, seventy-five bodies they buried there,
> All mostly 92nd men, who, I hope, are free from all care.

McGonagall's second offering at the Trades Hall was 'The Tay Bridge Disaster'. One wag in the audience inquired indecently if this was a 'new disaster', but the chairman soberly informed him that it was the 'old affair'. As the audience warmed to the occasion the poet was greeted at the close of his second composition with a volley of green peas. This salute called forth an impromptu couplet from the gifted bard which deserves to be immortalised. Smarting under the stinging shower he exclaimed . . .

> Gentlemen, if you please,
> Stop throwing pease.

When 'Bannockburn' was announced the 'gods' sounded the Scottish charge on a toy drum as the celebrated offensive against Edward's English began . . .

> Sir Robert the Bruce at Bannockburn
> Beat the English in every wheel and turn,
> And made them fly in great dismay
> From the field without delay . . .

The warrior poet was encored, and had to fight the battle all over again, slaying the opposition at least two at a time and nearly decapitating those nearest the stage in the process. An interval of five minutes was allowed to give him time to recover his breath, during which his unidentified son – probably William junior – appeared on the platform and mumbled some incoherent jargon in a weak, squeaking voice, which was completely drowned out by the shouts and laughter of the audience. A gentleman remarked that the foolishness of the father was more perfectly developed in the son – a remark which brought ironic cheers of assent. Both William and John made a few attempts to follow their father's footsteps after this humiliation, but usually faced an onslaught of missiles and abandoned their performances.

'The Rattling Boy from Dublin' concluded the Trades Hall entertainment and the 'Poet rattled away at the rattling song, amidst a rattling chorus, and rattling fire of green peas by the audience.' At the close, the chairman invited the audience to shake hands with the star turn, which resulted in a rush to the dressing room. Not for the first time the crowding pressure of admirers proved too much for McGonagall, who lost his temper. He drew his broadsword and drove his tormentors into the hall as if they were Edward's advancing English.[14]

A theme was developing of McGonagall taking his life in his hands at the end of each performance in Dundee. Little wonder then that as 1881 began he decided it was time again to take to the road. He had explored Perthshire and Fife. Locally that left Angus in the trilogy of Tayside counties. This time, Dundee's missionary poet spread his appearances over a period of five months, suggesting either spasmodic employment or being grounded at home by lack of expeditionary funds.

Evidence of how rural 'entertainments' were arranged is provided by a hitherto unpublished letter from McGonagall to a Mr Gardener, who was keen to attract him to Brechin. This described the contract he sought in an attempt to guarantee a peaceable performance . . .

Mr Gardener,
My dear sir, I received your letter of today and felt happy to think that you and your friends in Brechin are desirous for me to give a reading from my works, or an entertainment in the City, which I would be quite willing to do, sir. So as you and your friends comes to terms with me, well, sir, if the entertainment be a private one, my terms are £1 and all expenses paid, namely loading and railway conveyance, going and returning, and along with that a return ticket must be sent to me, and one half of the money. Besides you will require to find a respectable clergyman to occupy the chair on this occasion. Besides, sir, I will require a line signed and written by the Clergyman that consents to do so and sent to me before I go to Brechin. These are my terms. Sir, if it is to be a Public Entertainment I require a Clergyman in the chair and more money. Namely £3, and half of it in advance. These are my terms dear sir, which I must have before I budge. I am dear Sir, yours truly, Wm McGonagall, poet.'[15]

So there was no budging for less than £1 and expenses, some of it up front, as his name and notoriety spread in the 1880s. He had twice taken in as little as a quarter of that in Dundee, sometimes less. For risks to his safety at public performances he wanted danger money totalling a hefty £3. He was also anxious to ensure decorum – and thereby protection – through the reassuring presence of a minister, though chairmen of such meetings were usually just as keen for a giggle as the rest of the audience.

It was not McGonagall but his audiences who found themselves in mortal peril on his 1881 Angus tour, however. February brought an appearance in the Trades Hall, Arbroath as part of a programme of vocalists and actors. Attracted in particular by a top-of-the-bill appearance of the Dundee bard, the theatre quickly filled to capacity. Due on stage after a comic singer, McGonagall responded to repeated chants of his name by entering clad in tartan, with his trusty sword strapped to his side. His patriotic opening, 'Bannockburn', roused the audience to near hysteria and the poet to a different planet . . .

'Having got well through with his thrilling narrative he drew his claymore with which he commenced a vigorous onslaught on the foe. While doing so he ceased speaking for a few minutes, during which he walked majestically from side to side of the stage, making ferocious sweeps with his claymore, each of which was intended to do for a southerner. From a minute observation and tally kept we are assured that had Edward's forces been there, 128 of the flower of his army would have "bit the dust".'

Caught up in the act in the town where Bruce signed Scotland's Declaration of Independence, McGonagall's declamatory rendering of Bannockburn had the same rousing effect as sending Proud Edward's army home to think again at Hampden or Murrayfield . . .

> And beat them off the field without delay
> Like lions bold and heroes gay,
> Upon them! – charge! – follow me,
> For Scotland's rights and liberty!

It was all too much for the gentle country folk. 'At first the fiddlers made their escape from the front or got down under their seats, and

the little boys who were clustering behind the orchestra also retired
to a safe distance.' When the onslaught was over and the battle
won, Edward being now at Dunbar, McGonagall resumed his
narrative, much of which, however, was lost amid cries of 'Tay
Bridge' and so on. On the whole he had a warm though somewhat
boisterous reception. As usual his 'Rattling Boy' was particularly
popular, the whole audience joining in the chorus . . .

> Whack fal de da, fal de darelido,
> Whack fal de da, fal de darelay,
> Whack fal de da, fal de darelido,
> Whack fal de da, fal de darelay.[16]

McGonagall always provided value for money. His sell-out shows
were visual, theatrical, rollicking and unrestrained. You got what it
said on the tin – entertainment. And the boisterous Arbroath
performance drew an eloquent poem of praise from a satisfied
patron in the following Saturday's *Weekly News* . . .

> Upon the stage he stood alone;
> He seized a stick, for sword he'd none,
> And soon to battle we were shown,
> To fight wi' Poet McGonagall.
> Let Yankee laud Longfellow's cheek,
> Let Ireland boast her Tom Moore dear;
> Let England claim her Will Shakespear;
> But let us claim McGonagall.[17]

On a Thursday afternoon in April 1881, McGonagall walked down
to the station at Yeaman Shore and bought a return ticket to
Brechin. The travelling bard had agreed to perform in the cathedral
town's Crown Hotel. Alas the *Brechin Advertiser* had a po-faced
reaction to the great presence in its midst, reporting stuffily that
the evening's programme consisted of 'original dramatic readings'.
The pieces, it concluded dully, were 'introduced in a racy manner,
and altogether the entertainment was unique in its way'. In fact,
the behaviour of the people of neighbouring Angus reputedly

degenerated from teasing to trouble. McGonagall later complained that his hat was nailed to a table in Brechin, while his coat-tails were scissored off as a souvenir at Arbroath.[18]

The next stopover on the Angus tour took McGonagall to far-flung Montrose in the final days of April 1881. He appeared in the town's Masonic Hall, where he was met by an audience comprising 'a number of young men who designate themselves "the choice spirits" of Montrose.' As so often happened, keeping order was the order of the day and the show required the services of several resolute occupants of the chairman's chair. McGonagall entered, bowed to great acclaim, and showily demonstrated his workman-ship. And all seemed to go well, despite the now-familiar noisy accompaniment.

McGonagall was not daft. He usually had in his repertoire a song or poem cataloguing the attractions of the place he was visiting. Here, he sang the new composition 'Bonnie Montrose', which was rapturously received. It so moved one Montrosian that he jumped on the stage to declare that the mighty genius before them ought to be Poet Laureate, and that Tennyson should be called upon to resign – a regular reader of the *Weekly News* obviously. The climax was reached, of course, when The McGonagall, sword in hand, became The Bruce . . .

'The bump of combativeness became so simultaneously roused in the heads of all the choice spirits, that they commenced attacking the lecturer and each other from a bag of flour in possession of one of the choicest of the spirits. To add farther to the effects of this blinding mealy battery, the lights were put out, and confusion reigned supreme. On their being relighted, the appearance of the McGonagall and the flour-bag combatants was ghostly in the extreme; but all, except the great man before them, seemed to be wildly delighted with the ordeal which they had so gallantly passed through.'[19]

Although unreported and subsequently unrecorded, it is clear McGonagall's intermittent tour of Angus included other perfor-mances which presented further opportunities for flour to turn him into Hamlet's ghost or soot to transform him into Othello.

He had made a friend of a Mr Balfour during his short stay in

Montrose. Balfour asked the Dundee poet to remain in contact and to send him verses as and when composed. McGonagall performed this poetic postal service on the odd occasion, notably towards the end of his life. To Mr Balfour he wrote in May 1881 saying that he had given an 'entertainment' in Inverkeilor the previous evening, adding, 'The proceeds amounted to 3 shillings and 1d which was very good regarding the notice given.' The letter added that a second performance was to be given in Arbroath the following evening.[20]

McGonagall's wanderings of 1881 were not confined to the east coast. In high summer he left his wife and family once more and set off westwards by train for Glasgow. There he took up what must have been fairly basic accommodation in the corporation lodging house in Hyde Park Street. This time he did not immediately face the chore of finding a suitable or willing venue for his 'entertainment'. He had been invited to Glasgow for a private recital. He had mixed feelings about this, as he reported to his Montrose aquaintance in mid-July . . . 'I met with my friends in Glasgow on Tuesday as I expected and met with a hearty reception from them, but it wasn't very profitable. I gave an Entertainment to them and they gave me 5 shillings. There was only six of them, of course, but [it] was very good considering the number.'[21] McGonagall spent at least a week in Glasgow, composing a new poem on the city's beautiousness, though no record of any public performances survives.

The term 'choice spirits' used for the Montrose audience implies an element of inebriation at McGonagall 'entertainments'. Theatres and music halls were not the only public venues available to McGonagall. Where people more commonly met, and where the week's wages were spent, were the 300 or so public houses in 1880s Dundee. McGonagall was a militant teetotaller and a member of a temperance society. Nevertheless, he could ill afford to ignore the drinking dens where money flowed and potential customers gathered.

In his loosely faithful memoirs, McGonagall details this love–hate relationship with public houses. On the one hand he had to reconcile himself to abandoning some firmly held principles on alcohol by staging drop-in recitals in public houses. On the other, his pub entertainments tended to slow the pace of drinking and thus lowered profits, which made him unpopular with the city's land-lords. He believed publicans were a social evil. They thought him a profit-sapping nuisance. Worse, he felt they cursed entertainers like him and, left to their own devices, would have outlawed any entertainment which deflected patrons from the core duty of downing drink after drink. Later in life, he claimed publicans influenced a controversial decision by the town's magistrates to ban him from performing in public.

McGonagall also advocated personal prohibition – total absti-nence from alcohol – a principle that remained with him all his life. He blamed most of life's ills on drink and in *Biographical Reminiscences by the Author*, which first appeared in 1891, proclaimed to his flock: 'My dear friends, I entreat of you all, for God's sake and for the furtherance of Christ's kingdom, to abstain from all kinds of intoxicating liquor, because seldom any good emanates from it. Yet the Government tolerates such a demon, I may call it, to be sold in society; to help burglars and thieves to rob and kill; also to help the seducer to seduce our daughters; and to help to fill our prisons, and our lunatic asylums, and our poorhouses.'

Thus he likened booze to Babylon and encouraged readers and audiences to shun pubs and to give their money anywhere other than to the pockets of publicans. McGonagall also takes up this story as an introductory chapter in the second printing of *Poetic Gems* . . .

I was taken into a public-house by a party of my friends and admirers, and requested to give them an entertainment, for which I was to be remunerated by them, which was the case; the money I received from them I remember amounted to four shillings and sixpence. All had gone on as smoothly as a marriage bell, and every one of the party seemed to be highly delighted with the entertainment I had given them.

Of course, you all ought to know that while singing a good song, or giving a good recitation, it helps to arrest the company's attention from the drink; yes! in many cases it does, my friends. Such, at least, was the case with me – at least the publican thought so – for – what do you think? – he devised a plan to bring my entertainment to an end abruptly, and the plan was, he told the waiter to throw a wet towel at me, which, of course, the waiter did, as he was told, and I received the wet towel, full force, in the face, which staggered me, no doubt, and had the desired effect of putting an end to me giving any more entertainments in his house.

Whether it was because they dispensed drink or because his flow of income was interrupted as much as their tide of takings, McGonagall despised publicans, as his *Biographical Reminscences* makes clear: 'My dear friends, a publican is a creature that would wish to decoy all the money out of the people's pockets that enter his house; he does not want them to give any of their money away for an intellectual entertainment. No, no! by no means; give it all to him, and crush out entertainment altogether, thereby he would make more money if he could only do so.'

It irked him that he had little choice other than to seek out public houses for his shows. He believed that if there were more theatres in society than public houses, it would be a much better world to live in, at least more moral. So he railed at publicans' greed and advised his readers to spend hard-won wages elsewhere: 'Oh! my dear friends, be advised by me. Give your money to the baker, and the butcher, also the shoemaker and the clothier, and shun the publicans; give them no money at all . . . no matter whether your families starve or not, or go naked or shoeless; they care not, so as their own families are well clothed from the cold, and well fed.'

McGonagall's condemnation concluded with evangelical fervour: 'Shun the publicans as you would shun the devil, because nothing good can emanate from indulging in strong drink, but only that which is evil. Turn ye, turn ye! why be a slave to the bottle? Turn to God, and He will save you.'

These episodes indicate McGonagall's strong and consistent anti-drink stance. He also recalled in *Poetic Gems Second Series* the time he had delivered 'Rattling Boy' and 'Bannockburn' to a foot-tapping pub audience and had taken a 'handsome' collection when he noticed his walking stick had been taken away – 'the landlady guessed I would leave the house when I missed my stick, which was really the case'. On another occasion he was in the same public house entertaining a number of gentlemen, and had received a second collection from them. 'As soon as the landlady found out I was getting so much money, she rushed into the room and ordered me out at once, telling me to "hook it" out of here, and laid hold of me by the arm and showed me to the door.'[22]

Thus, reciting poems and selling broadsides exposed William McGonagall to hostility and mockery on Dundee's streets, in the town's theatres and music halls and on his visits to its public houses. How often must he have returned to Paton's Lane tired, hungry, and footsore – and virtually penniless – and sunk back in his chair and wondered if his decision to write poetry had been the biggest mistake of his life?

SIX

PATRONS AND PAYMENT

WILLIAM McGONAGALL spent the last 25 years of his life striving to win praise for his poetry and performance. Never did a letter leave his hand without the hope that a response would bring a blessing which could be used as a reference from a distinguished person to promote or sell his work. He wrote to the queen, to civic dignitaries and to wealthy philanthropists. He was resolutely hopeful they would respond publicly or in print, praising his poetry as worthy of broader appeal, thus providing the patronage required to widen its paying possibilities. Taken by him as approval, such routine acknowledgements were his green light for surmounting his penny broadsides with 'V.R.' in bold type, adding the royal coat of arms for good measure, and then flanking his printed poems with lofty endorsements from the likes of Lord Wolseley, the Duke of Cambridge, William Gladstone and various 'Majesties'.

Letters he sent in 1881 and 1882 continued this egotistically acquisitive herocracy. The difference on these occasions was that he launched a determined campaign to win the support of generals and statesmen, hoping his poetic tributes to their endeavours would capture their imagination and gratitude, and for glowing testimonials to be returned from the drawing room or battlefield. McGonagall was, after all, a professional poet. The free, if unflattering, publicity from local newspapers had largely dried up – though it would return. He required and determinedly sought income to house and feed his family and did not hesitate to apply the power of the pen to secure it. Money, he once wrote, was a necessary evil, especially when in short supply . . .

'I was very hard up for money at the time, and being rather at a loss how to get a little of that filthy lucre, as some people term it.

But, my dear readers, I never considered it to be either filthy or bad. Money is most certainly the most useful commodity in society that I know of. It is certainly good when not abused; but, if abused, the fault rests with the abuser – the money is good nevertheless. For my own part, I have always found it to be one of my best friends.'[1]

A few shillings here, a few shillings there, perhaps a guinea on occasion. Every penny of a limited and precarious income counted towards food and lodgings. He proudly reported Jean's delight with the four shillings and ninepence he had secured after avoiding three rascals near Camperdown Park. 'I gave all to my wife, and she was very thankful to get it, because the wolf was at the door.' It was intermittent income, but a pieceworker was used to that. The visiting muse had egged him on to write, but she had no control over sales.

Just how close were the wolves to Paton's Lane? Poems begat broadsides, which could be sold, so his poetry flowed between performances. So did the thinly disguised letters to the great and the good who were in a position to help him. In the autumn of 1881 he despatched another epistle to his esteemed queen. This contained a new poem on the royal review of troops in King's Park, Edinburgh, now Holyrood Park. The event was staged to commemorate the Scottish Volunteers. Nearly 40,000 soldiers marched before the queen, watched by an estimated 400,000 spectators. The problem was the weather. It rained on the parade from morning to night and everyone – including the queen – was drenched. The event passed into history as the Wet Review.

Crossing comfortably from stormy performances to squally weather, McGonagall felt compelled to stretch his poetic abilities to mark the occasion. He perhaps had another petition to the queen in mind, as the verses, dated 25 September, explicitly eulogise the monarch . . .

All hail to the Empress of India, Great Britain's Queen –
Long may she live in health, happy and serene –
That came from London, far away,
To review the Scottish Volunteers in grand array:
Most magnificent to be seen,

Near by Salisbury Crags and its pastures green,
Which will long be remembered by our gracious Queen.
And by the Volunteers, that came from far away,

Because it rain'd most of the day.
And with the rain their clothes were wet all through,
On the 25th day of August, at the Royal Review,
And to the Volunteers it was no lark,
Because they were ankle deep in mud in the Queen's Park,
Which proved to the Queen they were loyal and true,
To endure such hardships at the Royal Review.

McGonagall's 'Royal Review' noted with a favourite phrase that the occasion would 'long be remembered' by the queen. She was unlikely to forget it, reporting afterwards to an aide that her stockings were soaked and that she had stripped to the royal skin. These two, and another five similarly flattering stanzas, were parcelled up and posted to Buckingham Palace on 10 October for the queen's pleasure and, hopefully, a place in the royal library. Sadly, it was still not policy for manuscript verse to be accepted by the monarch, and the poem was returned to Dundee a week later accompanied by a note from her Private Secretary . . .

'General Sir Henry F. Ponsonby has received the Queen's commands to thank Mr McGonagall for sending the verses which were contained in his letter of the 10th instant, but to express Her Majesty's regret that they must be returned, as it is an invariable rule that offerings of this nature should not be received by the Queen.'[2]

The poem's homecoming was hardly a setback. McGonagall had hoped for more, but scarcely expected it. Unhindered, he brazenly labelled the penny version 'Patronised by Her Majesty' and unleashed it upon his public. For much of the rest of 1881, however, he stayed at home at 19 Paton's Lane and seems to have composed only a handful of poems. His routine day probably involved wandering Dundee's streets flogging his penny sheets and sixpenny pamphlets to existing and new customers. One man who knew him spoke of how he would approach shops and offices in the city, 'with a deferential air carrying a bundle of the latest effusion, sold his copy and went off to the next of his patrons, of whom, I believe, there were many in the town'. Confronted by the Dundee bard bearing his black-ribbon-wrapped tracts, Lewis Spence recalled, 'I noticed the price on the priceless little broadsheet, "one penny"; so, taking sixpence from my pocket, I placed it on the desk. "I have no change," said the poet sadly. "That," I replied, "does not matter." Raising his umbrageous hat with an air quite foreign to Dundee, he graciously thanked me.'[3]

McGonagall set his heart on gaining loftier patronage, writing in the autumn of 1882 to the veteran army commander Sir Garnet Wolseley with a copy of a new poem, 'The Battle of Tel-el-Kebir'. This engagement had taken place in far-off Alexandria and had involved a British expeditionary force commanded by Wolseley which had put a much larger Egyptian force to flight. Little wonder McGonagall felt obliged to mark the stirring ending of an anti-British rebellion with a theatrical 15-verse tribute, which began . . .

> Ye sons of Great Britain, come join with me,
> And sing in praise of Sir Garnet Wolseley,
> Sound drums and trumpets cheerfully,
> For he has acted most heroically.

And ended . . .

> Now since the Egyptian war is at an end,
> Let us thank God! who did send
> Sir Garnet Wolseley to crush and kill
> Arabi and his rebel army at Kebir hill.

Give Sir Garnet his due, he found time from being lauded across the country to send a good-natured reply, via an aide, to McGonagall. Headed Horse Guards, War Office, and dated 13 November 1882, it read: 'Sir Garnet Wolseley has to thank Mr McGonagall for his letter enclosing some verses on the battle of Tel-el-Kebir, which he is much pleased with.' With this ringing endorsement McGonagall rushed out an unusual four-page printed pamphlet containing

'Tel-el-Kebir' – the first of several thunderous 'Arab' poems – and his perennial favourite, Bannockburn.[4]

A kindred letter of acknowledgement followed from Camp Korti on the directions of Wolseley, thanking McGonagall for a new poem written to commemorate the battle of Abu Klea.[5] This was viewed by the poet as another thumbs-up from the general and duly appeared on printed versions of 'Abu Klea' and on many subsequent broadsides. He also sent a copy of his tribute to the fearless Gordon of Khartoum to the general's daughter, receiving a letter of thanks for the lines written in her father's memory. A letter of acknowledgement on behalf of the Duke of Cambridge duly arrived for a copy of the Gordon poem, and another from the Lord Mayor of London for the same verse.[6] McGonagall had no inhibitions about allowing his work to be seen by the important and influential. Call it confidence or conceit, he believed his poetry good enough to be placed before a wider audience than that available to it locally.

The following years brought significant new compositions. Among them was 'The Famous Tay Whale' in January 1884, a tribute to a docile giant which playfully gave the local whaling fleet the slip before – to the whalers' embarrassment – being caught off Inverbervie and ignominiously carted back to Dundee for public display.

There, during what whalermen would call the flensing process at John Woods' East Dock Street yard, the *Advertiser* reported: 'In the course of the dissecting operations an amusing diversion was caused by a long-haired gentleman in a black surtout and slouched hat calling the attention of the spectators to a poem, apropos of the whale, of which he proclaimed himself the author, and which he proceeded to recite with much gusto. He afterwards announced that the poem could be obtained on payment of the sum of one penny, and condescendingly sold a few copies at that figure.' Here was McGonagall 'striking while the iron was hot'. He later offered a copy of the whale poem to Dundee Museum to display beside the creature's skeleton. The offer was declined.[7]

In the poem, McGonagall confuses his continents by introducing an equatorial celebrity to the tale . . .

'Twas in the month of December, and in the year 1883
That a monster whale came to Dundee,
Resolved for a few days to sport and play,
And devour small fishes in the silvery Tay.

And they laughed and grinned just like wild baboons,
While they fired at him their sharp harpoons:
But when struck with the harpoons he dived below,
Which filled his pursuers' hearts with woe:
Because they guessed they had lost a prize,
Which caused the tears to well up in their eyes;
And in that their anticipations were only right,
Because he sped on to Stonehaven with all his might.

Showing few signs of combat fatigue, 'The Battle of El-Teb' followed in March 1884, in which the British Army defeated the forces of the Egyptian commander Osman Digna, known as Osman the Ugly. McGonagall sang the praises of the victory over 18 spectacular stanzas, bequeathing to the nation a memorable couplet in praise of General Graham . . .

Whose name will be handed down to posterity without any
    stigma,
Because, at the battle of El-Teb, he defeated Osman Digna.

Another epic in 1884 marked the death of Queen Victoria's favourite son Prince Leopold from the effects of a fall, its penny broadside incorporating a black mourning border. This poem was one of the first to feature a conspicuous dating tool in the poet's corpus . . .

'Twas on Saturday the 12th of April, in the year 1884,
He was buried in the royal vault, never to rise more.

Similarly, when four firemen died in Dundee the same month, the 'Clepington Catastrophe' tribute to the tragedy began with, ' 'Twas on a Monday morning in the year 1884/That a fire broke out in Bailie Bradford's Store . . .'

A further 60 ' 'Twas' poems followed, offering useful dating aids. 'The Clepington Catastrophe' also typifies poems produced on weighty subjects which begin sombrely but develop comical stanzas. In this case . . .

> But accidents will happen by land and by sea,
> Therefore, to save ourselves from accidents, we needn't try
>   to flee,
> For whatsoever God has ordained will come to pass:
> For instance, ye might be killed by a stone or a piece of glass.

And in that year's 'Tale of the Sea', McGonagall innocently veers off his solemn story to reveal how a shipwrecked crew's hunger got the better of them . . .

> He suddenly seized his knife and cut off poor Jim's arm,
> Not thinking in his madness he'd done any harm;
> Then poor Jim's blood he did drink, and his flesh did eat,
> Declaring that the blood tasted like cream, and was a treat.

Major local events boosted William McGonagall's yield. September 1884 brought 'The Great Franchise Demonstration, Dundee', which reported on that month's march in favour of the government bill which would have extended the vote to many working-class men. Representative of no one other than himself, McGonagall was not invited to take part in the march. His frustration at being publicly sidelined was duly recorded . . .

'I was prohibited from walking in the Franchise Demonstration. Which I always remember of me running along the line of processionists and trying to get a place amongst them, but it was in vain, and in my opinion the greater shame. And, my dear Friend, I was like to faint with shame to think I should be refused a place in that procession that I had composed a Poem about, why Sir, I look upon it to be one of the most degrading actions ever I met with while in Dundee.'[8]

Instead the poem consisted of what McGonagall could see from the back of a carriage owned by a theatre manager who

had noticed him running after the procession and offered him a lift
to Magdalen Green. The following month he nailed his egalitarian
and democratic colours to the mast again when he penned an
elegant appeal for women's suffrage. This anticipated one of the
major arguments of the Edwardian suffragette movement by
thoughtfully highlighting the inequity of women's taxation without
representation . . .

> Fellow-men! why should the Lords try to despise,
> And prohibit women from having the benefit of the
>   parliamentary Franchise?
> When they pay the same taxes as you and me,
> I consider they ought to have the same liberty.
>
> And I consider if they are not allowed the same liberty,
> From taxation every one of them should be set free;
> And if they are not, it is really very unfair,
> And an act of injustice, I most solemnly declare.

In supporting the steady expansion of education and voting rights
to the working classes, McGonagall captured late Victorian Liberal
optimism. He had expressed his commitment to political equality
and left his footprint on the pathway to the democracy Scotland
enjoys today. And if he had lived just six more years into the
Edwardian era, he would have waved his priestly hat and cheered
on the militant suffragettes chasing Winston Churchill through the
streets of Dundee.

Instead, by the mid 1880s, William McGonagall was suffering
from a serious illness and unable to carry out public engagements.
His worsening condition propelled him to seek help – not medical,
but financial. Money always seemed at the root of his problems. In
January 1885, he wrote to his 'best friend' Alex Hutcheson, an
architect who lived in Broughty Ferry, to ask for funds. 'I am still in
great difficulties at present. I thank you for the 26/- in stamps you
sent during my illness, but my dear friend I ask you again for the last
time for god's sake to lend me one pound to bring me out of my
present difficulties, and I promise I will pay it back 2 fold before I

die, if not I will take it to be a great insult, and I will never look you in the face again, my modesty will not allow it.'[9]

McGonagall is despairing in this appeal. The amount asked for is significant and suggests that the wolf was very close to his door. He would not have been alone in seeing eviction and the poorhouse on the horizon, however. Dundee had effectively stuffed its manufacturing eggs into one basket, and textile production endured a terrible depression in the 1880s. Factories closed or went on to short time. Wages were at their lowest for a decade. Jute was squeezed from traditional markets by cheaper Indian cloth and European tariffs and 'jobs for men were scarce'. [10] Besides, McGonagall's poor health probably restricted his daily routine and contributed to the financial strain on his household. His medical problems were raised in a poetic tribute to his doctor, composed in 1885. Here he divulged that he had been poorly and that part of the remedy presented to him was to give up poetry. This cure, ironically, was related to his readers in rhyme . . .

> Success to the good and skilful Dr. Murison
> For golden opinions he has won
> From his patients one and all,
> And from myself, McGonagall.
>
> He is very skilful and void of pride;
> He was so to me when at my bedside,
> When I turned badly on the 25th of July,
> And was ill with inflammation, and like to die.
>
> He told me at once what was ailing me;
> He said I had been writing too much poetry,
> And from writing poetry I would have to refrain,
> Because I was suffering from inflammation on the brain . . .
>
> . . . And I wish him success for many a long day,
> For he has saved me from dying, I venture to say;
> The kind treatment I received surpasses all
> Is the honest confession of McGonagall.

The letter to his architect friend and the dedication to his doctor suggest McGonagall was ill for long periods spanning 1884–1886, apparently so seriously that he added in his letter to Alexander Hutcheson, 'I entreat of you for Gods sake for to comply with my request for fear I relapse again and die, Believe me yours truly, William McGonagall, poet, write soon.'[11] From this point, William McGonagall's health owns a significant share in the story of his life and his concerns, which would have affected his ability to improve his income, may have contributed to his move, in March 1885, from 19 to 31 Paton's Lane.

He was also troubled by domestic matters early in 1885 when his daughter Margaret faced a charge at Dundee Sheriff Court of failing to educate her fatherless son, Andrew. Margaret did not appear and it was left to her mother Jean to tell the court that her daughter was 'unwell'. The fiscal insisted that she explained precisely where she was . . .

Mrs McGonagall: 'Well, she got work this week and she's in some mill. She did not want to leave work.'

Procurator (to Sheriff Cheyne): 'There is no getting these people to do anything except by the severest measures. This old lady even declined to tell the officer where her daughter lived.'

Mrs McGonagall: 'I don't know; when she left the house I said I would never go near her.'

Then, to the sheriff, Jean said that she kept 12-year-old Andrew and that he had been crying all day the previous day with a pain in his ear – clearly a hereditary complaint.

Sheriff Cheyne: 'Go away, go away, we will get your daughter.'[12]

From this short exchange it can be gleaned that Margaret had left home under some sort of cloud, leaving her son with his grandparents. It also illuminates the position of the workplace where, rather than give up precious jobs, women in Dundee were known to have their babies where they stood and to continue working.

Contributing to McGonagall's *annus miserabilis* was a pseudo-autobiography which appeared in 1885. This anonymous paper-wrapped booklet, *The Book of the Lamentations of the Poet MacGonagall, An Autobiography*, ridiculed him in print and must have caused considerable distress among the wider McGonagall clan. It was subtitled, *Dedicated to Himself, Knowing None Greater,* and this theme of self-aggrandisement gathered pace through its 16 fault-finding pages.

Lamentations began with a malevolent flashback to McGonagall's birth and parentage and informed readers how his father had jail sentences 'varying from 4 to 14 weeks' for misdemeanours. There was nothing remarkable about McGonagall himself 'internally or externally' and he prosaically courted, married and had sons and daughters 'without anything anywhere to indicate the slumbering volcano of genius which lay hid beneath my placid breast'. Thereafter the diatribe poked fun at McGonagall's poetic contributions to newspapers, his Balmoral trek and how his public performances had resulted in being 'pelted with pease, rotten apples, treacle, flour, and all sorts of abominable and unmentionable offal'. One short extract portrays its gratuitous irony: 'Poinding for rent has become so common with me that I begin to experience a sense of neglect if somebody is not hunting me for coin.'[13]

The Book of the Lamentations is neither attributed to an author nor dated. It was written by the respected Lever Soap agent for the town, John Willocks, who lived in Dudhope Crescent, and was published by him in 1885. A pencil note on the 85-page manuscript supplied to the printer suggests 300 copies were ordered by Willocks from an A. Mitchell, Seagate, at a cost of £3 5s. It was priced sixpence and if all sold Willocks would have doubled his outlay. But McGonagall was appalled at the largely spurious telling of his life. It is not known if the men had a history, or whether Burns aficionado Willocks was simply caught up in the local pastime of decrying the rival bard. Indeed, McGonagall may have agreed in principle to the autobiography as a means of raising funds before taking grave exception to how it turned out. Whatever, McGonagall was sufficiently horrified by *Lamentations* to consult a solicitor soon after its publication. The result was that Willocks was forced to withdraw the booklet. On 8 December 1885 Willocks sent John Thomson, solicitor, a humble apology and retraction . . .

'. . . Re alleged slander of Mr McGonagall and his relatives and beg sincerely to apologise to Mr McGonagall for any statement

This portrait of McGonagall, in his familiar tweed suit, was copied in 1891 for the frontispiece of *Poetic Gems Second Series*.

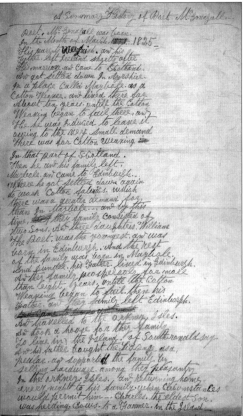

The pencilled autobiography *Summary History* provides the earliest-known information about McGonagall and his family. His purpose in writing it is unclear.

McGonagall's first recorded address in 1841 was on the Hawkhill, Dundee, seen here from the West Port. He moved to 44 West Port shortly after his marriage in 1846.

Right. This rare poster, now in the McGonagall Collection, establishes McGonagall as an amateur actor – or tragedian – as early as 1858.

Below left. The Theatre Royal in Castle Street is marked today by a small bust of William Shakespeare.

Below right. A manuscript copy of the 'Inauguration of the Hill o' Balgay', composed in 1878.

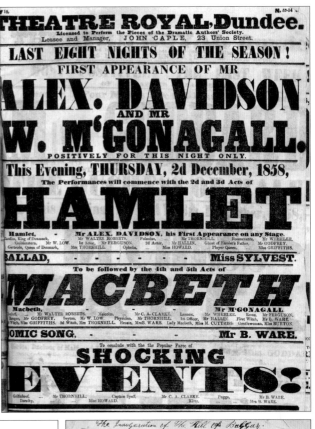

The back stairs of a typical Dundee tenement in McGonagall's time.

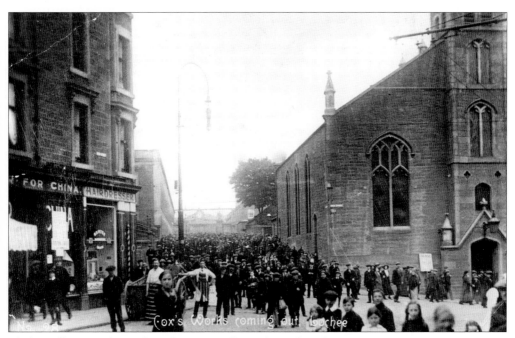

Clocking-off at a Dundee textiles mill. McGonagall spent his working days as a carpet weaver.

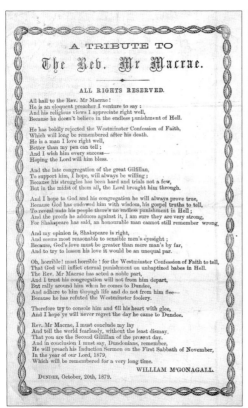

A TRIBUTE TO

The Rev. Mr Macrae.

All hail to the Rev. Mr Macrae!
He is an eloquent preacher I venture to say :
And his religious views I appreciate right well,
Because he doesn't believe in the endless punishment of Hell.

He has boldly rejected the Westminster Confession of Faith,
Which will long be remembered after his death.
He is a man I love right well,
Better than my pen can tell ;
And I wish him every success—
Hoping the Lord will him bless.

And the late congregation of the great Gilfillan,
To support him, I hope, will always be willing ;
Because his struggles has been hard and trials not a few,
But in the midst of them all, the Lord brought him through.

And I hope to God and his congregation he will always prove true,
Because God has endowed him with wisdom, his gospel truths to tell,
To reveal unto his people there's no endless punishment in Hell ;
And the proofs he adduces against it, I am sure they are very strong,
For Shakspeare has said, an honourable man cannot still remember wrong.

And my opinion is, Shakspeare is right,
And seems most reasonable to sensible men's eyesight ;
Because, God's love must be greater than mere man's by far,
And to try to lesson his love it would be an unequal par.

Oh, horrible! most horrible! for the Westminster Confession of Faith to tell,
That God will inflict eternal punishment on unbaptized babes in Hell.
The Rev. Mr Macrae has acted a noble part,
And I trust his congregation will not from him depart,
But rally around him when he comes to Dundee,
And adhere to him through life and do not from him flee—
Because he has refuted the Westminster foolery.

Therefore try to console him and fill his heart with glee,
And I hope ye will never regret the day he came to Dundee.

Rev. Mr Macrae, I must conclude my lay
And tell the world fearlessly, without the least dismay.
That you are the Second Gilfillan of the present day.
And in conclusion I must say, Dundonians, remember,
He will preach his Induction Sermon on the First Sabbath of November,
In the year of our Lord, 1879,
Which will be remembered for a very long time.

WILLIAM M'GONAGALL.

DUNDEE, October, 20th, 1879.

Above left. The printed version of McGonagall's tribute to the Rev David Macrae, dated October 20, 1879, was possibly his first-ever broadside.

Above right. Noted today for his trilogy on the Tay railway bridges, McGonagall also composed a fourth, titled 'The Testing Day of the Bridge of Tay'. It has not survived.

Right. The cover of McGonagall's first printed collection, which he issued in 1878 and proudly endorsed, Poet to Her Majesty.

Poetical Pieces.

POEMS AND SONG

BY

WILLIAM M^cGONAGALL,

POET TO HER MAJESTY.

CONTENTS.

THE RAILWAY BRIDGE OF THE SILVERY TAY.
THE INAUGURATION OF THE HILL O' BALGAY.
SONG—THE BONNIE LASS O' DUNDEE.
ADDRESS TO THE REV. GEORGE GILFILLAN.

Mr McGonagall holds in his possession an Acknowledgement from the Empress of India, dated, Buckingham Palace, sixteenth day of October, anno domini, eighteen hundred and seventy-seven, and signed by General Sir Thomas Biddulph.

GENTLEMEN WAITED UPON AT THEIR OWN RESIDENCES, AND READINGS GIVEN FROM THE BRITISH POETS.

Testimonials as Reader from the REV. GEORGE GILFILLAN, the Late Professor ISLAY BURNS, Free Church College, Glasgow, &c.

PRICE TWOPENCE EACH.

McGonagall was forcibly removed from the ceremony to unveil the Burns Statue in Dundee in 1880. His tribute poem has survived only as a fragment.

A spoof McGonagall 'autobiography' appeared in 1885. McGonagall secured an apology from its author and it was withdrawn from sale.

The exterior of 17–21 Paton's Lane in 1978, shortly before demolition. McGonagall moved to No 19 in 1873.

Above. An appeal to the hotelier Alex Lamb for help to pay outstanding rent.

Above right. An original manuscript of the song 'Loch Katrine', composed in 1886. McGonagall usually separated his stanzas with a thick ink line.

Right. McGonagall to A. C. Lamb in October 1886 asking for a £1 loan to help with printing costs 'to publish a 6d volume.'

Left. This dramatic pose recreates McGonagall's extraordinary stage performance of 'Bannockburn'.

Below. Some of McGonagall's most tempestuous performances took place in the 'village' of Lochee, a stronghold of the Irish weaving community.

'The Storming of Dargai Heights', composed in 1888, provides one of the most flamboyantly decorated of all McGonagall's penny sheets.

McGonagall in thoughtful pose, cloaked in a curious patterned robe, c1890.

The portrait was reworked by David Gray for the frontispiece of *Poetic Gems* in 1890.

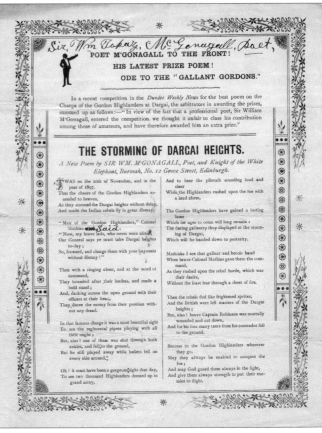

Sir Wm Topaz, McGonagall, Poet,

POET M'GONAGALL TO THE FRONT!

HIS LATEST PRIZE POEM!

ODE TO THE "GALLANT GORDONS."

In a recent competition in the *Dundee Weekly News* for the best poem on the Charge of the Gordon Highlanders at Dargai, the arbitrators in awarding the prizes, summed up as follows:—" In view of the fact that a professional poet, Sir William M'Gonagall, entered the competition, we thought it unfair to class his contribution among those of amateurs, and have therefore awarded him an extra prize."

THE STORMING OF DARGAI HEIGHTS.

A New Poem by SIR WM. M'GONAGALL, Poet, and Knight of the White Elephant, Burmah, No. 12 Grove Street, Edinburgh.

'TWAS on the 20th of November, and in the year of 1897,
That the cheers of the Gordon Highlanders ascended to heaven,
As they stormed the Dargai heights without delay,
And made the Indian rebels fly in great dismay.

"Men of the Gordon Highlanders," Colonel Mathias said,
"Now, my brave lads, who never were afraid,
Our General says ye must take Dargai heights to-day;
So, forward, and charge them with your bayonets without dismay!"

Then with a ringing cheer, and at the word of command,
They bounded after their leaders, and made a bold stand;
And, dashing across the open ground with their officers at their head,
They drove the enemy from their position without any dread.

In that famous charge it was a most beautiful sight
To see the regimental pipers playing with all their might;
But, alas! one of them was shot through both ankles, and fell to the ground,
But he still played away while bullets fell on every side around.

Oh! it must have been a gorgeous sight that day,
To see two thousand Highlanders dressed up in grand array.

And to hear the pibroch sounding loud and clear
While the Highlanders rushed upon the foe with a loud cheer.

The Gordon Highlanders have gained a lasting fame
Which for ages to come will long remain;
The daring gallantry they displayed at the storming of Dargai,
Which will be handed down to posterity.

Methinks I see that gallant and heroic band
When brave Colonel Mathias gave them the command,
As they rushed upon the rebel horde, which was their desire,
Without the least fear through a sheet of fire.

Then the rebels fled like frightened sprites,
And the British were left masters of the Dargai heights;
But, alas! brave Captain Robinson was mortally wounded and cut down,
And for his loss many tears from his comrades fell to the ground.

Success to the Gordon Highlanders wherever they go.
May they always be enabled to conquer the foe;
And may God guard them always in the fight,
And give them always strength to put their enemies to flight.

Faithfully Yours William McGonagall poet, and Tragedian.

V. R.

COMPOSED, 23rd MAY, 1884.

THE RATTLING BOY FROM DUBLIN.

A New Comic Song

By WILLIAM M'GONAGALL, 19 Paton's Lane, Dundee.

The Bard of Tel-El-Kebir, also El-Teb, &c., &c.

Patronized by Her Majesty and Lord Wolseley of Cairo; H.R.H. the Duke of Cambridge, The Right Hon. W. E. Gladstone, and General Graham; also the Nobility and Gentry, &c.

I'm a rattling Boy from Dublin town,
I courted a girl called Biddy Brown,
Her eyes they were as black as sloes,
She had black hair and an aquiline nose.

CHORUS—
Whack fal de da, fal de darelido,
Whack fal de da, fal de darelay,
Whack fal de da, fal de darelido,
Whack fal de da, fal de darelay.

One night I met her with another lad,
Says I, Biddy, I've caught you, by dad;
I never thought you were half so bad,
As to be going about with another lad.
Chorus.

Says I, Biddy, this will never do,
For to-night you've prov'd to me untrue;
So do not make a hullaballoo,
For I will bid farewell to you.
Chorus.

Says Barney Magee, she is my lass,
And the man that says no he is an ass;
So come away and I'll give you a glass,
Och, sure you can get another lass.
Chorus.

Says I, to the devil with your glass,
You have taken from me my darling lass;
And if you look angry or offer to frown,
With my darling shillelah I'll knock you down.
Chorus.

Says Barney Magee unto me,
By the hokey I love Biddy Brown,
And before I'll give her up to thee,
One or both of us will go down.
Chorus.

So with my darling shillelah I gave him a whack,
Which left him lying on his back,
Saying, botheration to you and Biddy Brown,—
For I'm the rattling boy from Dublin town.
Chorus.

So a policeman chanced to come up at the time,
And he asked of me the cause of the shine;
Says I, he threatened to knock me down,
When I challenged him for walking with my Biddy Brown.
Chorus.

So the policeman took Barney Magee to jail,
Which made him shout and bewail,
That ever he met with Biddy Brown,
The greatest deceiver in Dublin town.
Chorus.

So I bade farewell to Biddy Brown,
The greatest jilter in Dublin town;
Because she proved untrue to me,
And was going about with Barney Magee.
Chorus.

'The Rattling Boy from Dublin' was among McGonagall's favourite performance poems. This broadside version from 1884 is particularly handsome.

Only one McGonagall programme survives, possibly from his performance at the Cutlers' Hall, Murraygate in July 1879.

Right. The original manuscript of a McGonagall masterpiece, in which he anticipates Newport housewives rushing to Dundee by train for cheap jam and Lipton's ham.

Below. The billposters seen here in turn-of-the-century South Union Street would have proclaimed the venue, date and times of McGonagall's 'entertainments'.

The Newport Railway

Success to the Newport Railway,
Along the banks o' the Silvery Tay,
And to Dundee straightway,
Which was opened on the 12th. May,
In the year of our Lord 1879,
Which will clear all expenses in a very short time.
Because the thrifty housewives of Newport,
To Dundee often will resort,
Which will be to them profit and sport,
By bringing cheap Tea Bread and Jam,
And also some of Lipton's Ham,
Which will make their hearts feel light and gay,
And cause them for to bless the opening day
of the Newport Railway.

The train is most beautiful to be seen,
With its long white curling cloud of steam,
As the train passes on her way,
Along the bonnie braes o' the Silvery Tay,
And if the people of Dundee,
Should feel inclined to have a spree,
I'm sure t'will fill their hearts with glee,
By crossing o'er to Newport,
And there they can have excellent sport,
By viewing the scenery beautiful and gay,
During the live long Summer day,
And then they can return at night,
With spirits light and gay,
By the Newport Railway,
By night or by day,
Across the Railway Bridge o' the Silvery Tay,
Success to the undertakers of the Newport Railway,
Hoping the Lord will their labours repay,
And prove a blessing to the people
For many a long day,
That lives near by Newport on the bonnie
Braes o' the Silvery Tay.

Composed 1878. William McGonagall.
Dundee.

presented to Mr John Bell. With the Authors Compliments
Poet McGonagall.

Richard Pigott, The Forger.

Richard Pigott the forger, was a very bad man,
And to gainsay it there's nobody can.
Because for fifty years he pursued a career of deceit,
And as a forger, few men with him could compete.

For by forged letters he tried to accuse Parnell,
For the Phœnix Park murders but mark what befel.
When his Conscience smote him he confessed to the fraud,
And the thought thereof no doubt drove him mad.

Then he fled from London. without delay,
Knowing he wouldn't be safe there night, nor day,
And embarked on board a ship bound for Spain.
Thinking he would escape detection there, but twas all in vain.

Because while staying at a hotel in Spain.
He appeared to the landlord to be a little insane.
And he noticed he was always seemingly in dread.
Like a person that had committed a murder and afterwards fled.

And when arrested in the hotel, he seemed very cool,
Just like an innocent schoolboy going to School.
And he said to the detectives wait until my portmanteau,
And while going for his portmanteau, himself he shot. I've got.

Left. This is an example of how McGonagall would copy out poems, as if they were originals, to present as gifts, as in this instance, or to sell to customers.

Below. The Victorians at this busy market stall in Dundee would have witnessed the Poet of Paton's Lane on his broadside-selling wanderings.

Right. This tribute to the Rev Mackonochie, composed in 1887, shows the laudations typically incorporated into McGonagall's printed sheets.

Below. A bustling scene in Greenmarket, where McGonagall would have confronted the staring, baiting and finger-pointing youngsters who blighted his life in Dundee.

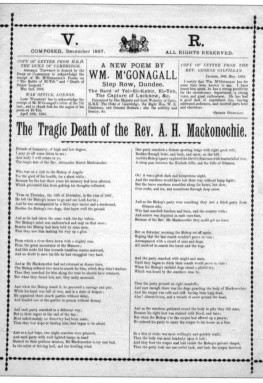

Originally Dundee Exchange, this handsome building was the scene of McGonagall's Music Hall triumphs in the 1860s.

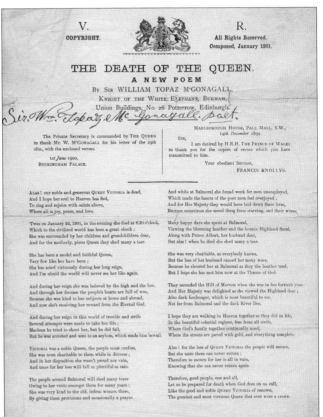

A letter from Potterow, Edinburgh to James Shand in Dundee enclosing copies of a poem rushed out to commemorate Queen Victoria's death in January 1901.

'The Death of the Queen' broadside is shown here with its author's flamboyant 'Sir Wm Topaz McGonagall, Poet' signature.

Right. This 'lecturing' portrait is untypical of a McGonagall performance, which would involve endless strutting to and fro across the stage.

Below. Another busy view of Dundee's Greenmarket, now the site of the Caird Hall.

Once situated in Perth Road, McGonagall's bar was frequented by members of the William McGonagall Appreciation Society as well as by McGonagall enthusiasts from around the world.

In the shadow of the triumphal Royal Arch, McGonagall set off by steamer in 1880 on his hope-filled peregrination to London.

Above left. This painting by Tom Mulholland adorns the wall outside the Local Studies department, which houses the McGonagall Collection at Dundee Central Library.

Above right. A memorial marking McGonagall's last resting place in Greyfriars Cemetery, Edinburgh was unveiled in 1999.

Right. A photograph of the poet in Dundee in his trademark long coat and 'priest's' hat, *c*1890.

made in the work in question calculated to injure his feelings and I undertake to sell no more of the book or cause any more of them to be printed and I also authorise Mr McGonagall or anyone acting for him to get the manuscript of the book from The Courier & Argus and to burn or publish from it as he sees fit.'[14]

Willocks did not keep his promise. Three years after McGonagall's death in 1902 he produced a new version of *Lamentations* and had it printed by John Durham in Dundee with the breathtaking title, *This is the Book of Lamentations of the Poet McGonagall, Portraying in His Own Unapproachable Style His Birth and Parentage, Early Struggles, Miraculous and Hairbreadth Escapes, with a Graphic and Characteristic Account Setting Forth, How, By His Inspired Genius and Indomitable Pluck, He Passed From Penury and Persecution Through a Knighthood into an Immortality of Fame.* Priced one shilling, and enlarged to 140 pages, the 'safe' 1905 printing cast a dark shadow over the late poet's life and work, but, happily, appears to have been produced in such small numbers that it quickly faded into insignificance and obscurity. Willocks' obituary said of him, 'He was a ready humorist and an accomplished raconteur.' Maybe, but he was neither a man of pity nor compassion.

McGonagall was determined to set the record straight. To the printers he went with his second manuscript autobiography, the *c* 1880 *Original Manuscript*. This was lodged with Luke, Mackie & Co. of 115 Murraygate, who added still-visible hand corrections to it and printed it as a 20-page pamphlet titled *The Authentic Autobiography of the Poet McGonagall, Written by Himself.*

This now-rare publication had steel-blue soft wrappers, carried an impressive cover quotation by Shakespeare and was priced at sixpence. Its contents covered brief elements of McGonagall's early stage career, his first poems to the *Weekly News* in 1877 and the *Evening Telegraph*'s review of his four-page *Poems and Song* in 1878. Much of it was given over to his Balmoral journey of the same year.

The Luke, Mackie booklet is undated. That nothing within it post-dates the Balmoral journey and that its text is unambiguously based on the earlier *Original Manuscript* suggests the booklet dates to before McGonagall's London trip in 1880 and certainly before the slanderous *Lamentations* of 1885. On closer scrutiny, however, this could not have been the case. Luke Mackie & Co. is recorded at 115 Murraygate only from 1885. The cover wording, *Written by Himself*, also suggests McGonagall was attempting damage limitation by offering an honest version of his life. Indeed, the title page also bears the advisory quotation, 'Truth is Stranger Than Fiction'. In any case, prior to the issue of Willocks' defamatory booklet in 1885, McGonagall had no reason to go to the expense of printing an account of his life. Thus it seems likely that *Lamentations* was circulated and withdrawn to be followed almost immediately by the rushed printing of *The Authentic Autobiography of the Poet McGonagall*, which had lain in manuscript form in the author's possession for some years.

As if to give Willocks a literary bloody nose to add to his wounded wallet, McGonagall upped production in 1885 with four battle poems in the spring and the start of his peculiar 'Jack o' the Cudgel' sequence of verse in June that year. The latter comprised what he termed first, second and fourth cantos of historical poems set at the time of the fourteenth-century Edward III. There is no record of a third canto, but the same title was adopted for McGonagall's sole surviving play, a medieval melodrama first performed in Dundee in 2002 and published by Birlinn in 2006 as 'Jack o' the Cudgel, The Hero of A Hundred Fights'.[15] Another unusual poem in 1885 was dedicated to his parents: 'A New Temperance Poem, in Memory of My Departed Parents, Who were Sober-Living and God-Fearing People', and was probably another response to Willocks' vindictive comments. It begins . . . 'My parents were sober-living, and often did pray for their family to abstain from intoxicating drink always', but quickly develops into a rant on alcohol abuse.

A change of theme followed in 1886 when William McGonagall's pen brought forth poetic narratives on a series of maritime calamities and heroics, including 'The Wreck of the Barque "Wm Paterson" of Liverpool', 'The Wreck of the "Columbine"', 'A Horrible Tale of the Sea' and 'Young Munro the Sailor'. These faithfully interpreted newspaper reports, or exercised the poet-doggerelist's ability to twang emotional heart-strings. On local affairs he offered his readers two straightforward scene-setters, Baldovan Mansion and Broughty Ferry. McGonagall was not the instinctive documentary writer often portrayed. He held a lifelong fascination with, and took pleasure from, the world around him. He wrote unhesitatingly, passionately and prolifically on lochs, rivers, the sea and the countryside. He praised parks and municipal shrubberies, recommended resorts for pure air and charted panoramas here and there that were always 'most lovely' or the 'most beautiful to be seen'.

Thus he seldom neglected local affairs and he clearly enjoyed his walk along to the Dundee Flower Show in 1886, which resulted in a colossal tribute from his pen in which he just avoids mentioning every participant. It begins in his familiar style . . .

'Twas in the year of 1886, and in the 2nd day of September,
Which the lovers of horticultural beauty will long remember,
Especially those that visited the Flower Show, on the
        Magdalen Green, Dundee,
Must confess it was really a most magnificent sight to see,
And the Mars' Boys band were there on Friday afternoon
And their instruments seemed to be in very good tune,
They discoursed sweet music until six o'clock,
While the people around them did flock.
There were also some beautiful Chrysanthemums, distinct,
All in full bloom, with a charming tint,
Some of them short and some of them tall,
And some of them belonging to Provost Ballingall,
And there were twenty-four roses distinct to be seen,
Belonging to James Cocker and Sons, Aberdeen,
Also some beautiful roses as ever sprang from the earth,
And some of them belonging to Dickens & Turnbull, Perth.

Over a century after it was composed, dedicated to the Earl of Dalhousie, and peddled as a penny tract, 'Dundee Flower Show' was given an appropriate public airing at the Dundee Flower and Food Festival at Camperdown Park in September 2005. Cocker's timeless roses were a blooming success then as in McGonagall's day. However, he must have had literary matters on his mind when referring to Perth horticulturalists Dickson & Turnbull as Dickens.

With this raft of fresh poems under his belt by the mid-1880s, and perhaps some financial settlement by way of compensation for Willocks' savaging, William McGonagall called into another print shop in late 1887. He felt a new collection of his work was required and it duly appeared as *The Autobiography and Poetical Works of William McGonagall, Dundee*, printed by Charles Mackie & Co. of 13 & 15 Peter Street. This booklet ran to a handsome 40 pages. Its grey, decorative cover bore a Shakespearean quotation and the asking price of sixpence. Inside was effectively the autobiography that had resurfaced two years earlier. He still did not feel obliged to include his 1880 London adventure, which had been ridiculed in *Lamentations*. Twenty-three poems spanned his first decade of production. They included his early 'Ode to the Queen' and 'Inauguration of the Hill o' Balgay', as well as the more recent 'Battle of El-Teb' and 'Dedication to Mr James Scrymgeour, Dundee', a champion of the working classes.

The copy of *Autobiography and Poetical Works* at Dundee Central Libraries is dated in McGonagall's hand 16 February 1887 and a brief review in the *People's Journal* three days later predicted long-lasting infamy for the literary genius the town had weaned . . . 'In this little pamphlet Poet McGonagall has gathered together the incidents of his life and the chief productions of his muse. The latter will place his fame upon a stable foundation.' The paper truthfully pointed out that Tennyson had never written anything like 'Bonnie Dundee' and that McGonagall's clairvoyant 'Address to the Tay Bridge' had 'foreseen the catastrophe in prophetic vision'. It is not known how many copies of the booklet were prepared, issued or sold. It may have been comparatively few, as McGonagall struggled to meet its costs. In September 1886 he wrote to A.C. Lamb, begging him to contribute to the bill anticipated for the sixpenny volume. In February 1888 financial arrears again prompted McGonagall to ask Lamb for £1, as his printer had demanded payment. In return he offered the hotelier his recitation sword or manuscripts of his poems. As old age beckoned, McGonagall became increasingly keen to sell original manuscripts to well-heeled collectors.[16]

McGonagall also continued to give random performances but

was justifiably reluctant, as someone approaching his sixtieth year, to face a barrage of missiles or physical violence. Instead, another great adventure was planned; the outrageous notion which befell him in the spring of 1887 to visit the United States. It is uncertain why he wanted or decided to go to America – though he said on his return it was partly due to the worsening behaviour of Dundee's youth. Presumably his hangers-on also told him the New World was where appreciative audiences on a vast scale would welcome his Scottish wit and wisdom. They would have egged him on, telling him fortunes were there to be made and that a showman of McGonagall's stature would soon shine brightly among the firmament of emerging stars on the other side of the Atlantic. Some probably chipped in for his travel costs – about £2 was required for a steerage return to New York. However he managed to pay for it, a two-way trip to America was quite out of the ordinary for working-class Dundonians. McGonagall himself was quite out of the ordinary, of course.

So on 9 March 1887 he took the train to Glasgow and spent the night in temperance lodgings in Broomielaw, leaving Dundonians to playfully bemoan his departure and quip that it would break the dear queen's heart to know he was leaving her shores in her Golden Jubilee year. The next day he boarded the SS *Circassia*, an Anchor Line steamer which could carry around 500 souls in saloons and steerage. She left Glasgow the following morning and arrived in New York 10 days later.

McGonagall recalled the trip for his self-congratulatory final autobiography in 1901, naming the chapter 'To New York in 1887'. Much of it, inevitably, can be taken with a pinch of salt, not least the start of the journey, when he discovered his instant popularity with fellow travellers: 'While at sea I was quite a favourite amongst the passengers, and displayed my histrionic abilities, to the delight of the passengers, but received no remuneration for so doing.' Recording events 14 years on, he still could not suppress the memory of an unpaid performance.

On arrival McGonagall faced an inquisition not unfamiliar to modern-day transatlantic travellers: 'When I arrived at Castle Garden, New York, I wasn't permitted to pass on to my place of destination until the officials there questioned me regarding the place in New York I was going to, and how old I was, and what trade I was; and, of course, I told them I was a weaver, whereas if I had said I was a poet, they wouldn't allow me to pass, but I satisfied them in their interrogations, and was allowed to pass on to my place of destination.'

McGonagall had no travellers' cheques, automated bank card, internet account or wad of US dollars. What he had was eight shillings, which he changed for American currency after persuading officials it was sufficient for his immediate needs. He then made his way to an address on 49th Street where an 'acquaintance' formerly of Dundee lived. No name of his host is provided, but this became his base for a six-week stay in New York.

Once settled McGonagall engaged the gears of finding work. 'But alas! 'twas all in vain, for they all told me they didn't encourage rivalry, but if I had the money to secure a hall to display my abilities, or a company of my own, I would make lots of money; but I am sorry to say I had neither.' His 1901 autobiography relates how he spent three days tramping around central New York plying theatre and music hall proprietors for work. Managers told him they could not give him a booking as there was patriotic hostility towards 'all British artists and how I had come at a very bad time'. He then tried hawking his poem sheets, but found the anti-British feeling persisting. 'The first day I tried to sell them it was a complete failure for this reason – when they saw the Royal coat of arms on the top of the poems they got angry.' An indignant McGonagall reported this experience to his host on 49th Street, to be advised to cut off the royal crests and to try again. But . . . 'I was astonished to hear him say so, and told him "No!" I said, "I decline to do so. I am not ashamed of the Royal coat of arms yet, and I think you ought to be ashamed for telling me so."'

McGonagall's exit strategy from America was pre-planned. He had beforehand consulted the wise hotelier Alexander Lamb and had been gifted a promise that if things did not go to plan, Lamb would telegram funds to pay his passage home. So it transpired. 'I told him for God's sake to take me home from out of this second Babylon, for I could get no one to help me, and when writing it the big tears were rolling down my cheeks, and at the end of the letter I told him to address it to the Anchor Line Steam Shipping Company's office, to lie till called for.'

Lamb kept his promise and sent £6 – twice as much as McGonagall expected – which allowed the disillusioned Dundee bard the luxury of a second-class cabin on the *Circassia*. He took part in another improvised concert on the return voyage, offering a part from 'Othello' and 'The Rattling Boy from Dublin' for an encore. He received 'thunders of applause' and was called upon to conclude the evening's entertainment, which he did by restaging 'Tel-el-Kebir'. Although no collection was taken for the participants, McGonagall recalled how he was visited in his cabin by an admirer who handed in a few shillings 'as a token of reward and his appreciation of my abilities as a reciter'.

Even a delay of three days stalled at sea with a broken piston did not lessen McGonagall's fascination with all aspects of the voyage. With Cromwellian acceptance of the godly providential, he viewed the coincidental ending of a storm as divine intervention. 'I said in my opinion it was God that calmed the sea – for, if the sea hadn't calmed down, the vessel would have been useless amongst the big waves owing to the engine giving way, and would have sunk with us all to the bottom of the briny deep, and not one of us would have been saved.' Thereafter he claimed he was looked upon as a prophet by his fellow passengers.

William McGonagall arrived safe and well at Glasgow after 14 days at sea. The next morning he took an early train for Dundee and was reunited with his family within sight of the continuing work on the new Tay Bridge. Though happy to be home, it must have been a difficult return to Paton's Lane. He had tasted the fruits of London and New York, sailed on steamships large and small and – like today's space travellers – had seen sights few contemporaries could even imagine. In his mind he was never 'a fixed part of the Dundee scene' as he has been described.[17] He was a man of the wider world and had witnessed its wonders. Yet his work, his poetry, had raised not one penny in London or a single cent in New York.

McGonagall recalled in 1901 that he sold the story of his intrepid

American adventure to a newspaper reporter, 'who gave me 7s. 6d. for it', but no report of his stay in the United States has been found. Instead, McGonagall agreed to keep a travel diary. The contents of this diary, detailed here for the first time since 1887, allow events described in the 1901 autobiography to be validated against contemporary jottings. It is in two parts. The first describes his outward journey and safe arrival in New York. The second, unfortunately, offers only brief notes on his stay in America before describing events on the return voyage.[18]

McGonagall's memories of the date of departure, 9 March 1887, and ship of conveyance, the *Circassia*, are accurate. He left the Clyde in heavy snow, with the wind blowing fiercely. His diary concentrates heavily on the meals he enjoyed and he frequently adds verses to describe the experience. On the second day, for example: 'Good dinner of potatoes and salt fish, which I have made a good meal of. Thank God for his mercies to me and all on board . . .

> After dinner I went to my bunk to have a sleep,
> While the Circassia ploughs on through the mighty deep;
> But I cannot sleep for the roaring tide,
> Dashing against the good ship's side.

In his bunk he listens to fellow passengers playing an accordion and fiddle, and the stirring sound of the pibroch: 'And as its thrilling notes strike my ear/It makes me think of old Scotland and my friends most dear.' He describes sea sickness, the snow-clad coast of Ireland, the Sunday hymns, calming seas and eventual sunshine, then the *Circassia* rolling fearfully and waves washing over the deck, but his creative concentration is dimmed, his physical frailty counterbalanced and his attention diverted, all by the riches of the food available . . .

'Just partaken of a good dinner – plum duff, beef, potatoes and broth. All on board highly pleased with the food . . . from the sublimity of the poet to the necessities of his appetite! What a descent!'

Doubtless he had been waiting for an opportunity to display his talents and the seaboard concert described in his memoirs was apparently in honour of St Patrick's Day and to raise money for the

Mariners' Fund, 'and of course I got nothing'. He appeared in Highland costume and delivered 'Bannockburn', 'Tel-el-Kebir', 'Address to the Tay Bridge' and the foot-stamping 'Rattling Boy'. There is a hint that he is homesick and missing his family. Yet he appears determined to make a go of it in the New World . . .

> Last night, as on my pallet of straw I lay,
> I thought of the Law hill and the silvery Tay,
> Where many happy days I spent,
> But now I feel rather discontent,
> And, while rocking to and fro,
> I let fall a silent tear
> When I think of Paton's Lane,
> And my family most dear.
> And what is the reason of my being here?
> I answer, 'Harsh treatment has banished me from my family
> and home,
> And now I am left to mourn alone.'
> Supper over. I am going to bed.

McGonagall arrived in New York on 22 March. His diary dwells little on his experiences there. It confirms his unsuccessful trawl of theatres and music halls where 'most of them laughed – yes, laughed at me'. He does not mention anti-British antagonism, though suspicion of British actors had existed since the Astor Place riot of 1849 in which fighting between immigrants and native New Yorkers left 25 dead. It would not have been lost on Americans that the genesis of the riot was a dispute between leading US and English actors over which of them was better at Shakespeare's major roles.[19] McGonagall's jingoistic popularisation of battles won across the Empire would have gone down like a lead balloon in a community with no love for the British. And broadsides endorsed by Lord This and General That would hardly have encouraged sales. Curiously, although McGonagall notes the ship's broken piston on the return voyage, his diary records 'all well' or 'nothing of importance' over subsequent days and his prophetic qualities are conjured up only for his 1901 autobiography. He confirms the second concert on board, in which he performed 'Bruce of Ban-nockburn', Hamlet meditating on self-destruction, 'Lord Ullin's Daughter' and 'The Rattling Boy'. Of those who took part, 'many of them acquitted themselves admirably, especially myself'. He also confirms he received a payment of five shillings 'as a presentation for my valuable service'.

Again his thoughts are shaped into rhyme, inspiration tending to visit him after a good dinner: ' 'Tis now 6 o'clock. Supper over. Tea, bread and butter, very good and fresh – daily – at least which I consider to be good and wholesome food.' A clumsy couplet concludes the diary: 'I am thankful to God that I am safe home again to Bonnie Dundee/For no other town like it can I see.'

William McGonagall's more familiar legacy of the journey to 'this second Babylon' is the 12-verse descriptive poem, 'Jottings of New York', extracts of which reveal his boyish excitement as well as his passion for numbers . . . from the height of the buildings to the thousands of people he came across . . .

Oh, mighty city of New York, you are wonderful to behold –
Your buildings are magnificent – the truth be it told –
They were the only thing that seemed to arrest my eye,
Because many of them are thirteen storeys high;

And as for Central Park, it is lovely to be seen –
Especially in the summer season when its shrubberies are green
And the Burns Statue is there to be seen,
Surrounded by trees on the beautiful sward so green;
Also Shakespeare and the immortal Sir Walter Scott,
Which by Scotchmen and Englishmen will never be forgot.

And there's beautiful boats to be seen there,
And joyous shouts of children does rend the air,
While the boats sail along with them o'er Lohengrin Lake,
And the fare is 5 cents for children, and adults ten is all they take.

Then there's the elevated railroads about five storeys high,
Which the inhabitants can hear night and day passing by;

Of such a mass of people there daily do throng –
No less than five 100,000 daily pass along;
And all along the city you can get for five cents –
And, believe me, among the passengers there's few discontent.

Though he had concluded seven years earlier that London's elegant
St Paul's could not be surpassed by any building in Dundee, the
New York landmarks fell short of what was most beautiful to be
seen in his home town . . .

And as for Brooklyn Bridge, it's a very great height,
And fills the stranger's heart with wonder at first sight;
And with all its loftiness I venture to say
It cannot surpass the new railway bridge of the Silvery Tay.

One of McGonagall's most unusual poems probably originated on
his return voyage from New York. He reported in his memoirs –
with a hint of rhyme – the presence of two icebergs in the North
Atlantic . . . 'a very big one, about ten feet high, which in the
distance has a very ghostly appearance, standing there so white,
which seemed most fearful to the passengers' sight'. His subsequent
poem, 'Greenland's Icy Mountains', one of his most eloquent
works, allowed scope to explore his twin appreciations of nature
and God among the crags, precipices and waterfalls of the icy Arctic
guardians. McGonagall's 'solemn silence and delight' describes the
serene fragility of the Arctic and the spirituality of its wonders.
Verses one and seven . . .

Greenland's icy mountains are fascinating and grand,
And wondrously created by the Almighty's command;
And the works of the Almighty there's few can understand:
Who knows but it might be a part of Fairyland?

And those that can witness such an awful sight
Can only gaze thereon in solemn silence and delight,
And the most Godfearless man that hath this region trod
Would be forced to recognise the power and majesty of God.

McGonagall's first performance after his return from the United States took place in the Comedy Theatre, Seagate. There he shared the evening bill with a short drama, a shorter farce and a Spanish dancer, and was announced on the handbill as 'Mr McGonagall, Dundee's Favourite Poet, Who will make his First Appearance after his Return from America, and recite Bannockburn In Full Highland Costume and give an account of the voyage.' He also arrived home in time to join in local celebrations for Queen Victoria's Golden Jubilee on 17 June 1887 and to witness the formal opening of the new Tay Bridge two days later. These events lubricated his inclination to compose two now-familiar verses within days of each other. First was his 'Address to the New Tay Bridge', in which he appeared to be much happier with the strength of Sir John Arrol's design . . .

> Beautiful new railway bridge of the Silvery Tay,
> With your strong brick piers and buttresses in so grand
>   array,
> And your thirteen central girders, which seem to my eye
> Strong enough all windy storms to defy.

Then came the 'Ode To The Queen On Her Jubilee Year', penned the month 50,000 gathered on his precious Magdalen Green to watch a fireworks display in her honour. He hoped with better grace this time that the ageing queen would at least reign a while before being allowed to 'die in peace' . . .

> Sound drums and trumpets, far and near!
> And let all Queen Victoria's subjects loudly cheer!
> And show by their actions that her they revere,
> Because she's served them faithfully fifty long year!

> She has been a good Queen, which no one dare gainsay,
> And I hope God will protect her for many a day;
> May He enable her a few more years to reign,
> And let all her lieges say – Amen!

And as this is her first Jubilee year,
And will be her last, I rather fear;
Therefore, sound drums and trumpets cheerfully,
Until the echoes are heard o'er land and sea.

And though it possibly passed him by, McGonagall celebrated in August 1887 the tenth anniversary of his apocalyptic conversion to poethood; the transformation from a life shaped by the search for work to one dominated by an unshakeable belief in his own genius – though during this extraordinary odyssey any pleasure in the vocation was diluted by the suffering endured from ridicule and rejection.

Fire then flood occupied McGonagall for the remainder of 1887. 'The Burning of Exeter Theatre', when 150 patrons lost their lives, brought no fewer than 16 pounding verses. The poem is a trademark gloomy narrative apart from the 'tion'-rhyming eighth stanza, where even McGonagall's potent pen could not do justice to the harrowing scene . . .

Alas! words fail to describe the desolation,
And in many homes it will cause great lamentation;
Because human remains are beyond all identification,
Which will cause the relatives of the sufferers to be in great
tribulation.

The scanning of the crowded news sections of the *Advertiser* then brought a tribute to those who had perished in a terrible flood in China. McGonagall was at such pains to strike appropriate pathos: ' 'Twas in the year of 1887, and on the 28th September/Which many people of Honan, in China, will long remember' . . . that he untypically screwed up a rhyming couplet . . .

All over the province of Honan, which for its fertility
Is commonly called by historians, the garden of China.

By this time William McGonagall was considered by all a bad poet, plumbing the depths of bathos with every desperate attempt to reach a rhyme. But somehow McGonagallese had captured and captivated an expanding audience and he had become the only household name among myriad aspirants flooding the town's newspaper columns with far better verse. Nor was his fame temporary or localised. Undeterred by the opinions of others, and with a joyous transparency in writing, he continued to pour out poems on subjects dear to him for the remainder of the 1880s, spurred on by a daily diet of 'terrible shipwreck' or 'awful accident' stories in the Press. There was one to a sunken steamer, another to a Glasgow fire, a funeral tribute to Ex-Provost Rough, another marking the death of a local doctor and a happier crop of stanzas describing the new Black Watch memorial at Aberfeldy.

McGonagall ended the decade the way it had begun, with public performances. Illness had restricted his appearances in the mid 1880s, but when an invitation to make his Glasgow debut came along, the adventurer's compass in his head pointed westwards. The programme at Ancell's Restaurant involved other performers, but a Glasgow newspaper commented dryly, 'He was the *pièce de résistance*, and he seemed to realise it.'

McGonagall wore a fearful Highland costume and was introduced in the customary complimentary terms by a Glasgow literateur in the chair. The paper could hardly contain its excitement: 'Then the poet took some lemonade, tightened his belt, sought the centre of the room, and recited his famous epic lay, "The Battle of Bannockburn". This poem, he admits himself, excited the patriotism of his countrymen more than any other thing he has written. When he recited it in a Dundee hall the place had to be fumigated afterwards.' The report concluded that the poet's works were sold to a large number of his admirers present, and his famed autograph was in great demand.[20]

Press reports tend to give the impression that McGonagall always performed his own works at these events. It is true that his more famous poems were in demand and there was generally a clamour to hear 'Bannockburn', 'The Rattling Boy' and 'Tel-el-Kebir'. McGonagall, however, consistently delivered a broad range of literary splendours at his 'entertainments'. One of his hand-written programmes has survived. This reveals the breadth of his repertoire and how he never neglected his Shakespearean roots. It is also a reminder that McGonagall included songs in his programme, and the lack of contemporary comment on his singing voice suggests it was passable. Written in black ink on a small sheet, but unfortunately undated, the 'programme' may be from his early Dundee appearance at the Cutlers' Hall in 1879 as it includes the works reported at that event. It lists 10 items and ascribes their authors . . .

1. New Irish Song . . . the Rattling Boy from Dublin Town. Author, Poet McGonagall.
2. Recital from Hamlet. Shakespeare.
3. Recitation, Lord Ullin's Daughter. Campbell.
4. Reading of a new poem entitled The Old Mendicant. Author Poet McGonagall.
5. Scene from Macbeth. Shakespeare.
6. Song. Follow the Dream. Author anonymous.
7. Recitation. Beth Gelert. Mrs Hemans.
   Recitation. The Battle of Linden. Campbell.
8. Reading. Balmoral Castle. Author McGonagall.
9. Bannockburn. Author McGonagall.
10. Song. The Bonnie Broon Hair'd Lass of Dundee. Author McGonagall.[21]

McGonagall's use of one of Thomas Campbell's most famous Scottish ballads and a work from the English literary figure Felicia Hemans points again to his extensive reading of poetry and literature. His inclusion of Shakespeare was to be expected. Luminary modern writers have hinted that some of the works McGonagall claimed as his own were composed by others to poke fun at him. Hugh MacDiarmid, for example, claimed in 1936 that 'The Rattling Boy from Dublin' 'is not an authentic McGonagall' and that 'he worked in a different vein altogether'. John Campbell, writing about 'Scotland's second most famous poet' in the *Guardian* in 2006, noted, 'There are poems in *Poetic Gems* that are much too refined to be his own work. One is the Bonnie Lass o' Dundee, which swings with such a regular beat that the reader's instinct is to sing it.'[22] Both men erred. 'Rattling Boy' was supplied by

McGonagall to the *Weekly News* in October 1878 and the paper commented that it was his 'new Irish song, having all rights reserved'. It was also introduced as his own composition at many public performances. 'The Bonnie Lass o' Dundee' was indeed a song and was written by McGonagall in 1877 as a tribute to his daughter Mary. In fact, both 'Rattling Boy' and 'Bonnie Lass' were included in *Complete Poetical Works* published by McGonagall in 1879, long before he was flattered by the playful compositions of imitators.

McGonagall may have determined his programme content, but one is left to wonder whether he had prior knowledge of the cheeky handbills which advertised his performances. His eyebrows must have risen like blinds when confronted with the specimen produced for the performance at the Mechanics' Hall in Brechin in 1887 . . .

'After a lengthened and most successful tour of the United States and a none the less successful re-appearance in the principal towns of the east of Scotland . . . the Unexampled and Incomparable Career of this Eminent and Versatile Literateur is a chapter in the history of Scotland's greatest men that is without parallel. His transcendent genius shines, the brightest star in Scottish poetry.' That was not the half of it. The poster went into literary overdrive in its merriment: 'All who hear and witness this alpha and omega of Literature should not fail to embrace this opportunity . . . Come in your hundreds and drink deep from this most marvellous well! Come All, and Hear The Great McGonagall.'[23]

This was a far cry from the problems that dogged McGonagall at home as his children became more difficult to control. Firstly daughter Mary found herself in court, accompanied by her father, on a charge of breach of the peace by swearing and using violent language to a Mrs Macgregor, wife of a ship steward. Mary pleaded guilty, but her father appealed on her behalf:

McGonagall: 'She is a well-disposed daughter; only her mother gives her drink at times. That is the cause of the breach of the peace. In my opinion there will never be peace in society until strong drink is abolished from the land.'

Bailie Perrie: 'Oh, that will do. (Laughter.) Five shillings or five days in prison.'[24]

Then, in June 1887 father William found himself accompanying son James to Dundee Police Court. James, a ropemaker and resident at his parents' home in Step Row, faced a charge of committing a breach of the peace in Perth Road while in a state of intoxication. He pleaded guilty and was fined 10 shillings and sixpence with the alternative of seven days in prison. The report of the case does not provide details of his offence, or whether the fine was paid.[25]

In March 1888, McGonagall was in the news again himself, writing to the *Courier* to complain about the 'severe snowballing I met with today'. Considerably frustrated, he went on: 'During the mill hour [lunchtime] I was passing along St Andrew's Street along by the foot of Queen Street and was attacked by a number of rough young men who were standing on the corner of Queen Street. I was forced to beat a retreat up Queen Street, and then pass along by the Cowgate. There again, Sir, I was attacked by a crowd of rough mill boys, also by mill girls, and I was struck on the right cheek by a snowball, which staggered me for the time being, and left a red mark behind it which has hurt my feelings very much. But thank God I wasn't struck in the eye.'

Within a week, the *Courier* had received two letters praising McGonagall's fortitude and wishing him safe passage on Dundee's streets. They were wasted words. McGonagall wrote again on 20 March to say he had been snowballed again, this time on Ferry Road by mill boys 'on the lookout for my coming'.[26]

As these troubled times continued, our hero found himself back in Dundee Police Court in May 1888. McGonagall was the complainant this time over an alleged assault in which he had lost a tooth. He had apparently been selling his poems in the Hawkhill when an altercation ensued with a shopkeeper over the Land League, an organisation which espoused direct-action tactics against land occupation and high rents. As with most of the affairs of the Prince of Poetry, the case found its way into the papers . . .

'Complainant deponed that he was struck a blow which knocked out one of his teeth, but in defence it was stated that McGonagall was not struck but merely ejected from the shop because he was flourishing his walking stick in a threatening manner. Much amusement was caused by the tragic attitude of the complainant while in the witness box, and at times he raised his voice to such a pitch that the procurator had to request him to speak in more moderate tones.' There was insufficient evidence for a conviction and the charge was not proven, although the *Courier* added a little colour to the proceedings by revealing that McGonagall had taken the disputed tooth out of his pocket to exhibit to the court. When the procurator asked him if he had pulled the tooth out himself, McGonagall answered in the affirmative:

Fiscal: 'Did you pull it out with your two fingers?'

McGonagall: 'Certainly, it was not with my head.' (Great laughter.)[27]

The baiting of McGonagall had become a local sport and was on the point of taking a sinister turn. Towards the end of the 1880s McGonagall enjoyed occasional work with Transfield's circus, an indoor circular circus ring located behind the Queen's Hotel in Nethergate and, afterwards, Baron Zeigler's Circus of Varieties on the same site, but refurbished into a theatre-style stage and seating. He was reportedly paid a handsome 15 shillings per performance. On one of these occasions the Paton's Lane poem-monger made a dramatic appearance in Highland dress to recite 'Bannockburn' . . .

'As soon as he reached the top of the ramp a jute bag struck him from above. It was filled with soot. He couldn't retreat. The Baron was at his back and said, "You've got to go on. If you don't go on they'll wreck the place." McGonagall never got round to saying his "Bannockburn". His soot-stained figure was assaulted by various missiles, including tins, rotten eggs and old boots. His act ended when a brick hit him in the stomach, and knocked him out cold.'[28]

On another occasion, eggs, herrings, potatoes and stale bread whizzed through the air towards the unfortunate bard. The first few lines of the poems were listened to, but when McGonagall raised his voice to a hoarse shout, 'the gravity of his hearers gave way, and derisive cheers broke forth from all quarters, accompanied by another shower of flour, eggs and bread'. [29]

Then, in January 1889, a large audience crowded into Baron Zeigler's circus expecting more of the same. He was advertised this time to give 'Macbeth as it should be played' – though he could have been advertised as a performing seal, as the audience expected more shooting practice than Shakespeare. No sooner had he appeared than he was greeted with a fusillade of all manner of missiles from every part of the theatre, which he tried to parry with his sword. For a few minutes he attempted to begin his repertoire, but the bombardment came so thick and fast that he was forced to retreat. The show was abandoned when a soot bag hit him in the face.

McGonagall's treatment – and the pre-planned barrage of missiles – drew the wrath of a contributor to Dundee's senior newspaper. In a strongly worded letter to the *Advertiser* he demanded to know where the police were when McGonagall was being targeted in such a dangerous manner. He went on . . .

'Is it legal that such scenes are being enacted? Is it right? The thing is evidently pre-arranged. Is McGonagall himself perhaps paid for allowing himself to be the butt of such horse play? I read that the vast crowd slowly dispersed evidently highly pleased. Alas! I am afraid much work of the School Board teachers, Sunday School teachers, mission workers and "slummers" will hardly countervail against such diversions. Was no hiss heard?'[30]

In actuality, McGonagall was an old hand at dealing with baiting, laughter and pretend scorn. He also had considerable pluck, battling through one hostile performance 'unflinchingly, despite the formidable fire to which he was subjected'. But what he did not expect, and hardly deserved, was the sudden change of attitude by the powerful men who regulated public performances in Dundee – the magistrates. In August 1889 the poet was due to return to Baron Zeigler's circus when, out of the blue, the magistrates peremptorily banned his appearances in all public places.

It was devastating news. To all intents and purposes, William McGonagall's career as a performance poet was over.

SEVEN

THE PUBLISHED POET

' "To be or not to be?" that is the question – whether I am to be permitted to perform in public places of entertainment or not.'

Thus, an outraged William McGonagall drew on the other William's greatest lines to petition readers of the *Weekly News* after his performance ban in August 1889. This had come about after two appearances at Transfield's Circus and two at Baron Zeigler's Circus of Varieties had resulted in chaotic scenes, with McGonagall retreating on each occasion under a hail of missiles. Protests in the Dundee papers followed, by readers outraged at the treatment of the poet, and by others who took a dim view of the public disorder at his fustian recitals.

Baron Zeigler – real name Burlington Brummel – appeared at Dundee Police Court that August to try to renew his public entertainment licence. He was told by the four presiding magistrates that Chief Constable Dewar had complained about the shows at the Nethergate circus, including 'several appearances of William McGonagall, who was received with showers of rotten eggs and missiles'. Brummel promised that McGonagall 'would not be exhibited this season'. And on the distinct undertaking 'to prohibit the appearance of the local poet' Brummel's licence was granted. In effect, the four bailies ruled that any theatre or musical hall proprietor who gave McGonagall a booking would risk losing their licence.[1]

McGonagall was both livid and confused, and from his pen the following month flowed a public attack on the magistrates who had abandoned him because of the rowdyism that dogged his professional path . . .

Fellow citizens of Bonnie Dundee,
Are ye aware how the magistrates have treated me?
Nay, do not stare or make a fuss
When I tell ye they have boycotted me from appearing in
    the Royal Circus,
Which in my opinion is a great shame,
And a dishonour to the city's name.
Fellow citizens, I consider such treatment to be very hard,
'Tis a proof for me they have little regard;
Or else in the circumstances they would have seen to my
    protection;
Then that would have been proof of their affection,
And how Genius ought to be rewarded.
But instead my Genius has been disregarded.
Why should magistrates try and punish me in such a cruel
    form?
I never heard of the like since I was born.
Fellow citizens, they have taken from me a part of my
    living,
And as Christians to me they should have been giving;
But instead of that they have prevented Baron Zeigler from
    engaging me,
Which certainly is a disgrace to Bonnie Dundee.

He was still banging on about disregarded genius years after the
poem on that theme had brought about his poetic awakening.
The fourth verse on the civic fathers also reminded readers who
it was that had immortalised the old and new railway bridges of
the Silvery Tay, which conveniently rhymed with the inauguration of the Hill of Balgay. And who was it who extolled the
advantages of the Newport Railway – as if anyone could forget
the lines that explained how it would clear its expenses by thrifty
housewives nipping over to Dundee for Lipton's ham? Still, he
was determined to quit Dundee because a) it could no longer
guarantee his protection, and b) it was preventing him from
earning a living . . .

Therefore I'm resolved from it to flee
For a prophet has no honour in his own country,
And try to live in some other town
Where the magistrates won't boycott me or try to keep me
   down.
No more shall the roughs of Bonnie Dundee
Get the chance of insulting or throwing missiles at me
For I'm going off to the beautiful west
To the fair city of Glasgow that I like the best,
Where the River Clyde rolls on to the sea
And the lark and the blackbird whistles with glee
And your beautiful bridges across the River Clyde,
And on your bonnie banks I'm going to reside.[2]

And off to Glasgow he went in September 1889 – though since
Mistress McGonagall, as he called her, remained at Step Row, this
was never intended to be his final farewell. Most likely he chose
Glasgow ahead of the other 'most beautiful' or 'bonnie' places
eulogised in poems on recalling the friendly reception and remuneration at Ancell's Restaurant the previous April. He had first
performed in Glasgow in July 1881 and had received 'a hearty
reception'. He also had fond recollections of an evening there prior
to his departure to New York in 1887 when, to quote his own
statement, he 'was treated like a prince'. And it seems he was
sufficiently irked by his treatment in Dundee to carry out expedient
editing of his 'Beautiful Glasgow' song of 1881. From his pen came a
new version, published, he said, 'By Particular Desire'. The particular desire was not only to satisfy Glaswegian tastes, but to give
Dundonians a poetic headbutt by adding a dissonant new verse.
Here, published for the first time since 1889, is the 'missing' seventh
verse of William McGonagall's 'improved' 'Beautiful Glasgow' . . .

I have mixed with all kinds of people – of low and high degree,
But the most unmannerly people are the people of Dundee,
The fact is, they don't know how to treat a poet,
But the Glasgow people does, and I do know it.

McGonagall's desire to escape the barbed baiting of bad-mannered Dundonians did not meet with success. By early November he was writing from rented lodgings in Glasgow to his friend A.C. Lamb to complain about poor weather and low sales of his penny broadsides . . .

November the 7th 1889, Rose Street, South Side, Glasgow, No. 40, care of Mrs Hendry, 3 stairs up.

My dear friend I am taking very bad with the incessant city's din and I find the climate here to be rather unhealthy for me. I am not liking the climate at all and I am not selling as many poems here as I expected, but no doubt I can make a living here. But I think the climate here, as I feel it, will soon put an end to my existence, therefore health is much better than wealth. I send you two copies of Beautiful Glasgow, a New Song, which I hope meets with your appreciation as hitherto. Give my best wishes to all my admirers in Dundee. You need not send me anything for the copies enclosed but if you wish you can do so, to Mrs McGonagall Step Row – no more at present, but remain yours truly, William McGonagall, poet.[3]

It would be fascinating to know if the 'Beautiful Glasgow' sent to Alex Lamb included the verse on the unmannerly people of Dundee to whom the elderly antiquarian had dedicated his life. Perhaps not. In any case, McGonagall soon brought his ill health home to Dundee, recalling in *Brief Autobiography* that, 'owing to declining health I had to leave the city of Glasgow'.

As 1889 moved aside for the incoming decade, he found himself once again attending surgery after hearing 'head noises'. He told his concerned journalist friend that he had suffered from them for a long time and that they had recently become intolerable. The problem was diagnosed as an air cavity blocked by 'intense' mental activity: 'The doctor put a tube up his nose and blew in it as if he were performing solo on the trombone. The pain was excruciating and McGonagall danced and roared and writhed in a sensation of agony worse than when in the throes of poetic fantasy.'[4]

His exalted ambitions remained undimmed, however. He had been encouraged to write a book as far back as 1877. Like so many other offers of advice, it was imparted then with tongue firmly in cheek by his long-time nemesis 'Old Stager'. McGonagall at the time had peppered the *Weekly News* with some of his earliest deranged poems. The paper, in turn, had won a promise from him to slow down, securing more success in that respect than the poet's doctor ever did. This was too much for Old Stager, who rushed into verse to implore McGonagall to press on at full steam ahead. Then the idea for a book surfaced . . .

> Though editors at time refuse,
> To pay due homage to your muse,
> Why, what of that? Just write a book,
> And see how *that* will make *them* look.[5]

The book idea stuck with McGonagall. He had published his first four-page pamphlet of poetry in 1878 and followed with another of 16 pages in 1879. His undated *Authentic Autobiography of the Poet McGonagall* in the mid 1880s was purposefully followed in February 1887 by *The Autobiography and Poetical Works of William McGonagall* – both 40 pages in length, but bound as pamphlets. Never lacking ambition, he would have cast envious glances at the more substantial poetry publications on the shelves of the town's circulating libraries.

McGonagall had a considerable body of work behind him by 1890. The previous decade had brought many familiar pieces, including 'An Address to the New Tay Bridge', 'Jottings of New York', 'General Gordon, The Hero of Khartoum' and 'The Famous Tay Whale' . . . enough for a book, if sufficient income could be siphoned off to meet costs. In any case, a book of poems was a fine way of getting back at the newspapers which had long given up publishing his poetry and the meddling magistrates who had blacklisted his public appearances. That effrontery had seen him huffily put up with Glasgow and its rain for a month, and a substantive collection of his work would be a nose-thumbing response to the boycott and deliver an ear-splitting message that

McGonagall was back. Besides, given his fragile mental and physical state, he probably felt it expedient to gather his poetic production under one metaphorical roof in case he was called suddenly to the next world.

Presumably forewarned of a sizeable printer's bill, however, McGonagall did the leg-work himself to find sufficient subscribers to cover costs. Such was his celebrity appeal in the town, it should be no surprise that 200 of the citizenry pledged support within a month. It was a remarkable response and the *Weekly News* was soon breathless with excitement: 'McGonagall is in the Press at last, and will be out soon. Now the orthodox "two hundred" have subscribed for the volume, it is confidently predicted that in a fortnight it will see the light, and it will certainly take the "cake" as the book of the season. Fact is, the book will be a casket of rare gems of rare poetry, by one of the rarest poets that ever lived.'[6]

The rare day arrived early in May 1890. *Poetic Gems, Selected from the Works of William McGonagall, Poet and Tragedian, with a Biographical Sketch by the Author and Portrait*, was placed before the public. And *Poetic Gems* was handsomely produced. Its pale-yellow cover was decorated with vignettes of flowers and illustrations of Highland scenes, the Bell Rock lighthouse and the female muses of science and poetry. It was printed for the author by Winter, Duncan & Co. of Castle Street, grandly ran to 96 pages and cost one shilling. The cover also featured the authorial lure, 'See my deep insight into Human Nature – McGonagall'. Inside, readers were confronted by a full-page illustration of the author, signed 'DBG' and dated 1890. Local artist David Gray had, in fact, faithfully copied a cabinet portrait of McGonagall for which he had sat the previous year. This depicted the poet in a heavy cloth wrap resembling a product from his Thomson & Shepherd loom. Below it, completing this dazzling opening page, was the boldly printed autograph, 'Faithfully yours, William McGonagall, poet and Tragedian'.

Poetic Gems contained McGonagall's most familiar works, including the Tay Bridge trilogy, his tributes to Edinburgh, Glasgow and Oban, his Christmas Carol and Goose, the battles of Bannockburn, Flodden and El-Teb, a few deaths, funerals, disasters and wrecks and the ever-popular 'Rattling Boy'. The contents were preceded by *Brief Autobiography*, a revision of the undated *Authentic Autobiography* of *c* 1885, but expanded to include his trip to New York in 1887.[7]

As usual, it was left to the *Weekly News* to ramp up the excitement: 'McGonagall is out at last in yellow covers, like "primroses in the spring".' Yet *Poetic Gems* was not immediately available on the shelves of local bookshops. McGonagall took it upon himself to collect stocks from Winter's to maximise profit, cutting out the 'middle man' in a manner Amazon might appreciate. The paper noted: 'It may not appear very dignified in the eyes of our cynical critics for a "poet" to hawk his own works from door to door, but McGonagall is practical as well as poetical, and has a thorough eye to the main chance.'[8] Within a month the paper was able to pass on the fantastic news that the book was flying off the shelves that it should have been on: 'McGonagall has scored a real success with his book . . . day after day shows a diminished number of copies in the poet's or the printer's hands.'[9]

Our hero must have had his pockets full as he peddled the slim volume as well as unsold broadsides on the streets of Dundee, a spring in his step as he sensed the promise of the new decade bringing him the acknowledgement he craved. Many more poems were to come, and as his little book found its way into nooks and crannies across the city and beyond, McGonagall penned one of his most unusual works, 'The Crucifixion of Christ'. This gospel narrative of 19 verses was, said the author, 'Composed by Special Request on 18 June 1890'. Its sponsor is unknown but 'The Crucifixion' raced to a dramatic and doom-laden message . . .

> And if you are not a believer, try and believe,
> And don't let the devil any longer you deceive,
> Because the precious Blood that Jesus shed will free you
> from all sin,
> Therefore, believe in the Saviour, and Heaven you shall
> enter in!

The solemn nature of the Crucifixion did not prevent the wag on the *Weekly News* seeing an opportunity to deliver a verbal thunderbolt to Dundee Presbytery. It was McGonagall's ambition, he supposed innocently, 'to deliver the last three verses from the pulpits of our city churches, when he would outshine all your prosy, humdrum, namby-pamby divines, who only "mouth the Gospel".'[10]

Godly intervention was exactly what McGonagall required to release him from the magistrates' ban. The town's newspapers were awash with reports of drunkenness, fights, wife-beating and worse. Yet what civic fathers feared most was the breakdown of public order among the incendiary working classes. Random mischief was adequately dealt with in the police court. Anarchy was a different matter. While it was not the case that every McGonagall entertainment guaranteed public disorder, a gambler would not have bet against one inciting the mill-hand hooliganism that the town's middle-classes tut-tutted at over their breakfast marmalade.

McGonagall's friendly scribe on the *Weekly News* – 'Johnny' of the *City Gossip* column – urged justice for a 'peaceable citizen, pursuing a legitimate business'. He suggested that magistrates find McGonagall an alternative source of income. Otherwise, he warned, the future of the showman hardly bore thinking about: " 'The poorhouse," I hear someone whisper. Perish the thought! It must never be said that Dundee allowed the most extraordinary man she ever produced to drift to that receptacle for waifs and strays of humanity.'[11]

McGonagall was advised to take his complaint to the Marquis of Lothian, the Scottish Secretary, and the highest authority in the land. And from his home at 48 Step Row, he did exactly that, writing to protest that the magistrates had prevented him from displaying his talents as a reciter and actor. Against anyone else's better judgement, he enclosed sample copies of three broadsides, 'Forget-Me-Not', 'Loch Katrine' and a 'Tribute to Henry M. Stanley', the explorer who had just been made a freeman of Dundee. McGonagall's letter of 30 August . . .

Honoured Sir, I take the liberty of writing to you to let you know how I have been boycotted by the Magistrates of Dundee. My dear Sir, I have been prevented by them from appearing in Baron Zeigler's Circus, Nethergate, or Circus of Varieties since 20th August 1889 up till the present year of

1890, and which holds good against me for some months to come. Unless the Magistrates change the License to allow me to perform, as it deprives me of my living comparatively so, besides being hurtful to my feelings and detrimental to my character, I appeal to you to see me righted and to see this wrong towards me requited, and I will feel delighted. My dear Sir, I only ask the same liberty as any other actor has got to be allowed to display my abilities when I get the chance to do so. If not, in my opinion it is an act of injustice. Whoever heard of a Poet being prevented from reading his own works? See copies enclosed, from such I make my living by selling and giving recitals when I get the chance.[12]

The reply from the Scottish Office in Whitehall was curiously dated three days before McGonagall had sent his appeal. The poet had confused his dates . . .

'Sir, – I am directed by the Marquis of Lothian to acknowledge receipt of your letter of the 27th instant and to inform you in reply that the matter of which you complain is not one for the interference of the Secretary for Scotland. Any further correspondence should be addressed to the Under-Secretary of State for Scotland, Whitehall.'

The reply, which survives in the National Archives of Scotland, suggests little sympathy for McGonagall. A minuted note on the front of the file reads, 'If the enclosed specimens are typical of his poetry I don't wonder at his being gagged.' Yet which other carper could have righted, requited and delighted their grievance in a single sentence?[13]

McGonagall was slighted, spited and disinclined to be fobbed off. On 30 August – a favourite date obviously – he sent another complaint to the Under-Secretary, explaining further the manner in which he was being boycotted by the bailies and nitpicking about the treatment he received compared to the honours showered on Shakespeare. This time, as if to raise the moral ante, he enclosed a copy of 'The Crucifixion of Christ'. The response from Whitehall was as brief as it was blunt: 'Sir, – I am directed by the Secretary of State for Scotland to acknowledge the receipt of your letter and enclosures.'[14] If the reply's non-committal brevity tested McGonagall's patience it also invoked a sense of outrage in the *Weekly News*, whose rebuke to the government anticipated a familiar twenty-first-century criticism . . . .

'Was there ever such a mockery and a sham as this last reply? Twenty words printed in the centre of a sheet of paper 12 x 6 inches – a waste of public money on paper . . . Red tape is still as rampant in Whitehall as ever. That is a pretty revelation of the way in which our high paid State officials discharge their duties. That's the return they make for their big salaries. Typewriters and printer's devils do their work, and they roll in their carriages and fatten on the blood and sweat of the toiling millions.' Plus ça change . . .

The paper recognised the justice of McGonagall's case and reported it unambiguously, forecasting political oblivion for offending magistrates if they failed to overturn their ban on the poet: 'The voice of the people must be heard, and if the people will but rise in their might they will make the Provost shiver in his robes and the Home Secretary shake in his shoes . . . A great meeting ought to be convened on the Magdalen Green . . . electors should make it one of the burning questions to blister the fingers of would-be candidates for Municipal honours.'

McGonagall himself stood up to be counted among those willing to mount the barricades of the proposed people's revolution. His personal rallying call to readers was conveyed in the following Saturday's issue . . .

Fellow citizens of the city of Dundee, I now lift my pen to ask of ye if ye are all willing to aid me in the present fight against the Magistrates of the city of Dundee. Perhaps you may not be aware of how I have been treated by them. If not, I take the liberty of letting ye know. Well, my fellow citizens and fellow electors of Bonnie Dundee. I have been prevented by them for more than a year past now – from the 20th August 1889, up to this present year of 1890, from appearing in Baron Zeigler's Circus of Varieties, whereby I lost a deal of money, besides being detrimental to my character, also hurtful to my feelings and against me getting engagements elsewhere, and depriving me of my living, comparatively so; and in the name of justice, fellow electors of Dundee, I ask ye if such a base inhuman action toward me is to be tolerated or not?

He was not quite done. It was time to drag brother bards into the quarrel: 'Fellow citizens, it is for ye to decide – "to be or not to be?" that is the question – whether I am to be permitted to perform in public places of entertainment or not. If ye allow the Magistrates to treat me so, wherein is your respect towards me? Therefore I appeal to ye for to see me righted. In the name of all that's good and just, fellow electors, in ye and God I put my trust. "Man's inhumanity to man makes countless thousands mourn" – Burns. "Vain man, dressed up in a little brief authority, plays such fantastic tricks that make the angels weep" – Shakespeare.' While the angels dabbed their eyes, he signed off with a rhyme: 'Therefore ye electors of the city of Dundee, I hope ye will all rally around me, and aid me in this Magisterial fight, and Heaven will defend the right.'[15]

Meanwhile, the rival *Courier* was proudly proclaiming, 'McGonagall in the Free Library'. The poet had sent a copy of *Poetic Gems* to the town's chief librarian in search of the usual public endorsement. Presumably to avoid any misunderstanding about authorship he inscribed on its flyleaf, 'I, William McGonagall, poet and tragedian, present this book of *Poetic Gems* to the Dundee Free Library for the benefit and edification of the readers. Hoping they will derive pleasure and profit from its pages. Believe me, yours sincerely, William McGonagall, poet, September 10th, 1890.'

If only profit had matched the pleasure that came his way from poetry. Still, he must have been quite dizzy with delight when a note was returned from the library: 'Mr William McGonagall, I am instructed by the committee to acknowledge receipt of the donation named below, and also to tender you their grateful thanks for the same.' It was signed by the chief librarian, J. McLauchan. The *Courier* rounded off the story with further good news: 'We understand that Mr McLauchan has informed the donor that the book will be adorned with a grained morocco cover, with gold bars across it.'[16]

Within a year, McGonagall had ordered a sequel to *Poetic Gems*. This was announced to the public in January 1891 and appeared in March bearing a striking red cover. It retained the name, *Poetic Gems*, etc, but carried the subtitle *Second Series*. 'Science' and 'poetry' had been elbowed out by cover muses of literature and art, with etched vignettes of a windmill and a yacht replacing the Bell Rock lighthouse and Highland landscape. It was similar in size and format to the previous year's publication, was again printed by Winter, Duncan & Co. of Castle Street and also retailed for a shilling.

The *Second Series* featured a new illustrated portrait of the author by D.B. Gray, dated 1891. This was a half-length study, looking to the left this time, and wearing a three-piece suit and tie, clean shaven and with hair swept back behind his ears. Below the portrait was the printed autograph, 'With the author's compliments, William McGonagall, Poet and Tragedian, 1891.'

Poetic Gems, Second Series contained 34 poems, including the new-comers 'Battle of Culloden' and 'The Battle of Sheriffmuir', and the printed debut of 'Jottings of London'. He did not this time include his *Brief Autobiography*, substituting it with *Reminiscences*, a treatise on roguish publicans and the perils of excessive drinking. A preface explained why a second edition was necessary: 'The first Series of these Selections was issued some months ago and is now out of print. Repeated enquiries for copies of it from Dundee and various parts of the country, which the Author was unable to supply, induced him to prepare this second series. To the Subscribers for it, and also to the Subscribers for the first Series, the Author returns his grateful thanks, and wishes them long life, health and prosperity. William McGonagall, 48 Step Row, Dundee, 17th March, 1891.' A copy of the second volume was also donated to the local library.

William McGonagall left the world his two compilations of *Poetic Gems* in 1890 and 1891, but otherwise produced barely a handful of poems at this time and seems to have drifted out of public life. He appears to have written only one new poem in 1891, to commemorate the Battle of Langside, unpublished so far, and few of his letters survive from that year. As the moratorium on public appearances continued, it is possible he decided a break from Dundee was necessary in order to secure an income to pay for everyday outgoings and his recent printing costs.

In March 1891, the *Weekly News* warned readers that McGonagall's love affair with Dundee was wearing thin. It uncompromisingly demanded: 'What do you think of that, you hard-hearted, scoffing, miserable jute-spinners? Will you never think shame for your hard-hearted neglect of poor McGonagall?'[17] The poet's realisation that his genius was better acknowledged and better remunerated elsewhere was soon shared with his journalist friend: 'I write to inform you that I am resolved to leave Dundee owing to the shameful treatment I meet with daily while walking the streets . . . I can get no protection in Dundee . . . I am resolved to leave when my own time comes. "No boasting like a fool, This deed I'll do before the purpose cool – Shakespeare". Believe me, yours truly, William McGonagall, Poet.'[18]

Although David Phillips in 1971 suggested that McGonagall did not leave at this time, there is a possibility that he moved for some weeks to Perth. The town's valuation rolls for 1891 indicate a 'Mrs McGonagall' renting one room on the fourth floor at 74 South Street. It was to South Street that the McGonagalls moved in 1894 – the reason being, perhaps, that they had lived there three years earlier. The property was in a poor part of central Perth, at an address occupied by 15 families, and probably viewed at the time as near-slum accommodation. Neighbours were hawkers and labourers and the rent, at £1 10s per annum, was the cheapest in the street.[19] A temporary move to Perth in 1891 would explain McGonagall's absence from Dundee newspapers for much of that year. It would also explain the poetry drought at this time.

McGonagall was soon active again in Dundee, however. His ground-floor flat at 48 Step Row, which he had taken in August 1887, was kept on as, in May 1891, he wrote anxiously from there to Alexander Lamb in an attempt to raise funds . . .

'My dear Sir, as I am thinking of selling all my manuscripts which, in number, is 100 and 42 great and small, I will give you the preference of purchasing them, if you feel inclined to do so, as I intend to sell them to the first person that gives me a fair bid for them, but looking to our long friendship, I would like that you would be the purchaser, an answer will oblige, yours truly, Wm McGonagall, poet.' It is not certain if a deal was concluded, although Lamb certainly had manuscripts in his possession at the end of his life – though not the large number mentioned by McGonagall in his letter. Around 50 manuscript poems survive from the Lamb collection at Dundee Central Libraries. Phillips suggests that several originals went to public auction in McGonagall's time, but raised only sixpence.[20] What appears certain is that, in 1891, the poet was passing through some sort of crisis.

Such was William McGonagall's parlous state of health and finances that in September 1891 he drew up a memorial to the First Lord of the Treasury in the hope of obtaining a pension to see him securely into old age. He had this appeal printed with the royal coat of arms surmounting its text . . .

'William McGonagall, who has been enlightening us with poetic effusions for the last fourteen years, is now in failing health, and has been forbidden by the doctors to compose any more pieces; he is now 62 years of age [offering a new birth date of 1829] and in poor circumstances; he has been a loyal and respectable citizen, and he prays that his Lordship will be generous enough to grant him a small annuity. God Save The Queen.' The four lines of pathetic poetry added to the appeal indicate the depth of his despair at this low point in his life . . .

> Pity the sorrows of the poor poet
> When he wants bread;
> Help him living
> For he requires no help when dead.

The petition was circulated by McGonagall in the manner of his peddled broadsides. That many citizens willingly put their names to it demonstrates the sympathy for him aroused in the town. By October 1891 it bore over 400 signatures. The *Weekly News* was impressed: 'The great McGonagall is still indefatigable in his hunt for signatures. He is intent on the business as though he were a political agent and getting a penny for every name he bagged. He has got over 400 to autograph his petition pension and, as he says, "most influential men, too, sir".' McGonagall added to his appeal by telling the newspaper, 'I have been forbidden to compose poetry; I have been forbidden to recite or to act on the stage. I have been told to live on the most nourishing food and take as much care as I can, and how can I do so without money?' The newspaper drew its own conclusion: 'The argument is unanswerable; McGonagall must have a pension.'[21]

In November the document was despatched to Arthur Balfour, the newly appointed First Lord of the Treasury and prime minister in waiting. During the daily anxious wait for a reply his friendly scribe urged readers to plug the gap left by government: 'All you rich men and women of Dundee who are ever ready to subscribe for pinafores and rattles or any little comfort for the savages of Kamtchatka or Timbuctoo, here is a very deserving object at your very door – a starving poet crying for bread.' [22] A response to the petition, if one came at all, is not recorded and there is no evidence that the poet received a state pension.

Full production was resumed at Step Row in 1892. The first item on McGonagall's agenda was perhaps the most remarkable offering of the entire year. In February he published a four-page prose essay titled 'Shakespeare Reviewed by William McGonagall, Dundee'. Curiously, the cover was subtitled 'composed 1878' and it has since been catalogued with that date, but no earlier reference to it has been found. [23] It was announced as a new publication by the *Courier* in mid February 1892, with copies available to purchase from the poet. [24]

Shakespeare Reviewed is an illuminating landmark in William McGonagall's literary corpus. It demonstrates his intimate knowledge of Shakespeare's works. But it also reinforces the manner in which McGonagall frequently felt it necessary to use literature to instruct the educationally or culturally underprivileged, or morally bankrupt. In the case of Macbeth, for instance, 'The poet lets us see that it is better to be with our condition of life – no matter how low it be – rather than act dishonestly.' McGonagall moralised endlessly in verse, not least in 'folksy' poems such as 'The Nithsdale Widow and Her Son', 'The Death of the Old Mendicant' and 'Jack Honest'.

Shakespeare Reviewed also identifies McGonagall's theatrical icons and places Shakespearean drama in the context of local experience. Combining eloquence and arrogance, he uses it to explain why Shakespeare was not 'appreciated' in Dundee . . . 'It is because the people are not thoroughly acquainted with the proper intonation of language; and until they come to understand how to read his works, they can neither derive any pleasure nor profit from them.' The author was just the man to enlighten the masses, his postscript explaining: 'Parties desirous of being taught Elocution may be waited on at their own residences by Wm McGonagall. Fees Moderate.' It is a measure of his self-belief – perhaps self-conceit – that this impoverished weaver felt competent to lecture townsfolk on the merits of the world's greatest literary figure.

Over a dozen new poems and songs were delivered in 1892, including the unpublished duo 'Hawthornden' and 'Too Late'. There were also sorrowful ballads, scenic sketches and additions to his 'temperance' and 'Arab' collections. His tribute to the huge procession on Lifeboat Saturday in September 1892 brought a revealing exchange between the poet and journalist 'Johnny' during a visit in the days after the event . . .

'I greeted him with, "A New Poem, Mr McGonagall; this will be about the lifeboat day is it not?" "No," he said, in a tone which, while free from the least tinge of anger, showed as plain as plain could be that it was wrong for anyone to assume that his poems are produced as easily as they make sausages, by simply turning the handle. "No, my dear sir. It is too soon for that yet. It requires thinking."'

Thinking took McGonagall exactly a week. And when the lifeboat poem was dropped off to the newspaper seven days later he was asked if it had been a difficult undertaking. 'Difficult, Yes it was rather difficult,' he replied. The columnist continued: 'Taking me into his confidence, which I hope I am not betraying, he lowered his voice to that pitch which is known as a stage whisper, and remarked, "Do you know a certain party asked me how I got all the trades to rhyme? [As usual, McGonagall had listed the

procession's participants.] I said to him that it was my business. I
told him that was my business, do you see?" That last sentence was
accompanied by a sudden contraction of his other eye, which
indicated that the poet had no immediate intention of parting with
the secrets of his trade.'[25]

'The Lifeboat Demonstration', another major poem hitherto
unpublished, amounted to a 'difficult' composition by a secret
method because McGonagall was not present at the procession.
For all his nod-and-wink delivery of the mechanics of composition,
he was nowhere near the event. He had stayed at Step Row on
Lifeboat Saturday to read the papers. He also failed to record
spectacular jute fires in Dundee in 1892 and continued to ignore
working conditions, the state of the unemployed and the 2,000
paupers on the town's poor roll that year. There was not even an
effusion to mark the burning to the ground of the Circus of
Varieties in April 1892, which put his spat with the magistrates
on the back burner for a while.

One poem which must have caused McGonagall an emotional
twinge in October 1892 was 'The Death and Burial of Lord
Tennyson', for which a funereal black border was ordered for
the penny sheet accompanying the tribute lines to the famous Poet
Laureate. This began . . .

> Alas! England now mourns for her poet that's gone –
> The late and the good Lord Tennyson.
> I hope his soul has fled to heaven above,
> Where there is everlasting joy and love.

And went on in familiar strain . . .

> He believes in the Bible, also in Shakespeare,
> Which he advised young men to read without any fear;
> And by following the advice of both works therein,
> They would seldom or never commit any sin.

Thus, tribute paid and moralising made, McGonagall next did what
he did best and completed his 'Death and Burial' with six stanzas of

brilliant reporting. He introduced the pall-bearers by name, those on the right of the coffin and those on the left. The chief mourners, he said, were the Tennyson family, and they were promptly identified. Next he described the graveside VIPs, including the queen's representative Sir Henry Ponsonby, who had previously returned his verses. Wreaths included one from the Gladstones.

Perhaps the most important quality of William McGonagall's work was this ability to communicate news through poetry. Literacy levels were historically poor. Many struggled to read the tightly-packed columns of the *Courier, Advertiser, People's Journal, Weekly News* and *Evening Telegraph* – a remarkable quintet of publications delivered to doorsteps, but all of which catered for the educated citizenry. Many people were not reached by the popular Press or were reluctant to pay for regular copies. McGonagall could access and inform them through the content of descriptive ballads. Funerals were an obvious topic and, for example, his readers would have learned from his lines exactly who turned up when the drink-bashing, pub-closing former Provost Rough was laid to rest . . .

'Twas on Friday afternoon, in November the 23rd day,
That the funeral cortege to the Western Cemetery wended
   its way,
Accompanied by the Magistrates, and amongst those
   present were –
Bailie Macdonald and Bailie Black, also Lord Provost Hunter
I do declare.
There were also Bailie Foggie, Bailie Craig, and Bailie
   Stephenson,
And Ex-Provost Moncur, and Ex-Provost Ballingall
Representing the Royal Orphan Institution;
Besides them were present the Rev. J. Jenkins and the Rev.
   J. Masson,
With grief depicted in their faces and seemingly woe-begone.

McGonagall's observations reached beyond mere couplets and bad verse. He was the People's Bard who wrote epics for declamation to the working classes. In his 'Clepington Catastrophe' of 1884, for instance, he left nothing to the imagination as he told the story of the four firemen who were killed when a wall collapsed in a Dundee warehouse . . .

> But brave James Fyffe held on to the hose till the last,
> And when found in the debris, the people stood aghast.
> When they saw him lying dead, with the hose in his hand,
> Their tears for him they couldn't check nor yet command.

Events worthy of his pen included parades, banquets, battles, calamities, sinkings and drownings. He chronicled fires, famines and floods, charred bodies, weeping widows and watery graves. There was horrific detail and, at times, sensitive observation. Thus his work instructed and informed as much as it amused. It was distinctive and memorable for its honest description of what actually happened as much as it was entertaining in its haphazard construction.

So there was less original thought in McGonagall's poetry than often stated. Instead he championed circumstances, facts and news, the gathered crowds and the word on the street. Local newspapers offered him the rules of the when-what-where-who-and-why world of journalistic reporting in pursuit of his raw material, but Hugh MacDiarmid was wide of the truth by suggesting he simply hammered out newspaper reports 'till he got rhymes at the end of his sprawling lines'.[26] McGonagall was never a plagiarist in terms of what he put down on paper. He never passed off the work of others as his own. And he offered 'front page news' a century before the *Courier* ever did. His nose for a story is demonstrated in poems such as 'The Miraculous Escape of Robert Allan', 'The Fireman', 'The Lifeboat Demonstration' and 'The Death of Lord and Lady Dalhousie', where his 'camera' rolled as . . .

> About eleven o'clock the remains reached Dalhousie,
> And were met by a body of the tenantry;
> They conveyed them inside the building, all seemingly
>   woebegone,
> And among those that sent wreaths was Lord Claude
>   Hamilton.

He could also bring readers soundbites of news from beyond routine patterns of travel. His poetic recording of the opening of the Black Watch memorial at Aberfeldy in 1887, for instance, describes events in familiar but distant Perthshire. His verse dates and places the ceremony, then lists the processional order, from the Glasgow Highlanders to the Taymouth Brass Band. He describes the monument, why it has been erected, speeches marking the opening ceremony and the banquet after it, and . . . 'So ended the proceedings in honour of the Black Watch, the bravest of men/And the company with one accord sung the National Anthem.'

Thus, mindful of the importance of information, McGonagall provided for some readers their only access to current affairs, though it had to be extrapolated and interpreted from within his obsessive pursuit of melodramatic rhyme. In a quarter-century of composition he consistently dwelt on matters of public interest – the topical material editors promptly promote to today's front pages.

For all this effort and output, McGonagall's love affair with Dundee had withered by 1892. The year had started well. When, in February, he spoke to the Dundee, Lochee & East of Scotland Society of Poets, the membership lined up to shake his hand. So pleased was his audience that, 'they secretly put back the clock hands an hour the longer to enjoy him'. The following month he enjoyed further success at a meeting of the Waverly Shakespearean Drama Club in Perth. At this gathering he was nominated for the Poet Laureateship and was told his verses should replace the 'trash' in local schoolbooks. The compliment must have swirled in his head, for he appeared unoffended by the slagging Dundee took from the waffling chairman (whose knowledge of Dundee enabled him to say that it was 'perhaps the most poetical city in the British Empire. (Laughter.) Almost every fifth man met on the street was a poet. (Laughter.)'). Later, just as the climax of 'Bannockburn' was reached, McGonagall in his patriotic passion hit the chairman a stunning blow on the head. Perhaps the criticism of Dundee was noted after all.[27]

Compare these successes to his next performance in Dundee. On 1 April 1892 he was invited to speak again to the Dundee, Lochee, Etc, society in the Imperial Hotel in Commercial Street.

McGonagall endured several annoying interruptions, and a journalist reported his growing frustration as the audience took an
increasing hand in the show. After 'incoming' peas during the
'Battle of Tel-el-Kebir', McGonagall announced loudly that he
would never give another entertainment in Dundee – which only
inflamed the situation. A crowd then attempted to carry the poet
shoulder high into the street. McGonagall was having none of it and
struck out with his cane. He was dragged down the stairs in the
ensuing scuffle and outside claimed he had hurt his head. A mob
gathered, the police were called, and in the care of a sergeant
McGonagall was escorted to the Nethergate and sent home on a
tram. Adding to his woes, he once again had to attend Dr Murison,
complaining of hearing noises. And once again he was advised to
give up composing poetry. He declined . . . once again.[28]

McGonagall suffered further humiliation in the autumn of 1892.
The Marquis of Lorne, son-in-law of Queen Victoria, was visiting
the area with his wife, the Princess Louise. McGonagall took the
opportunity to send him a copy of his Tennyson tribute. The reply,
on Glamis Castle notepaper and signed 'Lorne', said: 'I thank you
for your enclosure and, as a friend, would advise you to keep strictly
to prose for the future.' McGonagall was aghast at the response,
later described by the *People's Journal* as 'a short, sharp, cruel little
letter'. The paper demanded an apology from the Duke of Argyll's
son while McGonagall boldly branded the marquis and his kind
'a set of ignorant, unmitigated humbugs'. For once, though, something good came out of the exchange. A messenger arrived from the
Earl of Camperdown asking for three copies of the Tennyson
address. Recovering his poise, McGonagall charged him sixpence
– double the usual price.[29]

Sadly, there were further family difficulties in 1892. His children
James and Mary had appeared in court in the late 1880s. Now it
was the turn of son John to stray. In June he was charged with
assaulting a young woman in Step Row. The procurator told the
court that the girl had accused the youth of circulating stories about
her and that the only satisfaction she got 'was a blow'. John
McGonagall was fined 15 shillings, or 10 days in prison. The
following month he was back in court facing a charge of disorderly

conduct in Perth Road. He pleaded not guilty, but was convicted on evidence. This time he was fined 30 shillings or 20 days in prison.[30]

Small wonder McGonagall was demoralised with life in Dundee. Yet, as 1893 came along, the poet's pen swept across tragedies and triumphs, paid tribute to St Andrews and Aberfoyle, dwelt on the curious tale of a faithful dog called Fido and commemorated the great winter storm that hit Scotland and toppled the Balgay tombstones he had encouraged the citizenry to visit in an early effusion. And in March he was the lucky recipient of a promise of a new tweed suit from the admiring Borders merchant J. Graham Henderson, the owner of Weensforth Mill in Hawick. McGonagall was absolutely delighted and popped down to Henry's outfitters in Reform Street to be measured by a Mr Tocher. The *Weekly News* was beside itself at the prospect of McGonagall parading along the Overgate in an outlandish costume, but unhelpfully let it out of the bag that a tribute poem was the price to be paid: 'The donor mentioned that the suit would be ready by the time the poem was written, but when he made that promise he had no idea how rapidly poetry can be turned out.'[31] If the handsome present had a wonderfully stimulating effect on McGonagall's muse, it was merely a poor poet repaying the compliment the only way he could . . .

> Success to Mr J. Graham Henderson, who is a good man,
> And to gainsay it there's few people can,
> I say so from my own experience,
> And experience is a great defence.
> He is a good man, I venture to say,
> Which I declare to the world without dismay,
> Because he's given me a suit of Tweeds, magnificent to see,
> So good that it cannot be surpassed in Dundee.

And so on for seven eulogising stanzas.

The promised suit was due to be supplied by J.H. Henry, merchant tailor of 63 Reform Street. Henry's boasted in a contemporary advert: 'Splendid selections of the newest coatings, overcoatings, suitings, vestings and trouserings Always In Stock.' Made-to-measurings was another matterings, however, and, with a

notoriously fickle local VIP, delays with the order for Mr McGonagall of Step Row were doubtless to be expected.[32] Nonetheless,
readers around Scotland anxiously awaited its arrival, one from
Aberdeen addressing an ode to 'William McGonagall, Poetry
Manufacturer, Dundee' . . .

> When ye get yer new suit, will ye flit from Step Row,
> Leave Bonnie Dundee, an' yer friends ane an' a'?
> When ye get yer new suit, will ye swagger an' strut,
> Intae some famous barber's an' get your hair cut?[33]

It was worth the wait. The suit consisted of sound-barrier-loud
checked material made up in the style he favoured, frock coat and
square-cut waistcoat . . . 'said to be easily picked out half a mile off
in the busiest street'. To this was added his pudding-shaped hat and
lambskin gauntlets with – wait for it – the wool lining outside. The
suit was duly presented to McGonagall at a ceremony in Gilfillan
Memorial Church. The poet acknowledged the gift in appropriate
terms, remarking with pathetic earnestness that it 'came in a great
time of need'. Yet when he was asked to put it on – in other words
to give everyone a laugh – he refused indignantly and threatened to
walk out.[34] McGonagall obviously liked the suit. Later in 1893 he
wrote a second tribute to Henderson to commemorate his appointment as a judge at the World's Fair in Chicago. This made him,
according to the Dundee papers, 'the hero of the hour' in the
Borders.[35]

McGonagall also enjoyed that March a placid performance in
Reform Street Hall, convened by the manager of J.P. Smith,
drapers, Reform Street, with many Smith employees in the audience. The ban from Baron Zeigler's circus had not prevented the
staging of privately-organised events where he would receive a fair
hearing. Sometimes these groups gave themselves grand names,
intended in fun to circumvent the magisterial ban, but with the
added intention of capturing the poet's ego. The Dundee Select
Committee for Unearthing Gems was one such group. The latest of
the McGonagallian sects was the swiftly dubbed Hawick Tweed
Committee, which issued his invitation to Reform Street.

McGonagall duly appeared in the gifted tweeds. The chairman referred to some of the poet's familiar pieces, such as 'The Newport Railway' and 'The Silvery Tay', before presenting him with a mounted walking stick. The poet replied modestly that he accepted 'this beautiful stick' as a testimony to his abilities. McGonagall then recited 'The Rattling Boy', the 'whacks' in the chorus being emphasised by 'whacks' on the floor with his new stick. Another admirer then read an address from the committee recognising McGonagall as the Poet Laureate of Dundee and authorising him to go wherever he pleased and whenever he pleased, provided he conformed to the law. They earnestly offered to provide him with 'one of the strongest men in the city who was prepared to tackle any tormentor'. McGonagall replied that, although he took the address as a guarantee of goodwill, he believed it was impossible for the meeting to protect him when the constabulary of Dundee was unable to do so. McGonagall then drew cries of 'shame' when he announced loudly that the only way to secure such protection was, 'When you are persecuted in one city flee to another.'

He was eventually mollified and gave 'Bannockburn' in characteristic style and 'Macbeth' for an encore. To finish, a committee man handed McGonagall a tall hat, alleged to have been one which Gladstone wore when introducing an important bill. McGonagall, however, told them that he never wore and never intended to wear such a hat, and, while recognising their kindness, refused to accept it. He knew, of course, it would have presented too tempting a target for the town's snowballing youth.

McGonagall was so chuffed with the generosity of the 'gentlemen' that he knitted together seven stanzas as a tribute to the occasion – though he misdated the performance by a week. 'Lines in Memoriam Regarding the Entertainment I Gave on the 31st of March 1893 in Reform Street Hall, Dundee' finished with an expression of the poet's pleasure at an entertainment that did not sink into 'any slang chaff'. More especially there was satisfaction with the money that came his way . . .

> Because they showered upon me their approbation,
> And got up for me a handsome donation,

Which was presented to me by Mr Green,
In a purse most beautiful to be seen.
Which was a generous action in deed,
And came to me in time of need,
And the gentlemen that so generously treated me
I'll remember during my stay in Dundee.[36]

Between pleasantries McGonagall dropped a very public hint during the Reform Street show that he intended quitting Dundee. His growing disenchantment and weariness with the town had been articulated in a poem published by the *Weekly News* at the start of 1893 titled 'A New Year's Resolution to Leave Dundee', its single, long verse explaining his pique . . .

Welcome! thrice welcome! to the year 1893,
For it is the year that I intend to leave Dundee,
Owing to the treatment I receive,
Which does my heart sadly grieve,
Every morning when I go out
The ignorant rabble they do shout
'There goes Mad McGonagall'
In derisive shouts, as loud as they can bawl,
And lifts stones and snowballs, throws them at me,
And such actions are shameful to be heard in the City of Dundee.
And I'm ashamed, kind Christians, to confess,
That from the Magistrates I can get no redress.
Therefore I have made up my mind, in the year of 1893,
To leave the Ancient City of Dundee,
Because the citizens and me cannot agree,
The reason why? because they disrespect me,
Which makes me feel rather discontent.
Therefore to leave them I am bent;
And I will make arrangements without delay,
And leave Dundee some early day.

Now, in May 1893, in despair at his treatment in Dundee, McGonagall made a pathetic appeal to move to Perth. He wrote a letter to

J. Wallace Scott, secretary of Perth Lyric Club, which would have drawn tears from the eyes of the literary statues in both towns. He pleaded for one of its members to find him lodgings in the town: 'If they are willing to provide me, in a house, at their earliest convenience, I will leave when the house is prepared for me. I don't want ye to put out much money for furniture, say one bed to begin with, second-hand furniture, say . . .' The follow-up report added: 'It is understood several influential members of the club are doing all they can to secure for the poet "one bed" with the necessary "second-hand furniture" in Tullylumb Lodge.'[37]

There is no record of McGonagall leaving Dundee at this time, however. Whether he discovered that 'Dundee' rhymed with '1893', and realised it was too good an opportunity for a year's worth of comfortable couplets, or whether he had a change of heart, cannot be said.

Meanwhile, public announcements promoting William McGonagall to the county's vacant Poet Laureateship came thick and fast. One recommendation to the *People's Journal* probably raised a collective chuckle among the paper's flock: 'We have in our midst a man of gigantic intellect and Herculean brain-power . . . the Poet Laureateship could not fall into more honoured hands than that of Mr William McGonagall, poet and tragedian. Such an appointment would prove an incalculable boon to the nation.' Small wonder McGonagall began to see himself equal to the task. Tennyson had been appointed in 1850. He was made a peer in 1884 and died in October 1892, when he earned £72 salary plus a £200 annual bonus. Nice money if you could get it. The Dundee papers ruminated on who should be nominated to replace him. They decided it was a toss-up between two mainstream poets, Algernon Charles Swinburne and William Morris. The uppity *Advertiser* sniffed: 'No other name of sufficient qualification presents itself.'

It is difficult to say whether McGonagall considered himself a serious candidate for the position. He had often seen his name in print teasingly connected to the laureateship and there is a lingering impression that he kept his eye on the vacancy. At the very least he probably considered he was the unofficial Poet Laureate of Scotland, to the extent that he was taken for a sucker when an Edinburgh journalist called at Step Row bringing a letter, said to be from 'Lord Roseberry', inviting him to apply for the Laureate-ship. McGonagall was suspicious of this – not least because he probably expected the new prime minister to be able to spell his own name. He nonetheless parcelled off a bundle of his latest works in the hope of receiving the royal nod from the queen. He heard no more and, despite the *Advertiser*'s sure-footed punditing, Alfred Austin – almost anonymous since – was offered the vacant Laur-eateship after an awkward interregnum in which William Morris declined the post and Swinburne turned to drink.

As 1893 continued, McGonagall's irritation at the entertainment ban persisted and he could not be blamed for coupling 'Dundee' and 'disrespect me' in his lines pledging to leave the town after reporting he had to 'steel himself' every time he left his house. Instead of attracting universal sympathy, one 'Beautiful Poet' wrote to the *Weekly News* challenging McGonagall over half a dozen stanzas to carry out his public threat to leave Dundee. His friendly journalist 'Johnny' printed the rival's verse, but wondered aloud why some sad readers were bent on dragging the Step Row poet from his lofty pedestal. He especially resented the challenge from this imitator: 'Just look at the effusion that has emanated from the virile brain of an atribillous versifier who dares to set himself up in comparison with McGonagall. Imagine the thing! Does this would-be poet suppose that he will ever replenish his wardrobe by writing such poetry? Pah! No one would think of giving him a paper collar for such rhyme, far less a suit of the best tweed that the world can produce.'[38]

The rival's poem was titled 'Farewell to McGonagall' and its vinegary verse was as blunt as it comes . . .

> But though ye're gane an' far awa',
> Ye'll never be forgotten.
> Ye maun write us a verse or twa,
> For a' you've writ is rotten.

> A true rope roond yer noble brow,
> To drive awa' dull care;
> We'll decorate your learned prow
> Wi' a saw to cut your hair.

In tar we'll ha'e yer likeness ta'en,
Ere you mak' your exit,
And your farewell memorial
We'll hing in the ashpit.[39]

McGonagall treated the anonymous lampooning with scorn – but expressed mortification over a reference to his 'shambling' appearance. He complained to his friend on the paper, 'Why, I am noted for my majestic gait', and he attributed this to his military training. The paper raised an eyebrow at this and dragged its readers into a bracket to whisper, 'It will be news to most of my readers that McGonagall once wore the Queen's uniform, but it is a fact, and he was a full private in the Royal Perthshire Militia, and he tells me that he was the pet of the regiment.' In truth, the nearest McGonagall got to the Perthshire militia was probably a free feed at Queen's Barracks in the county capital.

McGonagall decided, or was persuaded, that a response was required to contradict the printed baiting. The paper's in-tray the following week contained his six-stanza rebuke under the title, 'Lines in Reply to the Beautiful Poet, Dundee' . . .

Dear Johnny, I return my thanks to you;
But more than thanks is your due
For publishing the scurrilous poetry about me
Leaving the Ancient City of Dundee.

The rhymster says, we'll weary for your schauchlin' form;
But if I'm not mistaken I've seen bonnier than his in a
  field of corn;
And, as I venture to say and really suppose,
His form seen in a cornfield would frighten the crows.

But, dear Johnny, as you said, he's just a lampoon,
And as ugly and as ignorant as a wild baboon;
And, as far as I can judge or think,
He is a vendor of strong drink.

He says my nose would make a peasemeal warrior weep;
But I've seen a much bonnier sweep,
And a more manly and wiser man
Than he is by far, deny it who can!

And, in conclusion, I'd have him to beware,
And never again to interfere with a poet's hair,
Because Christ the Saviour wore long hair,
And many more good men, I do declare.

Therefore I laugh at such bosh that appears in print.
So I hope from me you will take the hint,
And never publish such bosh of poetry again,
Or else you'll get the famous *Weekly News* a bad name.[40]

So McGonagall's quiver contained the barbed arrows of satire and irony. He also liked a joust, likening his rival's appearance to a scarecrow, warning him to meddle if he dare with a poet's hair – and labelling him a trader of society's most evil substance, the alcohol downed in vast quantities in the city's hostelries.

Thanks largely to 'Johnny' and the paper's million-strong readership, McGonagall's name and infamy were spreading. In the spring of 1893 he became probably the first showbiz personality in the world to present a trophy at a football match. He had been invited to a game between Arbroath FC and Oddfellows as a guest of the home side. He said he was 'very proud indeed' to be asked to Gayfield and passed on poetic advice as he handed the silver cup to the winning captain: 'Never attempt to drink the full of it of whisky/ Because it will make you rather frisky.' This own-goal of a couplet attracted raucous cheers. McGonagall then staged an impromptu show – the usual 'Bannockburn', 'Rattling Boy' and 'Tel-el-Kebir' – which was met with the late-Victorian equivalent of a 'champeee-oonn-ees' chant.[41]

In football parlance, a regular income continued to prove McGonagall's personal, but elusive, goal. In August 1893, his friend at Lindsay Street revealed to *City Gossip* readers that McGonagall was suffering 'mentally, physically and domestically'. He reported a recurrence of the inflammation of the brain diagnosed by Dr Murison eight years earlier and that the same doctor was attending him. Worse than that, 'There was not a bit of food in the house, and no money and no tick.' The report concluded: 'Dundee ought to blush with shame.' The following month he reported that McGonagall was in a very bad way and that his 'haggard looks, his hollow cheeks and sunken eyes' were causing concern.[42]

McGonagall was still at 48 Step Row – and still ill – in May 1894 when he despatched another plea for funds to the hotelier A.C. Lamb, his anxiety evident: 'My dear Friend, I beg to be excused for letting you know that I am very ill at present with bronchitis and have been confined to bed since the 3rd of May up till the present time and Dr Murison is attending me, and as I am in very poor circumstances at present, beyond my control, and no one to help me, I ask you for God's sake, to try and help me. Believe me yours truly, Wm McGonagall, poet.'[43]

Receiving 10 shillings by return, a thank-you letter to his hotelier friend followed four days later, along with confirmation that the injection of cash had acted favourably on his health: 'My dear and esteemed Friend, I have received the half sovereign today that you sent with the messenger to give me and I thank you very much for the same. It will do me a deal of good. It will buy for me some wholesome food. I am a little better today than I have been for some time past. I took two pills last night to make me sleep and found great benefit in doing so, and I will take the other two the [this] night – and I think with good care and rest my health will shortly improve with the help of God. I hope you are well and the family, I remain yours truly, William McGonagall, poet.'[44]

During this period of peaks and troughs, McGonagall called intermittently at David Winter in Shore Terrace to order printed broadsides. The records of this company are thin for the Victorian period. One supply ledger has survived from the 1890s, each of its pages badly stained by water damage. A single entry records dealings with William McGonagall. It is barely legible but it shows the numbers of poem sheets supplied in 1894 and the amount charged for them.

Thus on 6 February 1894 he was invoiced seven shillings for 400 verses, the same on 17 April, and again on 25 August and 29 September. One other undated entry during this period suggests an additional uplift of 200 copies – a total of 1,800 sheets of poetry for the year, at a cost of around 30 shillings. The only other readable portion of the damaged page suggests that McGonagall twice paid two shillings towards these costs. As a rule of thumb, then, he was being charged 84 old pence for 400 sheets, which he could sell at a penny each making 400 old pence. In other words the sale of a quarterly supply of 400 broadsides could potentially earn him around 26 shillings, or 33 shillings if Winter's turned a blind eye to payment for them. It was hardly enough to live on and he would have required several 'entertainments' to pay his way – placing him in an invidious position given the magistrates' ban. Given these figures, it is not difficult to discern why the consistent cause of William McGonagall's problems should have been lack of income.

Sales of broadsides must have been sluggish, as from Step Row in June 1894 was despatched a desperate appeal to the influential local MP Sir John Leng, which revisited his claim to receive a state pension . . .

My dear Sir, I beg to be excused for writing to you again, hoping you will be so kind as to try and get me a gift of money from the Civil List as I am in delicate health at present, and likely to be so. I have been ill with bronchitis since the 3rd of May and is very much reduced in body. . . . I get but very little sleep. That is owing to brain worry, which I will never get rid of, only by resting the brain, and getting plenty of nourishing food and change of air. Therefore my dear Sir, I will feel very much obliged to you to lay my case before the Premier Lord Rosebery. I don't think you need to be afraid to approach him. Hoping you will remember me, believe yours faithfully, Wm McGonagall, poet.[45]

No response survives from MP or PM and presumably the sickly McGonagall ruminated on his plans as the year progressed. Disheartened, disillusioned and disappointed as 1894 continued to bring him heartache and problems, William McGonagall finally made good his threat to leave Dundee.

It is not described in his autobiographies, but when the move finally came, McGonagall's hand was forced.

EIGHT

DESPAIR AND DEPARTURE

A QUARTET OF tipping points hastened William McGonagall's departure from Dundee in 1894. In probable order of prodding they were: worsening ridicule on the town's streets, the ban on his public performances, another sequence of court appearances and a family dilemma-cum-disaster.

Firstly, in an agonising insight into the despair he was feeling at this time, McGonagall interrupted proceedings at Dundee Police Court when he stomped into the courtroom carrying a heavy butcher's basket. Bailie James Perrie, known as the 'Provost of Lochee', asked him to explain himself. So he tried to: 'This is a serious matter,' he began, as the magistrate, procurator and clerks listened and everyone else in the room eavesdropped. 'I consider I have been subjected this morning to grievous insult. Observe how this is becoming a daily practice, gentlemen, and I am afraid to leave my own house in the morning for fear of abuse, which is rather hard.'

McGonagall stated that the previous week two youths pushing a barrow had started to call him names. He had taken possession of the barrow and held it for about half an hour as a means of punishing the pair. Then he had allowed them to take it. On that morning, however, a different pair of barrow boys had annoyed him. This time he had seized a basket from them – the exhibit produced in court. He did so, he said, in order that when the owner of the barrow called at the police station to collect it, officers could identify the guilty youths.

'Now,' continued the poet in the hushed courtroom, 'this custom of annoying me is destroying my head. It keeps up an eternal sound in my brain.' Expressing his exasperation at being repeatedly pro-voked, he warned that if the hounding persisted he was determined to leave Dundee for the good of his health. He was assured by Perrie that he would have the protection of the law. Thereupon he wished his sympathisers a good morning.[1]

We may smile, but such acute action in the police court was symptomatic of a man at the end of his tether. McGonagall was infuriated, frustrated and deeply disappointed that he could no longer go about his business in Dundee without intimidation. His letter of indignation to James Laskie over impudent staff in 1886 suggests the problem had existed for many years. But his impulsive courtroom appearance in 1893 was a cry for help. His life was in turmoil. It was ups and downs, downs more than ups. And it was going from bad to worse.

McGonagall called on his columnist friend at the *Weekly News* office and told him, 'Do you know what I am in the habit of doing . . . before I leave home every morning I say to myself, "I wonder if I am to meet with abuse this morning," and then I button up my coat and make a rush for the door. Would you believe it, Sir, I won't travel a hundred yards when I am assaulted, pointed at with the finger of scorn, and laughed at and giggled at by silly girls.'

His listener poured out the poet's dejection to the paper's claimed one million readers: 'With a tremor in his voice, and a big tear-drop glistening in his eye, the persecuted Bard assured me that if he had known all that he knows now before he began to write poetry, he believed he would have cut off his right hand to prevent him from composition.'[2]

The misery McGonagall endured in his last years in Dundee should not be underestimated. The relentless baiting really got to him. He was despondent to the point of depression and the daily hostility affected his health as much as his routine. His four 'circus' appearances bridgeing 1888–89 confirm the level of abuse he suffered . . .

On 21 December 1888, at Transfield's Circus in the Nethergate, he came under a 'withering fire of potatoes, apples and rotten eggs'. A well-aimed cabbage hit his head before his third and final retreat ended the show.

On 28 December, again at Transfield's Circus, 'bags of flour and eggs rained around' and he sought sanctuary behind the scenery.

On 30 January 1889, at Baron Zeigler's Circus of Varieties, the remodelled circus, he was struck by 'bouquets of vegetables, bags of soot and flour, and a ham bone'. He gave up when 'a liquid bombshell' hit him on the eye and burst its nauseous liquid on his face.

On 16 February, at Zeigler's Circus, he had hardly started 'Macbeth' when he was forced to run as if chased by the witches as 'bags of soot, tin cans, eggs and garbage' were flung at the stage.[3]

On the last of these occasions, a full house had the pleasure of seeing McGonagall on stage for only three minutes before he was forced to abandon his show. The violence he experienced was the cause communicated as the reason he had to leave Dundee . . .

'My Dear Friend, I write to inform you that I am resolved to leave Dundee owing to the shameful treatment I meet with daily while walking the streets. No farther gone today than a cab-driver called me an impostor and a pauper imposing on the people of Dundee. Moreover, I was attacked in Reform Street by a young man while entering a shop to sell my new poem. He drove up against me full force, and almost drove me through the shop door, and as he ran he kept shouting "Poet McGonagall! Poet McGona-gall!" as loud as he could bawl.'

Another letter: 'My dear Sir – I am thinking about leaving Dundee owing to the abuse I meet with daily. Just this morning I was set upon by two roughs down the Ferry Road and had to take refuge in a butcher's shop, and only that he came to the rescue it would have been serious. Then after leaving they followed me and threw mud at me and mouthed my name, derisively, until I had to take refuge again in a grocer's shop until they went away.'[4]

Adding to his woes, McGonagall was back in court in the spring of 1893 to act as a witness for John, his fifth son. John McGonagall appeared before the formidable Sheriff Campbell Smith accused of assaulting a William Harvie, a ropemaker, at his father's home at 48 Step Row. Harvie had suffered broken ribs in the incident, but the 28-year-old labourer had tendered a not guilty plea. His father then stepped forward. Sheriff Campbell Smith asked him how much money he could get to bail out his son. The answer came – 'I can get no caution, My Lord. It is not in my power seemingly to get money to bail my son out.' To this he was told, 'I will let him out for £2. You will have to try to raise that or he will have to stay a week in prison.'[5]

It is not known if bail was arranged or John was locked up in Bell Street for a week. He reappeared with his father seven days later to answer the charge. This time he admitted assault, but claimed he had acted in self-defence. William Harvie told the court his daughter Elizabeth was the wife of John McGonagall's brother Joseph. Harvie stated that Joseph McGonagall was confined to Westgreen Asylum at the time and he had called at Step Row to inquire as to his son-in-law's health. He claimed the door was slammed in his face and that John had followed him into the street, where the assault took place. When the police arrived they found John McGonagall hiding in a coal bunker.

For the defence the only witness was our hero. Having taken the oath, McGonagall proceeded in a loud voice and tragic gestures to testify that he had asked John to 'get rid of Harvie peacefully', as he did not want to see him. He said Harvie had struck John with a belt.

Witness: 'I consider my son was quite right to defend his own house, which signifies his father's house.'

Fiscal: 'Do not speak so loudly.'

Witness: 'Granted, I am of a tragic disposition (laughter) and must speak out. I came here to tell the truth. This man has been haunting me like an evil shadow, calling out to me, "Poet, Poet, Silvery Tay, Silvery Tay, bring out your sword an' I'll fight you."

'What would be the consequence, my lord, if I brought out my sword? He could not stand the strokes of that sword for five minutes. With one stroke of my sword I declare I could sweep fifty of King Edward's army into the Tay (great laughter).'

The sheriff found the charge not proven – probably to prevent further testimony.[6]

The mention of Westgreen Asylum, later Royal Dundee Liff Hospital, concerned William and Jean's second son, Joseph. Then aged 38, Joseph had spent several years at sea as a sailor. He had returned to Dundee and married Elizabeth Harvie and set up home at 298 Perth Road. In 1893 he was stated to be a labourer. The couple had three children, two of whom had not survived – 'wasted away'. Joseph was described as having a thin face, dark blue eyes and prominent cheekbones.

He had been admitted to Westgreen Asylum on 11 March 1893 suffering from melancholy – said to be hereditary – and in a frail physical condition. He had endured convulsive attacks and was said to weigh only seven stones. He was not suicidal, but regarded by medical staff as 'dangerous to others'. The first psychiatric report, signed by a Dr Tulloch, noted: 'He is intensely stupid and vacant: on being questioned he answered very incoherently and seems to have a very imperfect understanding of what is required. His wife tells me she is very frightened of him.' A second report, signed by a Dr Buist, added, 'He has been given to drink. Since the New Year he has been out of work, with a wife and young child to keep and not receiving sufficient nourishment.'

Joseph McGonagall spent the remainder of 1893, all of 1894 and part of 1895 in medical and lunatic wards at Westgreen. Reports suggest little improvement over the period, one saying that, 'he twists his mouth as if chewing out the words', another suggesting that he believed he was dead, 'and awaits his funeral'. There is a reference in an 1895 entry to the effect that he had been transferred to Dundee West Poorhouse. He died in that institution in 1901, aged 47.[7]

It is difficult to gauge how such a misfortune was regarded among the poorer working classes. Presumably mother Jean was heartbroken and Joseph's siblings confused and, to an extent, embarrassed. What must have been of particular concern was Elizabeth's fear for her safety. Dr Buist had added in one report: 'His wife tells me that he has taken violent outbursts and threatens her life.' This family adversity must have impacted deeply on a proud public figure like William McGonagall.

But the old sage of Step Row continued to write through this thick and thin. Among prominent compositions at this time was 'The Kessack Ferry Boat Fatality', which provided his patrons with a collectors' item. The hiccup here was that his broadside was dated

February 1894, while the tragic sinking had taken place on 2 March. Not for the first time, his cronies claimed McGonagall had second sight. He was having none of it though, and unflinchingly placed the mistake at the compositor's door: 'There's no man more likely to make mistakes than the printer,' he said, adding, 'Don't you observe that they have also spelt Kessock with an "a" instead of an "o"?' The clanger did wonders for sales: 'The fatality poem is going rapidly into circulation, a fact which is itself conclusive proof of the sustaining power of the Poet's genius.'[8]

During the course of this output, McGonagall schemed to move his family as far from Dundee as possible. He set his sights in a typically unrealistic way – contemplating a move to another town, another country or another continent. His first choice was Ireland. He announced in May 1894 that he would travel to the country of his forefathers, saying: 'When I go to Ireland they won't treat me as I was treated in New York. In the streets there, when they looked at my poems with the Royal coat of arms, printed on the top, the Yankies shouted, "To the deuce with that. We won't buy that here. You go home to Scotland." They won't tell me that in Ireland.'[9]

Having made up his mind to leave, he sent his friend 'Johnny' on the *Weekly News* a 'farewell' note containing a list of 33 poems he had composed in praise of Scotland. It is a pity that the paper did not publish the inventory in full, but among those mentioned were two completely unrecorded McGonagall compositions, 'Beautiful Craighall, Blairgowrie' and 'The Ancient Castle of Glamis'. Appended to this catalogue 'in the Poet's beautiful calligraphy' was the enigmatic addendum . . .

> Who composed these poems big and small?
> I answer McGonagall.
> Deny it who can,
> And, be it said, an Irishman.

Here was teasing proof by his own hand that McGonagall was not Scottish-born – unless, of course, he felt it expedient to say such a thing with a departure for Ireland imminent. McGonagall, however, postponed his journey to the Emerald Isle after his doctor insisted his health was not up to it. The unhappy poet then considered emigrating to Australia. In November 1894 he wrote to the Rev. Alex Henderson, who had left the ministry in Dundee the previous May to move to Melbourne, to investigate whether the McGonagalls could settle in Australia. Henderson replied: 'Do not think of coming to Melbourne. You have no idea how the depression has made its mark.' Henderson's negative urgency appears to have ended the matter.[10]

While illness in 1894 interrupted William McGonagall's routine of selling broadsides as much as his travel plans, he was still able to harness his talents into a commercial channel in the autumn of that year, earning £2 for 'Lines in Praise of Sunlight Soap', and composing a hopeful follow-up tribute to Beecham's pills. Ignored by many anthologies of his work – the Beecham's verse never previously published, for example – this duo of poems can be viewed today as pioneers of the radio or television advertising jingle. McGonagall's lines to Sunlight soap were probably sent to the firm's head office by the local agent for Lever soaps – ironically, one John Willocks!

> You can use it with great pleasure and ease
> Without wasting any elbow grease;
> And when washing most dirty clothes
> The sweat won't be dripping from your nose.
> You can wash your clothes with little rubbing
> And without scarcely any scrubbing;
> And I tell you once again without any joke
> There's no soap can surpass Sunlight soap.
> And believe me, charwomen, one and all,
> I remain yours truly, the Poet McGonagall.

One wonders if the lines were modelled on Jean McGonagall's homely household at Step Row, as only close observation could account for how McGonagall knew no woman looks well with a dripping nose. Nevertheless, the cheque did wonders for his morale and he could not be faulted for sniffing a pot of money at the end of the advertising rainbow. There was talk in the papers of a million bars of soap bearing his poem, and a million pennies in royalties for the poet. As he attempted to get his head around these fantastic figures, there were words of thanks for his new sponsors with a predictable 'can-I-have-some-more' theme, with his full address purposefully prominent . . .

Gentlemen, you have my best wishes, and I hope
That the poem I've written about Sunlight Soap
Will cause a demand for it in every clime
For I declare it to be superfine.
And I hope before long, without any joke
You will require some more of my poems about Sunlight Soap.
And in conclusion, gentlemen, I thank ye –
William McGonagall, Poet, 48 Step Row, Dundee.

With no royalties on the horizon, this unsung inventor of the advertising jingle next turned his attention to Beecham's pills. It is not known if he simply picked the subject at random or ransacked Jean's cupboards, delving among cough mixtures, castor oils, fruit salts or soothing syrups, before downing a handful of Beecham's additives and coughing up 'A Wonderful Medicine', with its brilliant opening line . . .

What ho! sickly people of high and low degree
I pray ye all be warned by me;
No matter what may be your bodily ills,
The safest and quickest cure is Beecham's Pills.
They are admitted to be worth a guinea a box
For bilious and nervous disorders, also small pox,
And dizziness and drowsiness, also cold chills,
And for such diseases nothing else can equal Beecham's pills.
They have been proved by thousands who have tried them
So that the people cannot them condemn.
Be advised by me one and all
Is the advice of Poet McGonagall.

It was a verse that amazed his friend in Lindsay Street, who scanned its lines before telling astonished readers that the poem was unique:

'We have not once met the expression "most beautiful to be seen".'[11]

McGonagall searched out every opportunity to take advantage of his fame. In September 1894 he crafted an ambitious request to the Tay Ferries committee of Dundee Harbour Trust to ask for free passage to and from Newport by steamer, 'when he felt inclined to brave the dangers of the Tay'. The poet drew attention to the fact that several of his poems had 'waxed eloquent' on the beauties of Newport and had 'sung of the beautiful banks of the silvery Tay'. Among them were 'The Newport Railway' and 'Beautiful Newport', composed in 1878 and 1892 respectively. Gilding his request further he boldly promised that if his plea met with approval he might write a few more lines on the area 'and so induce many more persons to cross the river and add to the revenue of the Tay Ferries'. There could even be 'some verses in honour of the convenor of the Tay Ferries', he hinted.

Unfortunately, McGonagall's letter enclosed examples of his work. The committee noted his request with much merriment and there was a move to ask the treasurer to read 'Beautiful Newport' so that they would have 'all the facts before them'. He wisely refused. After careful and serious consideration, the request was declined, the convener clearly inconsolable at the thought of missing out on immortality . . .

'I beg to inform you that your application has been considered in a Harbour Board meeting, with the result that members have refused to comply with your earnest request, much to my regret. I should have been pleased to grant you free trips between Dundee and Newport, but the majority of the members seemingly disapproved of the idea.'[12]

With heartbreaking irony, William McGonagall's 'ticket' to leave Dundee was 'bought' for him. In the last week of September 1894 he was summoned to Dundee Sheriff Court to answer an eviction order. There his factor, a Mr Sibbald, obtained a decree enabling him to eject the McGonagalls from his Step Row property. Incredibly, it was not because of failure to pay rent that the action was brought – though this likely occurred – but because the tenants above the McGonagalls had complained about the family's anti-social behaviour and had threatened to leave unless their goods and chattels – and themselves – were removed.

The *Weekly News* reported the unfolding drama: 'Several times the name of McGonagall was shouted in the Court, but that personage failed to appear to offer defence to the action. Accordingly Sheriff Campbell Smith gave decree in absence, the customary three days being allowed to the poet to leave the precincts of 48 Step Row.' McGonagall did not defend the action because he had already packed his bags and, earlier in the week, had taken the train to new lodgings in Perth.

As news of his departure from Dundee spread, the *People's Journal* rushed to explain: 'Poet McGonagall wishes the people of Dundee to understand that in consequence of their want of appreciation and harsh treatment he has resolved to shake the dust of Juteopolis off his feet and is for the future to reside in the Fair City.' And from his new lodgings at 57 South Street, the 'Perth Poet' declared, 'I will keep from the city of my persecution, so help me God', and defiantly wrote a new version of 'Beautiful Perth'.[13]

McGonagall recorded his decision to leave Dundee in Part Five of the rambling memoirs submitted in dollops to the *Weekly News* in the autumn of 1901, conveniently omitting the court's decision to uphold the eviction action. His memory recalled instead the move with his wife to 'a small garret in the South Street' in Perth – surviving today as the upper floor of a building which now incorporates a restaurant at street level. In 1894, 57 South Street was located between ice cream vendor Luigi Lizzati at No. 55 and a plumber's workshop at No. 59. It had three floors and their attic home. The highest recorded annual rent for 57 South Street was £5, but the McGonagalls are stated to have paid the inflated price of one shilling nightly, suggesting a temporary stay was intended. This is borne out by their absence from the Burgh of Perth Land Valuation Rolls for 1894–95.[14]

Yet McGonagall must have been deeply disappointed to leave Step Row, where some of his most powerful and pathetic poems had been created.

While in Perth, in mid October, McGonagall received an

invitation to speak to a group of 'admirers' in Inverness called the Heather Blend Club. From his railway carriage window he must have seen the bleak moorland and mountains witnessed on his sodden walk to Balmoral nearly 20 years earlier. It was a romantic journey then, despite its awkward and fruitless ending. Doubtless it was better still in the comfortable accommodation of a train compartment. Lost in admiration of the world around him, he was in the Highland capital before he knew it. He was met at Inverness station, shown to his lodgings, and found time for a walk before returning to the Gellion Hotel, where his evening audience had gathered in twos and threes until the assigned room was well filled. In due course the chairman launched into the usual preamble . . .

'Gentlemen! I feel proud to-night to be elected at this meeting of friends and acquaintances to hear the great poet, Mr McGonagall, displaying his poetic abilities from his own works and from other poets also, and I request, gentlemen, that we will give him a patient hearing, and I am sure if ye do ye will get a poetic treat, for his name is a household word at the present day.'[15]

McGonagall was not given to responding to such introductions. He certainly did not make a habit of it. But with a well-filled belly and the promise of a decent hearing, the 'household word' rose and said he was proud to be amongst such a 'select company'. Recalling the event for his 1901 memoirs he said 'Bannockburn' was no more than halfway through before, 'the cheering from the company was really deafening to my ears, so much so that I had to halt until the cheering subsided'.

'The Rattling Boy' was followed by 'Tel-el-Kebir' and a scene from 'Macbeth' – his tried and trusted programme. The night apparently passed pleasantly and without serious interruption and, when finished, the company good-humouredly lined up to shake hands with the bard, while the poet could be forgiven for looking beyond them to the shillings dropping into a collecting tin.

Two days after his homecoming, and still aglow with Highland hospitality, he composed a poem in praise of the Heather Blend Club and delightedly recorded that his performance had gone 'without any hubbub'. His pleasure at the food provided at the banquet also mirrored the studious documentation of meals enjoyed on the sea voyages to and from New York in 1887 . . .

'Twas on the 16th of October, in the year 1894,
I was invited to Inverness, not far from the sea shore,
To partake of a banquet prepared by the Heather Blend Club,
Gentlemen who honoured me without any hubbub.

The banquet consisted of roast beef, potatoes, and red wine;
Also hare soup and sherry and grapes most fine,
And baked pudding and apples lovely to be seen;
Also rich sweet milk and delicious cream.

And for my entertainment they did me well reward
By titling me there the Heather Blend Club bard;
Likewise I received an illuminated address,
Also a purse of silver, I honestly confess.

Perth offered an atmosphere far distant from the pressured days of 'Gentlemen, if you please/No more green peas', and other immortal or apocryphal lines such as 'Gentlemen, I beg/No more rotten egg'. The playful ribbing he encountered at literary dinners in Perth, Inverness, Glasgow and Edinburgh was a stark and welcome contrast to the verbal and physical peltings endured in Dundee. In Perth and later in Edinburgh he was the centre of attention among sophisticated literateurs whom he must have regarded as an agreeable diversion from the ear-thumping snowballs of Step Row.

Shortly before leaving Dundee, for example, he had been invited by the Lyric Club to perform at the Queen's Hotel in Perth. A supper followed and, as a tribute to McGonagall, it was ruled that the company should stop eating the moment the poet finished. Their ever-hollow guest recorded the stomach-stretching meal with considerable relish: 'There was Beef, Fish, and Potatoes galore/And we all ate until we could eat no more.' And so the Dundee bard was introduced by the chairman with the usual sprinkling of munificent compliments. Then – something new – a specially composed

'McGonagall March' was played on a pianoforte by one of the guests. Our hero then stood on the platform to deliver 'Macbeth', 'The Village of Tayport', 'The Faithful Dog Fido' and 'Bannock-burn'. And once again it was McGonagall's 'powerful delivery' and 'strong voice and great enthusiasm' and 'the dramatic force with which it was delivered' and 'the tones and expression' that were noted by the Press. Taken all together, 'The recital was not one readily to be forgotten.'[16]

But while his experiences of Perth drew a sharp distinction from the fusillades of peas and eggs of the abandoned home 22 miles distant, it quickly dawned on McGonagall that sales of broadsides were poor and invitations to perform few and far between. More-over, his stay there seemingly provided no surge of poetry from his pen. Only a handful of poems are known from late 1894 to early 1895. He reworked a version of 'Beautiful City of Perth' for local consumption, and an unpublished tribute to Kinnoull Hill, a beauty spot overlooking the town, appeared in broadsheet in late 1894. 'The Fair Maid's House', fictional home of Catherine Glover, heroine of Sir Walter Scott's novel, was also given a McGonagall makeover.

He may, indeed, have been subsumed by domestic affairs. In November 1894, once again before Bailie Perrie, his son John and grandson Andrew appeared at Dundee Police Court. They were charged with fighting with each other in Step Row. Andrew initially failed to appear and bail of five shillings was forfeited. John pleaded guilty, 'and prayed for a chance, as he was about to go to Perth to join his illustrious father'. Despite this appeal he was fined 10 shillings and sixpence, with the option of seven days in prison. When Andrew eventually appeared, the evidence was to the effect that the pair had been fighting in the midst of a surging crowd and that Andrew had an open pocket knife in his hand and had flourished it menacingly. He was found guilty and given the same sentence.[17]

Despite being well treated, Perth proved too modest for William McGonagall and he lived there only eight months, until the summer of 1895. He explained in 1901, 'My Dear Reader . . . I must now tell ye my reason for leaving the Fair City of Perth. It was because I found it to be too small for me making a living in.' There were simply not enough takers for his work in a town a sixth the size of Dundee. Yet he recalled in his final autobiography that the inhabitants of Perth were 'very kind to us in many respects'.

Dundonians would have raised a wry smile that the pretentious little neighbour along the Carse proved inadequate to satisfy the material needs of their bard. But what probably made up McGonagall's mind to move to Edinburgh was the prospect of better sales and paid work, such as the invitation delivered to 57 South Street in December 1894. This was yet another pseudo-literary set-up, of course, but McGonagall chose to read into it hope rather than hoax. 'When I opened it I was struck with amazement when I found a silver elephant enclosed, and I looked at it in amazement, and said – "I'll now have a look at this big letter enclosed." I was astonished to see that King Theebaw, of Burmah and the Andaman Islands, had conferred upon me the honorary title of Sir Wm. Topaz McGonagall, Knight of The White Elephant, Burmah, and for the benefit of my readers and the public, I consider I am justified in recording it in my auto-biography, which runs as follows . . .

Court of King Theebaw,
Andaman Islands,
Dec. 2, 1894.

Dear and Most Highly Honoured Sir, – Having the great honour to belong to the same holy fraternity of poets as yourself, I have been requested by our fellow-country-men at present serving our Queen and country in Her Majesty's great Indian Empire to send you the following address, and at the same time to inform you that you were lately appointed a Grand Knight of the Holy Order of the White Elephant, by his Royal Highness upon representation being made to him by your fellow-countrymen out here. King Theebaw, who is just now holding his Court in the Andaman Islands, expressed himself as being only too pleased to confer the highest honour possible upon merit . . . and with much eclat and esteem caused it to be proclaimed throughout his present palace and kingdom that you were to be known henceforth as Topaz McGonagall, G.K.H.O.W.E.B.

And so this carefully crafted hoax continued. McGonagall was assured of a warm welcome should he ever visit the Andaman Islands and was urged to quickly accept the high-status gong now on offer as a reward for his 'thrilling' poetry. Much to the recipient's dismay, His Majesty's representative added, 'King Theebaw will not injure your sensitive feelings by offering you any filthy lucre as payment for what you may compose in his honour after receiving the insignia of the Holy Order.'

McGonagall was duly invited to the University Hotel in Chambers Street, Edinburgh, then a popular meeting place of medical students, to receive his new honour. He was provided with a return rail ticket to the capital, hotel accommodation and drew a promise that entry would be by ticket only. And a handsome fee was forthcoming. This was more to his liking. The Order of the White Elephant was conferred on the poet and an illuminated address in Latin presented to him.

Thereafter, McGonagall crowned his broadsheets with the new title and included 'Topaz' in his autograph – often mistakenly assumed today to be his given middle name. He also titled his 1901 memoir *The Autobiography of Sir William Topaz McGonagall, Poet and Tragedian, Knight of the White Elephant, Burmah*. It is difficult to say if he adopted the title in fun, or whether he believed it might commercialise his work, or whether he was actually convinced it was genuine recognition of his genius. Back in Dundee his newspaper friend observed drolly: 'He seems to be annexing new titles at a rate calculated to give the editor of Burke's Peerage fits.'[18]

It is no surprise, then, that on 28 May 1895 William McGonagall and his wife left Perth and moved to Edinburgh permanently. He took lodgings firstly in an unnamed hostel in Leith and then moved to 12 Grove Street, close to Haymarket Station on the other side of the city. He may not have gone directly, however, as he appears to have used a Dundee publisher for a modest collection of poems around the middle of the decade – dating evidence provided by an

1895 Press comment: 'An important piece of intelligence is that the Poet contemplates the issue of a volume of his verses.'[19]

The flamboyantly titled *Poet McGonagall's Masterpieces* was his first publication since *Poetic Gems, Second Series* of 1891. A5-sized and with a blue cover showing the poet in his suit of tweeds, this slim pamphlet ran to twelve pages and featured eight poems. Although undated by the High Street printer John Pellow, the booklet included the Heather Blend Club tribute of October 1894, 'The Beautiful City of Perth' and 'The Fair Maid of Perth's House', and is thus likely to have been arranged around the time a move to Edinburgh was under consideration. *Poet McGonagall's Masterpieces* was subtitled 'First Time Published' and priced at sixpence. Two versions of the first printing appear to have been made, as there are small text anomalies between copies. Soon after, a second impression appeared. This bore the same title, with a new subheading, 'Fifth Thousand – Second Edition'. If this is an accurate total of printed copies, Poet McGonagall had a significant following in and around Dundee, or else he was preparing a substantial stock of masterpieces to take with him to Edinburgh.

McGonagall's fame had spread to the capital, of course. In late 1895 two performances there were advertised for which he charged a guinea, plus cab fares to and from Grove Street . . .

Waverley Hotel, Saturday first, at 3 and 8pm. The Great McGonagall will give his inimitable performance from Macbeth etc, Music, Songs, etc, by other Gentlemen. Admission 1/-, Reserved Seats 2/-, by tickets only, from Kohler & Sons, North Bridge.

Mr McGonagall and Party will appear in Morningside Hall on Monday, 5th November at 8pm. Tickets at Morningside P.O.

McGonagall apparently went out of his way to make the Waverley Hotel gigs memorable, procuring a Wallace tartan kilt and jacket for the occasion and wearing pink flashings, medieval shoes, and a velvet cap adorned with an eagle's feather. It seems his youngest son John was by his side during these performances. Not to be outdone by his father, Jock showed up in a scarlet jacket and military trousers. On his head he wore a Glengarry bonnet, 'and on his face a perennial smirk'. The same critic clearly took exception to any dilution of the father's genius: 'While the great poet was refreshing, the time between his turns was filled in by McGonagall junior, who was a great deal more self-conscious than the elderly bard, and not half so amusing.'[20]

The date for the Morningside show was 5 November, but there were surprisingly few fireworks for the crowd of 200. Edinburgh was all about sophisticated, amused audiences – and for the first time McGonagall was attracting many women to his entertainments. He was still a figure of fun among the capital's snobbish elite, but his reception there lacked the malice of raucous Dundee. In the capital his eccentricities were probably viewed with polite amusement. There was rib-pulling, but little hostility.

Indeed, the veteran tragedian's first week in the capital could not have begun better when he was visited by the elusive Henry Irving and his famous actress partner Ellen Terry. Adding to the excitement, the introductions were made by none other than *Dracula* author Bram Stoker, who worked then as Irving's secretary, and who had attended the Waverly Hotel matinee. How McGonagall must have loved the irony – spurned in London and now homaged in person by three of the greatest names in British society. Not only that, both Irvine and Stoker ordered and paid for copies of *Poetic Gems*, complete with McGonagall's autograph. When Irvine asked the poet if he found the hotel audience appreciative, McGonagall replied that they were 'fascinated' and 'would have listened to him all night'.[21]

In time, McGonagall became a familiar figure in Edinburgh's Old Town. He still wore his long coat and clerical hat. He was slightly stooped, sallow-faced but always clean-shaven and with a quiet dignity. One man who lived beside him recalled: 'We used to have a smoke in front of the G.P.O. when McGonagall would be coming along Waterloo Place. One postman, now dead, would take off his cap and say, "Come on, boys! Here is McGonagall", and we would all put in a copper before he went along Princes Street.'[22] And a shopkeeper in Market Street remembered: 'Many mornings,

especially during stormy or frosty weather, one of our first customers was the poet. His first request was usually to be allowed to
warm himself, and after that for a carrot, which he was very fond of.
He was always polite and civil.' Another observation noted that
McGonagall retained his abstaining habits in the capital: 'At the
smoking concert he would drink only a small port, in spite of
pressing, and when he left, an untouched glass of wine stood as a
monument to his temperance.'[23]

McGonagall's income, as always, was derived from performances
and sales of poetry sheets. In Edinburgh he doubled the price of
broadsides to twopence each – and the signing of the tracts 'was a
solemn rite for him'. They were normally autographed along the
top edge of the sheet with 'Sir William Topaz McGonagall, Poet',
or occasionally down the left-hand side. He also made use of
contacts to ensure the broadsheets had as wide a circulation as
possible. One recalled: 'I knew him well and often acted as his agent
in selling his verses. It was his wont to appear at the office counter,
to be greeted with, "Well, Sir William, what can I do for you?" He
would produce copies of his latest efforts and I would leave him with
the remark, "I shall take these to the Duke of Cumberland" – one of
the clerks squatted on a stool. A ready sale afterwards took place
and the composer was most grateful for the patronage.'[24]

At first he seemed content with his new surroundings, writing to
a friend in August 1896: 'Since I came to Edinburgh I must say I
haven't felt sorrow. Such wasn't the case in Dundee. No, my dear
Friend, the Dundee folk have yet a deal to learn before they are on
an equality with the citizens of Edinburgh, namely good manner-
ism, which is not to be found in Dundee.'[25]

Yet Edinburgh neither offered nor provided William McGonagall with a pathway to a comfortable retirement. Although few of
his letters survive between 1895 and 1900, it seems he followed his
Dundee practice of tramping the streets flogging his broadsides
and hoping for letters of invitation to evening gatherings. To this
end, he continued composing verse on a variety of subjects, often
with an Edinburgh flavour. They included, in 1895, 'Lines in
Praise of Professor Blackie', a new version of 'Beautiful Edinburgh',
'The River of Leith' and 'An Address to the Members of the

Phunological Society'. 'New North Bridge Ceremonials' followed in 1896 and 'The Military Review in Queen's Park, Edinburgh', in 1897. Among the 'Edinburgh' group is the unpublished 'Colinton Dell and Its Surroundings'. Its opening couplet, perhaps out of laziness, was also used in 1899 for 'Beautiful Comrie', the town name being substituted . . .

> Ye lovers of the picturesque, away! away!
> To the bonnie Dell of Colinton, and have a holiday;
> And bask in the sunshine and inhale the pure air
> Emanating from the beautiful trees and green shrubberies there.
> There the butterfly and the bee can be seen on the wing
> And with the singing of the birds the Dell doth ring;
> While the innocent trout do sport and play
> In the pools of water all the day.
> Therefore, lovers of the beautiful and who are fond of recreation
> Go visit the Dell of Colinton, without hesitation;
> And revel among the scenery on a fine summer day,
> And it will elevate your spirits, and make you feel gay.

The talk north of the Tay was that these poems did not match his previous work in 'quality' and that he might return to Dundee one day: 'He has not excelled his Dundee production. I think the atmospheric conditions of Edinburgh are not conducive to McGonagall's muse. I have heard on good authority that he has half an idea of returning to the city.' His friend on the *Weekly News* never forgave readers for forcing him to leave in the first place . . . 'The citizens of Dundee should clothe themselves in sackcloth and cover their heads with dust and ashes . . . the Poet asked for bread and the boys stoned him, and the publicans persecuted him. In vain the Poet sang of the beauties of the silvery Tay; he was laughed at and jeered on the streets and left to perish of hunger.'[26]

*   *   *

McGonagall certainly kept abreast of Dundee goings-on. When a poem titled 'The New Town Hall' was culled by the *Weekly News* from the *Montrose Review*, and printed in full as 'Wm McGonagall's latest effusion', the poet rapidly got in touch to claim it was written by 'some coward or enemy'. Judge for yourself . . .

> The city of Edinburgh is most beautiful to be seen,
> And in a better city I never yet have been,
> Dundee is very smoky, and Perth is poor enough
> So I will not go for to give neither of them a puff.

Clearly a forgery. McGonagall would never descend to town halls – he drew the line at bridges. Similarly, when the *Weekly News* received a Queen's Jubilee effusion from 'McGonagall' in 1897, it was quickly dumped in the doubtful tray. No wonder. Its lines included, 'The procession in London was of the best to be seen/But it would have looked better on the Magdalen Green.' McGonagall was no traitor and instantly dashed off a letter to Dundee to deny authorship. And when his own jubilee tribute was eventually composed, the broadside of the poem displayed as a sign of its authenticity and his authority an etched vignette of the queen – the only McGonagall printed sheet to carry an illustration.[27]

McGonagall did move – but only within the confines of Edinburgh, and possibly under the threat of eviction, given the state of his finances. In the spring of 1898 he transferred his wife and belongings from 12 Grove Street to a flat at 21 Lothian Street, now part of the Royal Museum of Scotland. And in mid 1899, he moved again to Munro & Sons Buildings at 26 Potter Row.

McGonagall still had much to exercise his muse. The Queen's golden jubilee in 1897 was rewarded with a 13-verse sounding of drums and trumpets – and still he had not clapped eyes on her. He covered a military review by another favourite, Lord Wolseley, and fires in Paris, Scarborough and in London, where a family of 10 died. There was a sprinkling of battle and wreck poems and a handful of 'handsome' this and that. He also produced, in 1897, 'The Beautiful Sun', a companion piece at last to the wonderful tribute to the moon penned 21 years earlier. Two of its 13 verses . . .

How beautiful thou look'st on a summer morn,
When thou sheddest thy effulgence among the yellow corn,
Also upon lake, and river, and the mountain tops,
While thou leavest behind the most lovely dewdrops!
Thou cheerest the weary traveller while on his way
During the livelong summer day,
As he admires the beautiful scenery while passing along,
And singing to himself a stave of a song.

There was still no return to Dundee, however. Perhaps huffily, he was avoiding his former parish after hearing that his old friend A.C. Lamb had loaned his collection of relics, books, pictures and manuscripts to the museum for an exhibition titled – of all things – 'Shakespeare, Scott and Burns'. Come 1898 there was a formal move to attract McGonagall for a starring performance at the Kinnaird Hall in Bank Street. A committee was formed to make it happen and McGonagall's chum on the *Weekly News* tried hard to encourage the effort, reminding readers how a previous administration had 'boycotted him from giving public performances in theatres, music halls and circumstances . . . but for that the Poet, as he told me, might have been living in Dundee to this day'. He called on the current council 'to remove the boycott once and for all', and added, 'I would go further. Let them invite the Knight of the White Elephant to cake and pudding in the City Hall.' Alas, neither the Kinnaird Hall show nor the free feed, which would have drawn McGonagall like a drunk to whisky, took place. The end of 1898 marked the fourth year McGonagall had not set foot in his former home.[28]

He continued to write poetry, with nine new effusions in 1898 which mainly marked calamities, fires and battles. The pick of them was 'The Burial of Mr Gladstone', written and issued as a broadside in May. It was a grave and solemn time and there was no one better than McGonagall to convey the nation's collected grief . . .

'Twas in the year of 1898, and on the 19th of May,
When his soul took its flight for ever and aye,
And his body lies interred in Westminster Abbey;
But I hope his soul has gone to that Heavenly shore,
Where all trials and troubles cease for evermore.

And so on, until . . .

> Immortal Wm. Ewart Gladstone! I must conclude my muse,
> And to write in praise of thee my pen does not refuse –
> To tell the world, fearlessly, without the least dismay,
> You were the greatest politician in your day.

This 16-verse tribute was subtitled 'The Great Political Hero' and was despatched to Buckingham Palace, receiving the customary bland acknowledgement. It was left to the *Weekly News*, as usual, to provide the praise the poet sought: 'His muse has as strong a wind as ever, though his ear may be dull of hearing and a Niagra [sic] roars in his head every day.'[29]

McGonagall's last-ever touring performance probably took place at Crieff in May 1899. The *Weekly News*, which by then boasted a circulation of 246,000 sold through 10,000 newsagents, told readers he received a 'tremendous ovation' as he walked from the railway station to the hall followed by a huge crowd of Crieffites. As usual McGonagall appeared in Highland costume and opened with his most recent composition, 'Beautiful Crieff', which had been re-viewed in the paper's 29 April edition – hence the invitation to the Perthshire town. He followed with 'Bannockburn', 'Tel-el-Kebir', 'Macbeth', 'Lord Ullin's Daughter' and a new Boer War poem, 'The Hero of Rorke's Drift'. A diploma in a gilt frame was presented and the poet was escorted out of the hall by a policeman, the terms of his engagement being '£2 and police protection'.[30]

Despite his professional approach to performances McGonagall was, by then, struggling with illness. He was in his seventies and, in a letter to Johnny in Dundee, explained his infirmities: 'I am in the same condition I was in when I left Dundee – still troubled with noise in my head and deafness, also sleeplessness, which leaves me rather weakly sometimes, and makes me feel rather dispirited no doubt; but still I am willing to fight it out to the last and die in harness.' Another letter in 1899 urged the Dundee MP Sir John Leng to continue to pursue state help for him. The topic of his much-needed pension is prominent in McGonagall's surviving correspondence.[31]

A more remarkable letter in June 1899 was addressed to the *Weekly News* with a plea for its publication. In this, McGonagall gave vent to his injured feelings about his treatment in Dundee . . .

> I have written to some of my best friends in Dundee since I left it, and has never as yet received a reply from them, which in my opinion is only false friendship; but in my time, Sir, I have met with more flattery than real friendship. Such is the world I live in, Sir, and with regard to me leaving Dundee, I must declare honestly that I was justified in doing so, when I was prevented from giving recitals of my own Works and Shakespeare, and I consider, Sir, that any Man of Spirit would have done the same had he been treated the same way as I have been, or perhaps he would have claimed damages from the Corporation, as I do now, because it has prevented me from getting engagements in some towns in Scotland. The reason is Music Hall Lessees and Theatrical Lessees thinks there's something bad about me, and how I am unable to please an Intelligent audience, allowing to me been boycotted by the Magistrates of Dundee.

Here was something new. He was blaming Dundee for a boycott that had spread beyond its boundaries. And he was raising the issue of compensation. Perhaps more importantly, he was admitting he was aware of false flattery and that it was the 'world I live in'. In other words, by 1899 he was under no illusion that he was setting himself up for the inevitable fall. This was not uppermost on his mind on this occasion, however. He continued . . .

'Such a shameful action, Sir, is enough to make the Angels weep, and for such a shameful action, by way of solatium, I claim no less than £2,000 and, hoping to retrieve the honour of the City, the Magistrates will see to it, if not, it will remain an everlasting blot in the History of Dundee.'

McGonagall was not talking peanuts . . . £2,000 in 1899 was equivalent to roughly £180,000 today. He was determined to win redress for the ban on public performances imposed almost a decade earlier. Although he does not say if his claim was in the hands of a solicitor, the *Weekly News* warned the civic fathers that they would take on a legal action at their peril: 'If they go to law to defend the action raised by Poet McGonagall the city will be eaten up root and branch.'[32]

The council did not respond, not even when the poet issued a three-day ultimatum for a reply to his statement. Neither was an under-the-table settlement arranged. He wrote again to the paper in July 1899 explaining his continued stay in Edinburgh, where, as if to show what Dundee was missing, he boasted that he had recently recited 'El-Teb' to 'no less than 13,000 of an audience' at Waverly Market. If true, it must have been of T in the Park proportions in those days . . .

'My admirers in Dundee, I will honestly confess to ye that my chief reason for leaving Dundee was through the Corporation boycotting me . . . I declare it to be one of the most shameful actions that was ever perpetrated on any man; me, my dear admirers, that lived in Dundee for 60 years and more. I hope ye will all rally round McGonagall, the bard of the Silvery Tay.'[33]

The next Dundee 'admirers' knew of the poet was an astonishing Boer War news story in November 1899, titled 'McGonagall on the War – Attacks Rudyard Kipling'. McGonagall was ending the century with a pot-shot at Britain's leading writer for allegedly insulting British soldiers in a war poem, 'The Absent-Minded Beggar'. Outraged by its condescending remarks McGonagall rallied his troops . . .

'In my opinion a soldier ought to be respected because he is the people's protector from our foreign foes in time of danger, and as for Rudyard Kipling calling a soldier a beggar in his new poem, I consider it to be a great insult to the British army . . . I think he should be compelled to apologise for saying so . . .'[34]

The debate did not go unnoticed in the Dundee papers, which abandoned impartiality and batted for their bard: 'Sir William is not a man to fear Kipling, or any other, when he thinks they deserve a drubbing. That scathing letter which Mac dashed off in the height of indignation made Kipling's ears tingle.'[35]

As his annoyance brewed, McGonagall penned a powerful response – 'In Praise of Tommy Atkins' – a six-stanza poem which he sent to the Prince of Wales, gaining a favourable acknowl-edgement by return. This contained the counterblast . . .

> Success to Tommy Atkins, he's a very brave man,
> And to deny it there's very few people can;
> And to face his foreign foes he's never afraid,
> Therefore he's not a beggar, as Rudyard Kipling has said.

Though unable to shake off a bad bout of influenza at the end of the century, McGonagall continued writing. He was now well into his seventies, and there was a tendency to search war news for the bones of his effusions. In 1900, for example, he printed broadsides for 'Relief of Ladysmith', 'Battle of Corunna', 'General Roberts in Afghanistan', 'The Funeral of the Late Prince Henry of Battenberg' and 'Lord Robert's Triumphal Entry into Pretoria'. Yet he told 'Johnny' on the *Weekly News* in May 1900 that, 'I don't think I will be able to go about much longer to help myself by selling poems'. Indeed, in June he sent his friend the original manuscript of the 'Relief of Mafeking' poem because he 'was unable to publish it through lack of money'. Johnny, to his credit, continually urged his readers to help McGonagall, and from time to time was able to forward postal orders from sympathetic readers.

The last years of William McGonagall's life were spent in discomfort. We know something of this period from correspon-dence between McGonagall and one of his patrons in Dundee, the banker James Shand. A total of 10 letters survive from Edinburgh to Shand at the Union Bank in Dundee.[36] Most are short and convey pleasantries and usually three copies of the poet's latest work. The letters expose McGonagall's continuing struggle with illness. 'I am still keeping weak', he wrote on 16 January 1901. Yet he was sufficiently invigorated by the death of Queen Victoria that month to pen his 14-verse tribute, which began: 'Alas! our noble and generous Queen Victoria is dead/And I hope her soul to Heaven has fled.' This was forwarded to the new king while the throne was still warm, receiving acknowledgement from his private secretary, Sir Francis Knollys. Naturally, the reply was seen by McGonagall as a continuation of the Royal Letters Patent granted by her late majesty, and viewed as authorisation to continue to print the lion and unicorn on the top of his broadsheets. The poem was duly reprinted in the society magazine *Truth*, thereby introducing the bard to bemused London readers.

As 1901 continued, McGonagall's illness took its toll, made worse, inevitably, by the death of his son Joseph. He was unable to generate income and reported his distress to 'Johnny' on the *Weekly News*. This led to the creation, in April, of the McGonagall Appreciators' Contributions, or MAC, of which Johnny became honorary treasurer. The idea was that readers sympathising with McGonagall's plight would send donations – sixpence was recommended – to the paper to be forwarded to the poet. Sadly, the fund did not catch the public's imagination. Johnny reported on 20 April: 'I have got a lonely little shilling.' Even when McGonagall wrote from Edinburgh suggesting that, to avoid confusion, the title of the fund should be changed to The Poet McGonagall Fund, readers remained reluctant to assist. By 11 May only the same couple of sixpences occupied Johnny's tin, and there was a feeling, he reported, that the people of Dundee had not forgiven the poet for his parting shots and his move to Auld Reekie.

Fifteen penny stamps donated by the Carnoustie Boot Works eventually boosted the fund to the grand total of two shillings and threepence. This sum was remitted to the poet with apologies for the meagre amount. Surprisingly, he was genuinely grateful and from his new lodgings at 5 South College Street came a couplet of thanks: 'The more the dole the small/It was useful to McGonagall.'[37]

On 20 July, from South College Street, he wrote to James Shand: 'You will have the chance of getting my autobiography in the Dundee *Weekly News* by instalment, commencing Saturday the 27th. No more at present, believe me yours sincerely Wm McGonagall, poet, thanks for your last remittance.' Sure enough, McGonagall's story was placed before readers for the next six weeks. His friend announced it thus: 'The Great Sir William is going to tell his own story in our columns. I can assure you that this is the real, true story, and no fiction, written in his own hand, and in his own inimitable style.'[38] He had to be kidding. The memoirs were in McGonagall's own hand and style sure enough, but they were as much a great work of fiction as fact. Nonetheless, they seemed to go down well, attracting nostalgic comment and sympathetic odes from readers and, shortly after their conclusion on 31 August, they reappeared in a small sixpenny pamphlet as *The Autobiography of Sir William Topaz McGonagall, Poet & Tragedian, Knight of the White Elephant of Burmah*. This comprised 18 pages, had blue paper covers and an illustration of McGonagall at his desk, quill poised.

In Edinburgh, though, McGonagall's health failed again at the start of 1902, as did his finances . . . .

'No. 5 South College Street, Edinburgh, January 1902.

'Dear Mr Shand, I hope to find you well, but I am in a very poor state of health at present. I am suffering from a severe attack of bronchitis. I am very weakly. I have been confined to bed for a fortnight, but thank God I am able to be out again, but I am in arrears with my quarter's rent which troubles me very much. It is due on the 2nd February. I am in arrears 11s and I have a hard Factor. Excuse me for letting you know this, believe me yours truly, Wm McGonagall, poet.'

Then, in the summer month of June, came the news from South College Street that his daughter Mary, who had moved to Edinburgh with her son – another William – to live with her frail parents, had passed away. Her father erred in his calculation of her age, however. Mary was around 42 in 1902.

'No. 5 South College Street, Edinburgh, June the 18th 1902.

'I hope to find you well. I am sorry to inform you that my Daughter died yesterday at 5 o' clock. pm. Of course she has been ill for years past, age 30 years past, but I hope she has gone to that heavenly shore where parting is no more. I am still in my ordinary health, believe me yours, William McGonagall, poet.'

The family also mourned in 1902 the loss to meningitis of one of William and Jean's grandchildren, James, the eight-year-old son of James and his wife Grace Hendrey. A further loss was William's first great-granddaughter Mary Ann, who died the same year of measles, aged 14 months.

William McGonagall continued to write poetry as he entered the final weeks of his life. 'McGonagall's Ode to the King' was penned in June 1902. It bore all the hallmarks of his undiminished passion for poetry – and continued his habit of prematurely killing off any monarch within reach of his pen . . .

> Oh! God, I thank Thee for restoring King Edward the
>   Seventh's health again,
> And let all his subjects throughout the Empire say Amen;
> May God guard him by night and day,
> At home and abroad, when he's far away.
> My blessing on his noble form, and on his lofty head,
> May all good angels guard him while living and when dead;
> And when the final hour shall come to summons him away,
> May his soul be wafted to the realms of bliss I do pray.

The last poem William McGonagall ever wrote was also dedicated to the new king. This marked his spectacular coronation in August 1902. Johnny, still looking out for the veteran poet, reported to readers who had grown old with McGonagall's exploits: 'I had an idea that the Poet McGonagall had been either ill or at the Coronation. Well, he has been both. The influenza had licked him up, but in the midst of all his many infirmaries, he has produced the great Coronation poem. The Poet Laureate does not have a look in. The printing has been a triumph, with headings, inscriptions and copies of letters from Royals and other notorious personages, including His Majesty King Edward.'[39]

Verses one and two of the surviving fragment of McGonagall's final 'triumph' . . .

> 'Twas in the year of 1902, and on August the 9th, a
>   beautiful day,
> That thousands of people came from far away,
> All in a statement of excitement and consternation
> Resolved to see King Edward the VII's Coronation.

The Coronation ceremony was really very grand,
There were countesses present, and duchesses from many a
    foreign land,
All dressed in costly dresses, glittering with diamonds and
    gold,
Oh, the scene was most beautiful to behold.

His last 'most beautiful' committed to paper, William McGonagall's death took place at 5 South College Street, Edinburgh, at 4pm on 29 September 1902. His passing was registered on the St Giles Registration Office death certificate by his widow Jean King, who was present at his death. The cause of death was given as cerebral haemorrhage, as certified by Dr J.A. Schoolbread. The spelling on the certificate is 'McGonigall'. Ironically, Jean McGonagall was apparently not able to sign her name, and appended a cross on the register.

McGonagall was laid to rest in an unmarked pauper's grave in historic Greyfriars Cemetery. Research has not revealed in which part of the burial ground he lies. By 1902 this lovely cemetery, known for its poignant memorial to executed Covenanters, was already subsumed by lines of tenements and was all but forgotten about, save for its most famous resident, the dog Greyfriars Bobby.

William McGonagall's move to Edinburgh was one he apparently never regretted. His very last lines in his final autobiography, written a year before he died, expressed no apology for abandoning Dundee: 'Since I came to beautiful Edinburgh, and that is more than six years now past, I have received the very best of treatment.

'I may say I have been highly appreciated by select audiences, and for their appreciation of my abilities I return them my sincere thanks.'

NINE

McGONAGALLISM – THE LAST LAUGH

W ILLIAM McGONAGALL is probably the best-known Dundonian ever. His name is a byword beyond the city for bad
poetry, and his writings live on to be recognised and recited
throughout the world. Seldom a day passes but his poems are
celebrated somewhere in relation to awfulness. They are what
connect this larger-than-life character to today, and he would be
tickled pink to know he is causing a stir a century and more after his
death.

Headlines about William McGonagall are no recent phenom-
enon, however. In his own lifetime he was swamped with tribute
odes, parchments and diplomas, suppers and dinners, gifts of
clothes, money and trinkets. He had a musical march composed
in his honour and was immortalised on an Edwardian postcard. He
was proposed for a state pension, promoted as a Poet Laureate and
recommended for a knighthood. He filled newspaper columns and
was a household name. This was extraordinary recognition for a
failed and ridiculed poet for whom women would make up flour
bags for their men to hurl during his 'entertainments'.

And, since his death in 1902, William McGonagall's reputation
has been both enhanced and diminished by a deluge of good and
bad anthologies, comic or complacent imitators and a clutch of
clever and clumsy celebrations. He has been the subject of shelves
of books, articles and heavyweight investigations. He is remembered in the town from which he was evicted by a housing complex
named for him, and a seat next to the statue where he was treated
'like a dog'. A memorial in his honour was described as the worst in
Scotland and a pub bearing his name changed its name. Appreciation societies have been founded and foundered in the four corners
of the world, where websites now relay his story in microseconds.

He has been parodied and popularised by the Goons, Pythons and Muppets, J.K. Rowling, Terry Pratchett and Philip Pullman, and his story taken to absurd levels by the great Spike Milligan.

All this has put William McGonagall on a pedestal, although the cherished intention to do exactly that – to see a statue of our hero unveiled in Dundee – remains unfulfilled.

Yet McGonagall's death in September 1902 was neither the signal for an outpouring of mourning, nor any public show of regret. In fact his remarkable life was dismissed in all-too-brief obituaries and was all but forgotten as the country grieved for war losses and focused on the concerns of a new century. It was not until the 1930s that his memory was awakened and his poetic star again began to sparkle.

The man mainly responsible for reviving interest in William McGonagall was one-time journalist and author Lowden Macartney. By the 1890s some of McGonagall's printed poem sheets were on sale in the Poet's Box, a bookshop which operated over the years from various locations in the Overgate. This small retail kiosk flourished in the 1880s under a J.C. Scott, was run in the 1890s by J.M. Oates, by which time it had published a catalogue listing around 200 pamphlets, and was taken on by Macartney early in the twentieth century from a site at 181 Overgate. One visitor there noted: 'It wasn't a big shop. I remember the bell tinkled when you opened the door. Inside, the counter was buried in boxes of songs at a penny each . . . I seem to remember he had McGonagall originals, on pink and green paper.'[1]

Macartney installed a hand-operated press in the gas-lit back room of the Poet's Box. It was there that many new songs were printed on single sheets. He had taken an interest in McGonagall from his early days when he worked on the *Dundee Advertiser* and the *Weekly News*. He recalled how each new McGonagall offering had been 'greeted with amusement' by staff on the papers 'and gave occasion for much merriment'. Yet the shuffling, elderly poet was 'encouraged' to keep his effusions coming and in no sense was he an unwelcome visitor.[2]

Macartney owned a collection of McGonagall broadsides and, in 1934, arranged with the Glasgow printer J. & D.R. Burnside to produce the slim, paper-wrapped booklet, *Select Poems of McGonagall, With Comments on His Works and Sketch of His Life*. Its pale orange cover bore a sketch of the Dundee bard in thoughtful pose and 'clerical' hat. Inside was a brief interpretation of McGonagall's work and excerpts from his autobiographies, including details of his metropolitan and transatlantic adventures. Twenty-two poems were included for the asking price of sixpence. Burnside expanded the selection to 35 poems for a reprint titled *The Real McGonagall*, published in 1945.

As to why he felt that publishing the first collection of McGonagall's work for 30 years was necessary, Macartney explained, 'The growing and insistent demand, not only in this country, but also in the Colonies and various parts of America, for a collected edition of McGonagall's "poems" is the chief reason for the brochure now presented to the public.' Despite the assertion that his booklet was, 'the only attempt yet made to convey a comprehensive idea of the peculiar and extremely interesting individual', Macartney restricted his comments to McGonagall's poetry.[3]

A trio of notable writers also picked up the McGonagall baton and ran with it onto the pages of pre-war books on Scotland's culture and identity. The first was Neil Munro, who recalled for readers of *The Brave Days* that McGonagall's poetry was worthy of review 'before it becomes wholly a creature of myth'. Munro described a McGonagall performance in Glasgow, but was apparently bamboozled by the veteran bard. On one hand, 'It was not a harmless, innocent character I had been expecting, but rather a crafty merry-andrew deliberately playing up to the conception his employers of the time being had formed of him.' On the other, he felt McGonagall was 'hypnotised by the unaccustomed glory of these proceedings and incapable of realising that his leg was being pulled'. Writing in 1934, the noted literary critic William Power also described seeing McGonagall on stage in Glasgow. The Dundee poet was then an old man, 'but with his athletic though slightly stooping figure and his dark hair, he did not look more than forty-five'. As usual McGonagall's repertoire was accompanied by whistles and cat-calls, which were followed by showers of apples and oranges. Power left the hall early, 'saddened and disgusted'. His short scrutiny of the poet in *My Scotland* concludes: 'He was a decent-living old man, with a kindly dignity that, while it need not have forbidden the genial raillery that his pretensions and compositions provoked, ought to have prevented the cruel baiting to which he was subjected by coarse ignoramuses.'[4]

A third writer, Hugh MacDiarmid, was completely disparaging about McGonagall in his 1936 cull of Scottish 'eccentrics'. MacDiarmid claimed McGonagall was not a poet at all and 'knew nothing of poetry'. He chose instead to lazily convert newspaper reports into rhyme. McGonagall's appalling verse, he said, was the combination of three factors – his laziness, his peasant conceit and where he lived . . . 'Dundee was then and has since been the great home and fostering centre of the cheapest popular literature in Scotland'. In short, McGonagall stumbled upon his rhymes and 'having once performed the miraculous feat of knocking a bit of journalese into rough rhyming verses, he naturally conceived an inordinate admiration for his own powers'. MacDiarmid was thus not a fan. From a mere photograph, for example, he published a peculiarly savage description of the poet: 'An appalling portrait, a fish-belly face, as of something half-human struggling out of the aboriginal slime. All the incurable illiteracy, the inaccessibility to the least enlightenment, and the unquenchable hope of the man are to be seen in the eyes.' It was, MacDiarmid concluded, a face 'to make one despair of humanity'.[5]

While reviving interest in the poet, the views of Munro, Power and MacDiarmid were both partial and polarised. He was to be recalled either for the awfulness of his work, or for the cruelty he endured, or for his touching compassion. However, their contributions were valuable in keeping McGonagall in the public consciousness at a time of great social and political upheaval when the between-the-wars unemployment in Dundee alone exceeded 30,000.

McGonagall was also rediscovered in the 1930s in a sequence of reader recollections in the *Edinburgh Evening Despatch*. Most of these dwelled on the poet's time in Edinburgh and whether he 'knew what he was doing' – in other words, was he as daft as his poetry suggested? One, from a feminist-leaning 'Mrs S', went under the heading 'Poet or Blockhead': 'As a business woman dealing with the public, I feel sure no member of my own sex could have been so grossly stupid as this man appears to have been . . . wherein lay the amusement in hoaxing such a lazy blockhead is now difficult to see. A most distressing exposure of their own sex!' Generally, however, these reader anecdotes, while taking McGonagall's story to a new generation of Scots, largely depended on hearsay.[6]

Dundee was not left behind in the 1930s renaissance of the world's worst poet. Local author George Martin covered McGonagall's eccentricities in his *Dundee Worthies* of 1934, but, fittingly, it was David Winter & Son who led his revival on a national stage. In 1938, Winter's reproduced the 1890 edition of *Poetic Gems* as a word-for-word facsimile and found it had a best-seller on its hands. Reviews appeared across the country and once again McGonagall became a familiar name. William Smith, eventually the firm's managing director, recalled *Poetic Gems* finding its way into 'the kitbags and haversacks of a small band of Dundee admirers, and was read in hammocks, desert tents and Nissen huts and declaimed from impoverished concert platforms on windswept northern isles, tropical beaches and jungle clearings.'[7] It was just like old times and Winter's churned out *Poetic Gems* then *More Poetic Gems* (1962), then *Last Poetic Gems* (1968) for the next 60 years, at times outselling Robert Burns, with *Poetic Gems* passing its half-millionth sale in 1977.[8]

Come the 1940s, McGonagall was championed by Lewis Spence, a writer who had known him quite well. Born in Broughty Ferry in 1874, Spence became a well-known journalist, folklorist, poet and patriot. He spent his first working years as a cub reporter on the *People's Journal* before emerging years later as a powerhouse poet and author of a bewildering array of books. His memories of McGonagall were exposed in an enjoyable magazine article in 1947. He recalled meeting the great man as a 17-year-old and regarding him with curiosity. At the time McGonagall was 'stricken in years' with a 'sallow and wrinkled face'. But 'a pair of sparkling black eyes, undimmed by age, quizzed me sharply'.

Spence depicts McGonagall as a person of intelligence and humility. He recalls discussing poetry with him and asking him what he thought of Swinburne. To this McGonagall had replied: 'A marvellous command of music, young sir, but he fails to touch the heart, as does our peerless Lord Tennyson.' This was one of many conversations he had with McGonagall, and, 'frequently I was to marvel at the way in which a man who could perpetrate doggerel so abject could yet assess the abilities of authentic poets so aptly'. Contrast this with MacDiarmid's view that McGonagall 'knew nothing of poetry'.

Thus Spence recalled McGonagall to his 1940s readers as someone who had suffered abuse merely because of his natural eccentricities. But he was also a man of considerable knowledge, capable of holding his own in a conversation: 'He was in every sense a good and worthy person. Indeed, a native goodness and strong sense of decency and right conduct revealed themselves in his speech and bearing . . . His conversation in private was most rational and not at all self-important or stagy. He expressed himself justly and in an educated voice and manner . . . but what chiefly impressed me was his invariable meekness and modesty of demeanour, his anxiety for the poor and his warmth of utterance on their behalf.'[9]

Next into the frame was *The Goon Show* gang – Peter Sellers, Michael Bentine, Harry Secombe and Spike Milligan – who introduced McGonagall's verse into their zany 1950s television series, before stumbling into forming a McGonagall Club in London. Spike's fascination with McGonagall has been dated to the third series of *The Goon Show* in November 1952. Four days before the series began the *Radio Times* reported, 'Mr Sellers also hopes to bring along occasionally one of the great authors of the day – Mr William McGonagall, poet and tragedian.'[10]

Spike's portrayal of William J. MacGoonigal inadvertently prompted a revival of wider interest in the genuine poet's work and kept his name to the fore in the 1950s. He later launched a one-man crusade to spoon-feed McGonagall to a worldwide audience. First came his succession of madcap books with Jack Hobbs, *The Great McGonagall Scrapbook* (1975), *William McGonagall: The Truth at Last* (1976), *William McGonagall-Freefall* (1978) and the improbably titled *William McGonagall Meets George Gershwin* (1988). Though hugely entertaining, these can be swallowed with a pinch of salt in terms of biographical relevance. Milligan's *pièce de résistance* was the 1974 film *The Great McGonagall*, featuring him as Mac and fellow Goon Peter Sellers, in a soprano voice, as Queen Victoria. McGonagall would have exploded with indignation at the film's royal premiere when an exuberant Spike fell over and destroyed a life-sized cardboard replica of Queen Victoria while reaching forward to shake hands with Princess Margaret. In true *Goon Show* tradition, everything went wrong. Spike had to apologise to the princess because the book accompanying the film was not available. Then the projection reel got stuck. And, finally, nobody had thought to tell Princess Margaret that *The Great McGonagall* contained a full-frontal nude scene. Oops.

Thus, royal recognition finally came, albeit a century late, for William McGonagall. Cruelly rebuffed as he tried to gain an audience with Queen Victoria in the summer of 1878, at least the husband of a successor had the grace to acknowledge his genius. During a royal visit to Dundee in 1977 the now-demolished Windmill Bar caught the eye of the Duke of Edinburgh as the royal couple – as they do – drove down the Hilltown. He turned and said something to the queen. The staff were baffled and sent a McGonagall-style verse to their summer residence at Holyrood asking what had passed between them. This prompted a return poem from the duke in McGonagallese, which was sent Biddulph-style to the bar. Headed 'Palace of Holyroodhouse, 24 May 1977', and titled The Windmill Bar, the duke's middle verse of three went like this . . .

> I recall very well the pub on the hill
> Which now I see was the old Windmill.
> It wasn't the crowd coming out of the door
> That caught my eye at quarter past four,
> 'Twas the Ann Street windows attracted my stare,
> I wondered if anyone could be living there.
> Then seeing the smiles on your customers' faces
> I reckoned your pub was one of those places
> Where the noise of good cheer drives off all dull cares
> And makes it impossible to live up those stares.

Mac would have given the duke pass marks for his witty ending and raised two cheers for the ' 'Twas'. The lines were hardly tortuous, though, and wanted McGonagall's unsteady hand to knock them out of shape. It is said that the queen enjoys his work, as did the late Queen Mother, who once revealed to the actor John Cairney that she was 'a zealous admirer' of the poet, before reciting the opening lines of the elegiac 'Railway Bridge of the Silvery Tay'.[11]

McGonagall would have cast a wary eye over today's media. Not for him *Big Brother*, but he would have been a terrifying TV panellist. He would naturally insist on a slot in the Royal Command Performance. Yet if he were on our screens, it would perhaps only be to find his eccentricities again being exploited. The BBC was an established broadcaster by the 1930s but did not discover McGonagall until 1947 when it presented a radio 'tribute' to 'the worst poet in the world'. The programme failed to draw a chuckle from some listeners. Ahead of her time, one Edinburgh resident pointed out that McGonagall earned his living playing the fool 'like many BBC stars'. Another listener wrote to express 'a strong disgust' over the corporation's treatment of the Dundee bard and how he had felt 'a painful wave of shame' as he listened.[12]

One of the first television programmes telling McGonagall's story, aired by STV in 1962, also resulted in negative feedback, this time from Grace McGonagall Hickey, the poet's granddaughter. Mrs Hickey, then aged 62, was the daughter of James, William and Jean's fourth son. She particularly objected to presenter Jack House's reading of a false couplet, 'Two birds sat on a barrow/One was a speug, the other a sparrow', which McGonagall never wrote despite repeated attributions to him.

In 1965 Grampian Television produced *The Ups and Downs of William McGonagall*, with a biographical script by Alastair Borthwick which had young William reaching Dundee via Edinburgh, Ayrshire and Orkney. BBC cameras rolled again in 1997 when Dundonian actor Jock Ferguson played McGonagall on the very stage from which the great man had once entertained inebriated audiences. By then the Pierre Victoire restaurant in Castle Street, it was the Music Hall in McGonagall's day and situated upstairs from David Winter, where his poems were printed. That event featured a

McGonagall Supper which, by tradition, offers dessert first and starter last in a backwards take on a Burns Supper. The following year radio journalist Jimmy Black produced *The Real McGonagall* for BBC Radio Scotland. And in 1981 the national pop radio station Radio 1 broadcast something unusual, even for it, when two McGonagall classics were read on *The Noel Edmonds Show* by David Phillips. Edmonds was so impressed he described the poetry as 'positively appalling'.

McGonagall's poems have also been recorded and distributed as vinyl records, tapes, videos, CDs and DVDs – the best of them probably John Lawrie's declamatory reading of 'The Tay Bridge Disaster' in 1965. Perhaps the weirdest recorded tribute occurred in 1958 when Dame Edith Evans, one of the greatest English actresses of her time, recited 'The Tay Whale', backed by 120 musicians of the London Philharmonic Orchestra. This raising of Britain's cultural bar by which McGonagall's comic poem was set to music was for the Interplanetary Music Festival at the Royal Albert Hall. Apparently the audience reaction was every bit as predictable as its Victorian counterpart's – they were in stitches for the duration of the epic.

Some of the greatest names in theatre have taken McGonagall's story to new audiences. Tom Fleming played the poet at the Gateway Playhouse in Edinburgh in 1960. This was achieved with a tartan motoring rug around his shoulders, a table and chairs for props, and by linking poems with excerpts from *Brief Autobiography* and *Reminiscences*. A documentary play called *McGonagall! McGonagall!* by Roy Kendall had its world premiere at Dundee Repertory Theatre in Lochee Road in March 1969. It was directed by James Lovell, with James Copeland taking the lead role. The *Courier* revisited the caustic comments of publishing predecessors by reporting: 'It lacks dramatic impact, lacks drama.'

In 1971 the Scots actor John Cairney staged a one-man, one-hour McGonagall play at the Edinburgh Festival, which later toured. When the play came to the Little Theatre in Dundee in August that year, a man stood up in the second-back row, pointed a finger at Cairney and shouted, 'Mr Cairney-McGonagall, I'll give it to you straight.' He then accused the actor of charging 70p for entry under 'false pretences'. At the top of his voice he shouted that the back rows had not received a bridie, the Forfar delicacy promised with the admittance ticket. 'All we've got is pie in the sky', he shouted, before returning to his seat. At the end of the performance Cairney told the audience, 'I came to Dundee as an actor, not a caterer.'[13]

The same year A.B. Paterson's play based on the poet's life was performed in Anstruther. In what some might have considered a tasteless gimmick, Victorian Dundee smells – including jam and marmalade – were floated through the hall. In 1972 the former Dundee Rep director Robert Robertson wrote and acted a short production taking the form of McGonagall telling the story of his life. It was staged at the Traverse in Edinburgh but, once again, its reviewer remained distinctly unimpressed: 'He failed to get beyond the outer skin of the poet and make a guess at the workings of his mind.'[14]

Perth Theatre followed with 'Hero o' A Hundred Fights', a Cliff Hanley dramatisation which borrowed its title from the 'Jack o' the Cudgel' sequence and, in 1984, 'How Handsome to be Seen', Dundee Rep's Youth and Community Project, was a merrily-named observation of the poet's life by Carl McDougall. A Fringe play, 'An Audience for McGonagall', written by Donald Campbell, was staged at the Netherbow in Edinburgh in 1987, and in 1991, Dundee Rep staged 'William McGonagall: Made from Girders', with a script by Chris Balance. To mark the centenary of McGonagall's death, Ballance also wrote 'The Great McGonagall Entertains', a one-man play which had its premiere at the Steps Theatre in Dundee in September 2002, with John Shedden in the title role.

Various William McGonagall appreciation societies flourished in the post-war period. One of the earliest was the Edinburgh University McGonagall Society. This group was established in 1962 'as a gesture against the Burns cult' and took the enlightened view that a bad verse book would encourage poetry. In 1963 the students produced a typewritten *McGonagall Yearbook* using rudimentary Gestetner duplication. It included translations of the bard's work into Greek and Latin and an article written in Finnish. In true McGonagallian style, one page was printed upside down.

Dundee's appreciation society, whose membership exceeded 100 in the mid-1990s, met for many years in McGonagall's, a pub in Perth Road. Among club highlights, its members in 1993 followed in the footsteps of McGonagall's 1879 Fife tour and, the following year, sent members to retrace McGonagall's trip to New York. In the summer of 2000 four hardy members spent 16 hours walking to Balmoral Castle to re-create the poet's 1878 crusade. In 1977 Sir John Betjeman, the Poet Laureate, agreed to be one of the Dundee society's honorary presidents, a post he was 'delighted to accept'.[15]

McGonagall enthusiast William Smith recorded McGonagall societies or groupings in far-flung corners of the world including Johannesburg, Krakow, Moscow, Toronto, Mombasa, Bangkok and Hong Kong. A World Congress of McGonagall societies was apparently considered in the late 1970s. One of the largest overseas fan clubs was The William McGonagall Society of Japan. This was formed in 1977, originally in Hiroshima then run mostly from the English department at Tohoku University in Sendai. Its honorary president was Spike Milligan and most members were ex-pats though it included seven Japanese at one point. One of the more enthusiastic members, a K. Sugahara from Kyoto, dwelled long and hard on 'The Rattling Boy from Dublin', before pointing out its poetic limitations in the society's short-lived newsletter:

'The neuter rhyme ending "-ass" is employed in four sequential lines (stanza 4), but only in two sequential lines in stanza 5. This gives an -aform structure of six sequential lines whereas most of the lines in the rest of the poem are conventional couplets. The chorus as befits the "incremental rest" is alternate ab ab rhyming. I can find no other instance of this in *Poetic Gems*.'[16]

William Smith was one of several individuals who promoted McGonagall in the manner of 'Johnny' of the *Weekly News*. Smith first learned of the poet in the 1930s when, as a 14-year-old message-boy for David Winter & Son, he delivered copies of *Poetic Gems* to Lowden Macartney at the Poet's Box: 'When I joined the firm, an old printer, Charles McLean, could recall being sent as a boy to McGonagall's home with printed broadsheets – and often the gift of a half-sovereign as well. It must have been a godsend on some of the many occasions when "the wolf was at the door" as the poet himself would put it.' Smith, later managing director, was not alone in wondering why David Winter, founder of the firm which kept McGonagall's work alive for a century, was not honoured with a few lines from the bard.[17]

Modern-day McGonagall champions have included one-time Dundee bookseller Frank Russell, long-time appreciation society chairman Alex Gouick, Canadian scholar Gord Bambrick, who has given McGonagall studies an academic edge, David Kett, custodian of and authority on Dundee's McGonagall Collection, Chris Hunt, who has introduced internet users to his work, artist Peter Trust and actor Jock Ferguson. Leaving aside Spike, celebrity fans have included Winston Churchill and President Eisenhower and, among literary and acting luminaries, Charlie Chaplin, W.C. Fields, Sir Harry Lauder, Sir Alec Guinness, Dick Van Dyke and Barry Cryer. Sheikh Yemani, who held the world to ransom during the oil crisis of 1973, was also a McGonagallite. Each would have received a begging letter in the poet's day.

McGonagall would be proud to learn he has also been remembered at a number of 'entertainments'. A William McGonagall Centenary Supper took place in the Angus Hotel, Dundee, in 1977 to mark the 100th anniversary of his first published poem. The event was organised by Dundee Junior Chamber and chaired by Kenneth Malcolm, one of the leading lights of the local appreciation society. BBC journalist Fraser Elder gave the address to the Dundee cake and author Jack House proposed the Immortal Memory. Another dinner took place in the Angus Hotel in January 1980. This time Elder chaired the evening assisted by Robin Hall, half of the singing duo Robin Hall and Jimmy MacGregor. The star of the show was William 'Amethyst' Connolly who replied to William Smith's Immortal Memory with controlled lunacy and the couplet, 'Oh shining town on the Silvery Tay/You've made all your streets go the same way.' Over 500 guests raised £3,500 towards the building of the new Rep Theatre in Tay Square, while the after-dinner shenanigans were broadcast by the BBC. A new theatre for Dundee would have been a project close to McGonagall's heart.

The highlight of the millennium year was the McGonagall 2000 Exhibition at Dundee Central Libraries which featured examples from its wonderful collection of original letters, manuscript poems, broadsides and photographs. But no previous focus on William McGonagall reached the levels achieved on the centenary of his death in 2002. Several events took place under the auspices of the McGonagall Festival, an initiative organised by the City of Discovery Campaign through a festival committee. A major highlight was the tribute unveiled to McGonagall at Riverside. Here, the first verse of the poem 'which made me famous' – 'The Railway Bridge of the Silvery Tay' – was etched in stone on the public walkway close to the bridge.

The centenary, which was also celebrated by motions in the Scottish Parliament and the House of Commons, did not pass without acrimony of the kind the poet witnessed as a public balladeer. The first printed punch-up began when a national newspaper claimed the city had commemorated the world's worst poet with Scotland's 'worst memorial'. The report pointed out that the inscribed verses on Riverside Drive included a misspelling of the word 'beautiful', which was instead spelled 'beatiful'. Dundee City Council responded by saying the £10,000 tribute included deliberate misspellings. It fumed: 'The meticulous research carried out prior to commissioning this project revealed that McGonagall himself had misspelled the word "beautiful" in his poem – a fact which this report seems to have deliberately ignored.' It pointed out that of the poem's seven verses, five included the misspelling and added, 'Far from being criticised for a spelling mistake, the planners who researched this project deserve credit for the thoroughness and accuracy of their preparation.'

Perhaps McGonagall misspelled 'beautiful' in one manuscript copy of the Tay Bridge poem. But he quickly corrected it in versions sent for public airings to both the *Weekly News* and *People's Journal*, as well as in his printed works, including *Poetic Gems*. It would have been appropriate and reasonable for the council to have done likewise.[18]

The next war of words surrounded Dundee's pre-eminence in the commemoration of the centenary of the poet's death. This resulted in a growing movement in Edinburgh to claim McGonagall as its own. At the height of the McGonagall Festival in 2002

academics in Edinburgh resubmitted the claim that McGonagall
was born and died in the capital and that, therefore, they and not
Dundee had the rightful claim to his name. The point was driven
home publicly. At exactly the same time as the Riverside sculpture
was unveiled, a ceremony took place in Edinburgh to dedicate a
plaque above the doorway to McGonagall's one-time lodgings in
South College Street.

The centenary year ended with another inter-city spat when the
Christmas card from Edinburgh's Lord Provost to Dundee City
Council controversially showed a photo of the plaque to McGonagall's memory in Greyfriars Cemetery, with four verses of 'Beautiful
Edinburgh' printed alongside. It paid tribute to McGonagall as one
of Edinburgh's 'critically-acclaimed' literary figures. The card
struck a dull note with the McGonagall Appreciation Society in
Dundee, but when the society accused Edinburgh of hijacking the
poet, the capital's Lord Provost Eric Milligan retorted: 'Hijack
McGonagall – I'm not having that. I have his book in front of me
and he states he was born in 1830 in Edinburgh. He moved to
Paisley and then to Glasgow before settling in Dundee, where he
did spend a large part of his life. He died in Edinburgh in
September 1902 and is buried at Greyfriars Churchyard.' Mr
Milligan got the death part correct – possibly because his council
forebears had unceremoniously lowered the 'critically-acclaimed'
poet into an unmarked pauper's grave.[19]

The biggest rammy of the 2002 centenary arose through an
otherwise innocuous tribute to McGonagall on Grampian TV's
Artery series. Among those taking part was a talented trio of
Taysiders – Don Paterson, Bill Herbert and Douglas Dunn, three
of Scotland's greatest living poets. Dunn, professor of English at St
Andrews University, editor of the *Faber Book of Twentieth-Century
Scottish Poetry* and a past winner of the Whitbread Book of the Year
Award, set the cat among the pigeons with a televised tirade against
the Dundee poet. McGonagall, said Dunn, was someone who
should be erased from history. 'To celebrate William McGonagall
as a poet is certainly an insult to people like myself who have spent
most of our lives pursuing the art of poetry.' He described the
centenary celebrations as 'utterly wrong-headed' and added: 'The

man was an idiot from birth, totally self-deluded. His poetry is appalling. I think it's cruel to remember a man like that. Dundonians are very canny people, and they know a fake when they see one. I don't know if Dundee does celebrate McGonagall with all its heart. They may celebrate McGonagall opportunistically. I don't think celebrating it is quite the thing to do. You could commemorate it – if you built a monument and buried it. If he was alive today, he wouldn't be allowed to walk the streets.'[20]

Dunn's hostility drew fierce criticism. W.N. Herbert defended his fellow Dundee poet: 'In a sense what McGonagall was doing was a kind of journalism – he was the Kate Adie of his day. It was wonderful how he could be inspired by absolutely anything.' City of Discovery Campaign chairman Mervyn Rolfe, a past Lord Provost, was less diplomatic and labelled Dunn purist and facile: 'I think he is being cruel to suggest something like building a monument and burying it – he is also being stupid, silly and facile. It's a bit disappointing to see a recognised poet being so purist about it.'[21]

Dundonians were also dismayed by Dunn's downbeat opinion. One letter to the *Courier* summed up the general reaction: 'If you go the length and breadth of the country asking people who McGonagall was, at least two out of every five would be able to tell you. Do the same for Professor Dunn and I doubt if you'll find one in a hundred.' Another reader commented: 'The people of Dundee were not stupid. They knew William was a funny, harmless character trying to scrape a living, and they had more compassion than Douglas Dunn.'[22]

The literary elite has always found it difficult to get its collective head around this weaver poet and tragedian. Much in the way that Jack Vettriano pictures generate turned-up noses from the art cognoscenti, so McGonagall has struggled to gain wider acceptance. Gradually, however, mainstream reference books and journals that regard themselves as 'learned' have finally lived up to that title by welcoming the Bard of the Silv'ry Tay. Turn to *Chambers Biographical Dictionary* – 'His poems are uniformly bad, but possess a disarming naivety and a calypso-like disregard for metre which never fail to entertain'; to the *Times Literary Supplement* – 'The only memorable truly bad poet in our language'; to the *Oxford Dictionary of Quotations* – 'Alas! Lord and Lady Dalhousie are dead, and buried at last/Which causes many people to feel a little downcast'; to *The Oxford Companion to English Literature* – 'His . . . unscanned doggerel continues to entertain' – and, lo and behold, the Knight of the White Elephant is, at last, grazing with literature's great and good.

Individual McGonagall poems have also been the butt of criticism from the cultural elite. When Chris Hunt included McGonagall's full-length play, 'Jack o' the Cudgel – or the Hero of A Hundred Fights', in his 2006 anthology of McGonagall poems, it was ridiculed by Gerard Carruthers, a senior lecturer on Scottish literature at Glasgow University. Reviewing the piece ahead of publication, Dr Carruthers called the work a 'blunt instrument of a play' and criticised McGonagall as 'a writer of indefatigable ambition, singularly unmatched by even a smidgen of talent'. Apparently elevating McGonagall to the honour of beating the Wright Brothers into the air, the *Courier* described the play's subtitle as 'Hero of a Hundred Flights'.[23]

Physical mementoes of McGonagall are less common than memories or observations of what his poetry stood for. His homes tended to be in the poorer parts of towns, and have mostly failed to survive modern-day clearance. This is especially true of his Dundee lodgings. His first, in Hawkhill, was located near the car-wash service close to the Whitehall Theatre on the north side of today's busy thoroughfare. Much of this area was cleared in the 1960s, while his *c* 1850 West Port tenement bit the dust during the 1970s Dundee Project clearance.

There was an attempt, however, to preserve his house at 19 Paton's Lane. The block housing numbers 7–21 was due for demolition in 1974 but its clearance was averted when Dundee District Council announced an effort to restore it. Work had to be halted in 1979, however, when structural engineers discovered problems. Bill Crabb was then the consultant surveyor for the Scottish Special Housing Association, which was involved in the attempt to preserve the block. He recalled: 'When the interior was stripped out it was obvious that the front and back walls were not tied in to the interior cross walls, so the structure was very unstable and dangerous. The remedial works involved extensive steelwork and delays and I remember preparing a probable cost for the work and reporting it to SSHA. It was decided that the additional cost would be better spent on new houses, so the tenement was demolished and the proposed main development site increased.'[24]

No. 19 Paton's Lane was levelled in the first week of April 1980, thus sharing the same fate as the previously bulldozed No. 31. It was also hoped that McGonagall's house at 48 Step Row, where the poet lived between 1889 and 1894, could be preserved but it, too, eventually had to be demolished.

McGonagall's Edinburgh addresses fared better. He did not occupy the fine Georgian ground-floor flat which survives at 12 Grove Street but perhaps took a basement room or lived in the block's garret. The exact location of his rented flat here is unknown. His next accommodation, from May 1898, was at 21 Lothian Street, overlooking McEwan Hall. Sadly, this street survives today only from No. 29 upwards. The site of McGonagall's former home at No. 21 is now part of the Royal Museum of Scotland extension. The tenement at 26 Potter Row, which he occupied from the summer of 1899 to June 1901, was demolished to make way for Marshall Street. He lived on the corner block, opposite a school, on a site now occupied by a Japanese restaurant. His last address was at 5 South College Street. This house survives in the ownership of Edinburgh University. Above its door is an oval plaque with the words, 'William McGonagall, Poet and Tragedian, died here, 29th September 1902.'

Among other physical reminders of his life are a number of memorials. In 1972 the Scottish Burns Club and Scottish Heritage Association donated a commemorative seat just behind Dundee's Burns Statue, at the foot of the steps to the old reference library in Meadowside. The two organisations also gifted a bench in McGonagall's honour to Greyfriars Cemetery in 1975. In October 1999 the poet's final resting place in Greyfriars was finally recognised with a black granite plaque in a ceremony attended by his great-great-grandson William McGonagall, great-great-great-granddaughter Mary Ross and the Lords Provost of Dundee and Edinburgh. For Dundonian Mary Ross, the memorial marked the end of a long struggle to pinpoint her ancestor's resting place.

She said, 'His relatives have been unable to pay their last respects because we had nowhere to go. Now we can, along with thousands of his fans from all over the world.' Generally, McGonagall's descendants have kept a low profile, though they have been ever-supportive of the illustrious poet in their family.

The unveiling of the Edinburgh memorial sparked fresh appeals for a similar dedication in Dundee. Eventually permission was secured for a memorial on the site of his demolished tenement in Paton's Lane. A sum of nearly £1750 was raised and a bronze plaque positioned on a street-facing wall at the sheltered housing complex on McGonagall Square. It was formally unveiled in September 2000. The black marble plaque at 5 South College Street was added in 2002.

Given the recent history of inter-council argy-bargy, it might be considered ironic that Dundee's civic fathers nowadays clutch McGonagall to their collective bosom after their predecessors contributed so much to his unhappy departure from the city. While many Dundonians appear unequivocal about the value of promoting McGonagall as a desirable image for the city – not least in light of the poet's continuing impact worldwide – he has appeared at times unappreciated in council chambers or the beneficiary of couldn't-care-less attitudes.[25]

During moves in the early 1980s to erect a statue at the Sinderins, for example, a high-level reluctance to accept the poet as an ambassador for the city materialised. When a report by the council's chief planning officer suggested that 'a sculpture of McGonagall would be acceptable' for the proposed site on the junction of Perth Road and Hawkhill, the councillor heading the planning development committee 'suggested that the reference to a sculpture of McGonagall being acceptable should be deleted from the report'.[26] Similarly, in a letter detailing plans for Dundee's Octocentenary celebrations in 1991, a council convener played down the idea of a McGonagall poetry competition: 'Given the stated unhappiness of many people with McGonagall as a relevant part of Dundee's Cultural Heritage, I feel that any activity linked to McGonagall should, as agreed, be kept low key. Further, the way it is handled and marketed should also be carefully considered.'[27]

One way the unresolved debate over what the local authority believes McGonagall means to the city has manifested itself is in deliberations over whether the city should erect a statue to its most famous 'son'.

Statues of people who have left their mark on the city and beyond provide a sense of bearing and identity. They can instil civic pride, provide a link to the past, a salute to individual excellence and offer an educational element for younger generations. Historically, however, there has been a miserly selection in Dundee. Until Desperate Dan and Admiral Duncan came along in recent times, Dundee was rationed to the four Victorian figures stationed outside the McManus Galleries.

The argument that McGonagall should be rescued from obscurity and commemorated on a plinth has rumbled on for many years. The poet himself was aware of the importance of statues and was all in favour of them . . .

> Beautiful city of Edinburgh!
> Where the tourist can drown his sorrow,
> By viewing your monuments and statues fine,
> During the lovely summer-time.

His poetic wit also touched Glasgow's statuary . . .

> And as for the statue of Sir Walter Scott that stands in George
>   Square,
> It is a handsome statue few can with it compare.
> And most elegant to be seen,
> And close beside it stands the statue of Her Majesty the
>   Queen.

And, of course, he wrote of the Burns Statue in the heart of Dundee, which began, 'This statue, I must confess, is magnificent to see/And I hope it will long be appreciated by the people of Dundee.'

The first serious attempt to erect a McGonagall statue was made by Junior Chamber Dundee in the late 1970s. Inspired by

McGonagall enthusiast Kenneth Malcolm, the chamber had already staged a successful exhibition of the poet's memorabilia in the Angus Hotel. It also went some way towards winning approval for the Magdalen Green bandstand to be used as a permanent McGonagall memorial, but this initiative fell through. The statue proposal, intended for a site at Seabraes, overlooking the Silv'ry Tay and close to the poet's former homes, was a far more ambitious project. By 1979 the chamber had raised £184 for the statue and had arranged for it to be sculpted by James Boyle, then serving a life sentence at Barlinnie Prison in Glasgow. After months of searching, a suitable block of sandstone was discovered in a disused quarry at Coupar Angus, and taken to the Glasgow prison. There was disappointment, though, when Boyle, who had famously turned to art while in prison, reported that a seam had been found running through the stone. The project appears to have been abandoned in September 1980, when Boyle was moved to Saughton Prison.

Driven by the McGonagall Appreciation Society the idea of a statue was revived and reached funding talk towards the end of the 1990s. Again nothing concrete came of it. And, in 2002, a local MSP called on the Lottery Heritage fund to ensure a statue could be built. This drew a stylish poem of support from one-time doyen of the House of Lords, Baroness Strange of Megginch . . .

> If we want a statue for bonny Dundee,
> What better figure could we hope to see
> Than that of our poet William McGonagall
> Who did Dundee's events chronicle.
> He was a handloom weaver and a traveller who went to Balmoral
> To see the Queen as she walked in the heather floral,
> And further afield to Edinburgh, London, and New York too,
> And he died in the year of Nineteen Hundred and Two.
> He loved Dundee, and I hope he may
> Be long remembered by the shores of silvery River Tay.[28]

Even without a statue, William McGonagall walks tall in today's world – from regular mentions on Terry Wogan's radio programme to being often parodied in *Private Eye*. J.K. Rowling named Minerva

McGonagall after him and Terry Pratchett introduced the battle poet Gonagale in *The Wee Free Man*. Some 107 years after his death, his presence continues to permeate our literary and artistic lives. And, largely thanks to the brilliant McGonagall-Online website, the one-time Poet Laureate of Paton's Lane retains widespread affection across the world.

How he would have revelled in this revival. And no one but himself would have 'Googled' his name more often . . .

GULLIBLE FOOL OR SHREWD ROGUE?

WILLIAM McGONAGALL's extraordinary life can be cut and pasted into a lonely paragraph without resorting to a single rhyme.

McGonagall had a poor start in life. He arrived in rapidly industrialising Dundee in the 1830s as one of a large, and largely uneducated, immigrant Irish family. He spent the next 60 years there. He worked as a weaver, began a long love affair with Shakespeare and ham-acted in amateur theatricals. He became a writer through reading and imposed his mutilated poetry upon an unwitting *Weekly News*. He sought venues on reading tours to ply his tragedian trade before trying his luck as a performance poet in London and America. As his notoriety grew he won bogus attention in sell-out gigs and appealed for endorsement with poetic laudations to the mighty. Between times his much-parodied poetry flowed from his miserable domestic surroundings in Paton's Lane and Step Row – an output now known to number around 270 titles, most of them printed on single sheets and sold for a penny. He soon became someone to be laughed at, hoaxed and victimised – even as he grew old and infirm. This led to him abandoning Dundee to settle eventually in Edinburgh, where he remained until his death from a cerebral haemorrhage in 1902.

Today the reputation of this often derided and misunderstood worthy floats all over the world, his immortality reinforced by the notion that he was bonkers. He stands in graceful isolation – awful enough to be called great – the pre-eminent bad poet of the English language, and possibly any other. Yet if the curtain on the 'real' William McGonagall is pulled back, a fascinating picture emerges of a giftedly bad showman in a compelling class of his own.

Bearing in mind that William McGonagall's character and

bardic status were shaped by his upbringing, social circumstances and events in his life, this concluding chapter will sum up briefly his poetry, his performances, his poetic ineptitude and, perhaps most poignantly, the illness and possible psychiatric problems that blighted his later life.

MCGONAGALL'S POETRY

William McGonagall's continuing appeal is mostly limited to the thudding rhymes cemented to the end of every second line – as he pursued the rhyme-at-all-cost school of mawkish poetry. The apparent badness of everything he committed to paper has transcended time, literary convention and artistic boundaries.

Some 270 poems and songs by William McGonagall were recorded during the course of this work – remarkably a tenth of them unpublished in any previous book. The poems began in 1877, as much a response to galloping mechanisation and de-skilling in textiles as the result of an overnight vision. Over the next quarter of a century they made McGonagall a legend in his own lifetime.

His poetic themes are well known. There are two dozen maritime disasters, a dozen historical epics, the same number of funerals and tributes to worthies, half a dozen fire tragedies and about 50 battle poems, from the medieval conflicts at Bannockburn and Cressy, through to the Crimean War and Indian Mutiny to his last works marking the Second Boer War. When neither shipwreck nor battle awoke his muse, he tramped around Scotland composing his 'Beautiful' and 'Bonnie' poems. These tributes inspired him to pick up his pen over 30 times. He moralised in two dozen tales and condemned drink in another half dozen. Apart from a couple of exceptions, McGonagall avoided the Scots vernacular style. In adopting 'high' English for his poems, he bypassed suggestions of provinciality or a lack of education, while taking a powerful personal stance by using 'proper' language. Indeed, he probably came to regard the Scottish dialect as vulgar.

The formulaic opening lines are sufficient to reveal that McGonagall's poetic output was not good, but that he had a storyteller's instinct in the tradition of Irish bardic poems dating back hundreds of years. He told tales from beginning to end, got his facts accurate, and somehow cajoled them into rhyme in a virtuoso way that refuses to be imitated. He knew his target market and possessed a persuasive sales pitch. He had an unerring eye for important subjects and coerced them into narrative mode in poems that almost read as prose.

What cannot be so easily understood is why McGonagall emerged a prominent poet so soon after self-admittedly taking up verse. In his time there were an estimated 200,000 amateur poets in Victorian Scotland anxious to see their poems in print. Thanks to the Burns cult, 'anyone who could rhyme "louse" with "mouse" thought they had the talent to become a poet.' Dundee newspapers that found their way to Paton's Lane were already awash with rhymes of suspect quality on every plausible subject.[1]

What turned McGonagall's bad verse into famous anti-poetry was, initially, its appearance in these papers. Editors recognised poor poetry and viewed its publication as an opportunity for a few patronising quips in the interests of reader entertainment. McGonagall, of course, offered spectacular opportunities for columns of tongue-in-cheek cleverness. The difference was that McGonagall came back for more after every put-down. What was said about his poetry passed over him. The fact that his verses appeared in print signalled to him their suitability, durability and potential profitability. He was not to be persuaded that they were in any way inferior to the verses published alongside them and did not care that people thought his poems were unintentionally amusing.

McGonagall appears to have been genuinely convinced of his own abilities and of his talent. And, motivated by this formidable self-belief, he regarded those who ridiculed him as ignorant of his true genius. His self-assurance and persistence were pivotal as to how his profile emerged.

Another key contributing factor to McGonagall's notoriety was his decision in 1879 to place his work for sale in the form of printed sheets. He was not alone among amateur poets in seeking a commercial return, but McGonagall's compositions rapidly attracted a trendy following via publicity in the *Weekly News* and the *People's Journal*. This exposure allowed his production to increase and his performance repertoire to expand beyond the works of

Shakespeare and the mainstream poets. Reports of these shows alongside reviews of his latest works acted to advance his name to an ever-widening audience.

The subjects of McGonagall's poems also contributed to his public persona. Leaving aside hoaxes by the hoi polloi or the ridicule of the working classes, or even his own attempts to rise above himself, McGonagall possessed a documentary eye and the pen of a reporter as he scrutinised current affairs and hammered newsworthy themes into crudely rhyming verse. He was instrumental in unpretentiously conveying local and national news to folk with limited literacy skills and less awareness of the here and now. He became the voice of the masses, the poet of the streets, passing on the who-what-when-where-how bread and butter of current events.

Looking back from today's media circus of citizen journalists and rolling website news, McGonagall's poetry offered a surprisingly accurate image of the times in which he lived. The celebrities, scandals, soap operas and heroes of conflicts were his poetic territory. Thus it was also McGonagall's 'difference' as a commentator/reporter which also stood him apart from other hopeful versifiers.

In 1894 McGonagall was asked which of all his poems made him most proud. He replied that it was 'The Destroying Angel or The Poet's Dream'. Thus the last McGonagall lines in this book are devoted to stanzas from his 'greatest work', an extraordinary composition in which he has a vision that pubs across the town are set on fire by an abstaining, avenging angel . . .

And in a sweet voice she said, 'You must follow me,
And in a short time you shall see
The destruction of all the public-houses in the city,
Which is, my friend, the God of Heaven's decree.'
So with the beautiful Angel away I did go,
And when we arrived at the High Street, Oh! what a show.
I suppose there were about five thousand men there,
All vowing vengeance against the publicans, I do declare.

And so the angel of his dream, clothed in white, led the procession through the streets on a cloudless night, and in her sweet voice told the crowd . . .

'That by God's decree ye must take up arms and follow me
And wreck all the public-houses in this fair City,
Because God cannot countenance such dens of iniquity.
Therefore, friends of God, come, follow me.'
And while the Angel was thus addressing the people,
The Devil seemed to be standing on the Townhouse Steeple,
Foaming at the mouth with rage, and seemingly much
    annoyed,
And kicking the Steeple because the public-houses were
    going to be destroyed.

'The Destroying Angel' was regarded as such a controversial poem that McGonagall was advised by David Winter & Son not to include it in *Poetic Gems* in 1890 – 'They pointed out it would raise up against him a host of enemies.'[2] It continues . . .

Then from the High Street we all did retire,
As the Angel, sent by God, did desire;
And along the Perth Road we all did go,
While the Angel set fire to the public-houses along that row.
And when the Perth Road public-houses were fired, she
    cried, 'Follow me,
And next I'll fire the Hawkhill public-houses instantly.'
Then away we went with the Angel, without dread or woe,
And she fired the Hawkhill public-houses as onward we did go.

So, with the Devil taking out his anger on the ancient Steeple, the procession burns, in turn, the Scouringburn, Murraygate and High Street pubs. Then, with smoke billowing over the town, McGonagall wakes up. The drinker's nightmare had been but the poet's dream.

As for his worst 'poem', there is one outstanding candidate. While on his ill-starred journey to America in 1887 McGonagall received a letter from a fellow Scot and his wife, who had recently suffered the untimely death of a beloved child. The grief-stricken parents, hearing that McGonagall was in New York, wrote to him asking if he would compose 'four sacred lines' to commemorate the death of their departed little daughter, which they would carve on her tombstone. With his usual urbanity the Dundee bard came up with these touching and pathetic lines . . .

> Here lies little Mary Jane,
> She neither cries nor hollers,
> She lived but one and twenty days,
> And cost us forty dollars.

PERFORMANCES

McGonagall is remembered for the words he wrote down on sheets ripped from a quarto notebook. His 270 compositions form that permanent legacy. However, the foregoing chapters suggest he regarded himself as more showman than dedicated poet. His creative arena was the stage and much of his poetry was written to support public performance. 'Rattling Boy', 'Bannockburn' and 'The Battle of Tel-el-Kebir' were among those penned for rousing the rabble. Later, poems such as 'River of Leith' and 'Lines in Praise of Professor Blackie' were composed expressly to be performed in Chaplinesque style to student fans in Edinburgh.

Thus, it is important to re-emphasise that McGonagall was a performance poet, and not one to be confined to the pages of a book. It was his powerful voice, facial expressions and theatrical gestures which drew crowds to performances from the 1850s, and these appearances over the subsequent half-century seldom passed without incident. 'All we can say is that McGonagall must be seen and heard before he can be fully appreciated', said the *Weekly News* in 1880. A report of an entertainment in Perth in 1892 noted: 'It may be questioned if any other living tragedian could speak the part with the same effect. His intonations of the voice, his dramatic positions, and his facial expression all marked him as one who had formed his own idea of the part.' Such was his deafening performance that a crowd gathered in the street outside 'and cheered him over and over again'.[3]

McGonagall's act confronted antagonistic audiences with such self-belief and delusions of fame that he became a must-have ticket. In turn, audiences were promised a fantastic night out, a bellyful of laughs for their admittance money and the opportunity to circumvent accepted behaviour by chucking everything bar the kitchen sink at the top-of-the bill performer. So it was the Great McGonagall they wanted to see, hear and insult – and what he was actually reciting did not particularly matter. If patrons kept time with 'For I'm a Rattling Boy from Dublin Town' and managed to reach the whack-fal-de-da chorus in unison, so much to the good. McGonagall cared not if his recital was drowned out by the whistles, cat-calls and foot stamping, and his self-mocking act usually rose above the tumult.

As for being a soft target, he displayed glorious resilience and unblinking determination despite deplorable hooliganism that would today attract an ASBO. Poet McGonagall was made of stern stuff and his poetry was designed to be the same – to be read aloud with an air of grandeur and absolutely no inhibitions.

POETICAL INEPTITUDE

One eyewitness – and only one – claimed to have seen McGonagall exit from a stage with a sly smirk on his face, almost as if he was laughing up his sleeve as others laughed at him. Otherwise McGonagall watchers usually agree that William McGonagall was without humour, a conclusion drawn from his being fireproof to satire, oblivious to insult and, of course, his legacy of unembroidered verse. Alan Dunsmore said, for example, 'He styled himself William McGonagall, poet and tragedian, having no truck with comedy.' Thomas Disch noted, 'Never suppose, because you find his verse hilarious, that McGonagall ever meant to be funny.'[4]

McGonagall's performances were humourless, and were so for a purpose. His inscrutable mannerisms were as much act as trait. But that is not the same as saying that McGonagall could not raise a smile. His humour is found in dollops among his poetic output, letters and interviews. 'The Famous Tay Whale', for instance, to which he added three exclamation marks on the printed penny version, was anything but a serious account of events. Like most

Dundonians, the irony of the cash-on-doorstep mammal appearing in Britain's premier whaling port while the fleet was tied up would not have been lost on him. He must have giggled with the rest of the town as countless men grabbed their stowed equipment and set off into the estuary for unsuccessful after unsuccessful attempt to land the monster.

So, on the contrary, it is not difficult to discover William McGonagall's humour. He was the man, after all, who could raise a laugh from a funeral, and who reminded Dundonians in one of his earliest poems that for leisure they could stroll through Balgay Park, 'and read the epitaphs on the tombstones before they go home'.

Indeed, by the 1890s McGonagall was handing out a business card which read: 'William McGonagall, Poet, Tragedian and Comedian, at liberty for Public and Private Entertainments, At Homes and Garden Parties. Address: 12 Grove Street, Edinburgh.' The card was finished off with a fantastic couplet from 'Address to the Moon', which not even a rigidly humourless poet would have viewed as his best . . .

Shine out, fair moon, upon the slates,
So that the fisherman may see to catch his cods and skates.

The addition of 'Comedian' to McGonagall's repertoire of skills suggests he was well aware that the 'entertainments' offered in his old age were viewed with high amusement by his Edinburgh audiences. It was a purposeful commercial decision to include the designation on his calling card – much in the way that the music hall posters used to play upon the hilarity value of his act. And he lived up to the act, judging by the report of one Edinburgh performance: 'Never once throughout the entire appearance was there a smile on his sombre countenance. Perhaps he was no fool when he had our guineas in his pocket. Be that as it may, the money so spent was a good investment.'[5]

Thus, by the 1890s William McGonagall was certainly aware of what was expected from him, and it is not beyond the bounds of possibility that, rather than being an unconscious humorist, he was the master of intentional mistakes and crafted buffoonery in the manner that, say, Tommy Cooper or Les Dawson were in more recent times. Cooper was a connoisseur of the botched trick that got laughs. Although the hallmark of his act was to get tricks wrong, he was in reality an accomplished magician. Dawson was king of the modern deadpan comedians. Among his stage specialities was his terrible piano playing, concealing the fact that he was an accomplished musician. Both possessed the ability to raise laughs with the thinnest of gags, a trademark bewildered look and extraordinary timing.

McGonagall also had a world-weary, lugubrious style that made people laugh. His straightfaced magnanimity was an enduring quality. He stood in front of hostile audiences attired in cheap Highland dress while reciting poetry that jettisoned the conventions of rhythm, harmony and measure. He must have heard their sniggering and noticed their pointing fingers.

So he is portrayed today as a tragic buffoon oblivious to the mock-respectful derision which confronted him. In private, however, William McGonagall was modest of demeanour and a compassionate person. He was a gentle soul who cared deeply for the underprivileged and often demonstrated his anxiety for the poor. This personal life rarely found its way into his poetry or his role as a performance poet.

People who knew him remember him as a sensitive man, 'a good and worthy person' and 'a man of surprises' – indeed, a 'decent-living old man with a kindly dignity'. One recalled that, 'A native goodness and strong sense of decency and right conduct revealed themselves in his speech and bearing . . . His conversation in private was most rational and not at all self-important or stagy. He expressed himself justly and in an educated voice and manner.'[6]

McGonagall's poetic ineptitude probably began as an innocent conceit. In time it became a deliberately conceived and craftily pursued funding tool, where he accepted the irony of an audience ovation or the ridiculing reviewer for what they were, a part of his act.

His patrons, after all, had as keen a sense of the ludicrous as he had.

ILLNESS AND POSSIBLE PSYCHIATRIC PROBLEMS

Kurt Wittig, a German literary critic, once claimed that the continuing popularity of *Poetic Gems* would 'be an interesting problem for a psychiatrist to study'.[7]

Psychologically, it can be argued that William McGonagall saw himself as something he wasn't. He seldom had a realistic grasp of his place or role in society. He identified himself with Shakespeare's tragic heroes or those portrayed in his poems. Later he tried to appeal to social levels above his own, seeing himself as an elite poet and viewing sycophantic flattery as a means of rising above himself. He imagined his audience as society's glitterati, when in fact it was everyone and anyone – mostly workers, students and ridiculing youngsters – who anticipated a laugh at his expense.

The vulnerability of this 'heroic failure', seen in self-inflicted ridicule and rejection, can perhaps be explained by the insecurity that poverty brought. He was a character full of contradictions, one sometimes able to put a happy spin on his calamities, while at other times crying for help. 'There goes Mad McGonagall' – he quoted in pathetic lines on the flak he endured on Dundee's streets. Was McGonagall mad? How else could he have endured the slights, rebuffs and ridicule for so long?

Where further expert research is required, however, is on the extent to which illness affected his character and his lifestyle. Poor health is a theme which weaves a thread through the nine chapters of his story. As early as 1879 he complained of being bodily frail. He reported hearing head noises throughout the 1880s, and in 1885 wrote anxiously to Alex Hutcheson to send him money 'for fear I relapse again and die'. He saw several doctors, one of whom diagnosed inflammation of the brain, while another reported an air cavity blocked by intense mental activity, and caused McGonagall intense pain by blowing vigorously through a tube up his nose 'as if he were performing solo on the trombone'.

The head noises persisted day and night for many years and his death was predicted by the *Weekly News* as early as 1890 – 'he has, like the old swan, sung his last song'. A decade later it was reporting to its readers that McGonagall, by this time in Edinburgh, was 'suffering from a bad cold, chest disease, sleeplessness, deafness and noises in his head – yet he is thankful he can get about and do a little business'. His friend Johnny pleaded for help: 'For two months now he has been laid on his back with influenza . . . his doctors have forbidden him from composing any new poems till his head gets right. How is he going to raise the rent to save him from the factor's crash? Send contributions to 26 Potter Row, Edinburgh.'[8]

Although he lived to the ripe old age of 75 – given as 62 on his death certificate – William McGonagall's demeanour and extravagant behaviour suggest the possibility of a lingering mental condition or cognitive impairment which impacted on his lifelong journey.

Posthumous psychoanalysis is fraught with difficulties, but McGonagall's health imbalances and idiosyncratic personality raise the possibility that he suffered from a chronic brain disorder, such as Asperger's syndrome or autism. Equally his over-valued ideas and grandiose notions of his genius point to manic-depressive psychosis.

People with Asperger's, for example, show significant difficulty in social interaction and restricted, stereotypical patterns of interests and behaviour. This adequately describes McGonagall, who made people laugh, but seemed to remain insensitive as to why. While preserving linguistic and cognitive development, as McGonagall did to his self-educated limits, atypical use of language has been reported among those with the disorder. With astonishing inflexibility, for example, McGonagall began over 60 poems with the same word, 'Twas.

The lack of demonstrated empathy is said to be possibly the most dysfunctional aspect of Asperger's syndrome, while not recognising a listener's feelings or reactions is another form of social awkwardness associated with it. McGonagall, of course, seemed inured to insult, his deadpan response to ridicule being his greatest character statement. He neither appeared concerned by verbal derision nor flinched before fusillades of missiles, and displayed other abnormalities associated with the autistic spectrum, including literal interpretations, pedantic language, loudness in pitch and oddities in intonation and rhythm. Recently, too, scientists discovered compelling evidence that autism may in some cases be linked to inflammation on the brain – a complaint McGonagall stated on numerous occasions.[9]

The possibility of an organic brain disease, Autistic Spectrum Disorder or Asperger's – or perhaps even a mild biopolar illness – may have played a part in how William McGonagall's life developed, mostly in the sense that he carried on regardless of audience or public reaction. Further research in this area would be welcome.

It cannot be said, however, if illness prevented him from realising he was being duped at the elaborate ceremonies designed to 'recognise' him with spurious titles, or made him miss the irony conveyed in chairmen's opening remarks or the parodying newspaper columns which launched his career.

A coin can be tossed on this. On one side he had no idea what was going on, either because of illness or an inflated sense of genius. On the other, McGonagall was exploiting for his own ends the humour people experienced in his poems and performances. Thus, his poetic ineptitude and insensitivity to humiliation can be explained by the ever-present prospect before him of starvation.

In other words, William McGonagall did what he did as a means to an end . . . survival.

REFERENCES

INTRODUCTION

1. Henderson, Hamish, 'William McGonagall and the Folk Scene', in *Chapbook*, Vol. 2, No. 5 (1965), p39; MacDiarmid, Hugh, *Scottish Eccentrics*, London, Michael Joseph, 1972, (reprint of 1936 edition), p70; William McIlvanney quoted in Smith, Gavin, 'White Elephant', published in *Scotland Magazine*, No. 5, November 2002, p1.
2. *Scotland on Sunday*, 10 February 1991.

CHAPTER ONE

1. Luke, Mackie & Co. first appear at 115 Murraygate in the Dundee Directory for 1885–86.
2. *People's Journal*, 4 October 1902; the *Courier*, 30 September 1902; the *Scotsman*, 9 October 1902.
3. Anon. [Willocks, John], *This is the Book of the Lamentations of the Poet McGonagall, An Autobiography, Dedicated to Himself, Knowing None Greater*, Dundee, nd, (1885), p1.
4. Smith, James L. (ed), *The Great McGonagall, Poetical Pearls from the Pen of William McGonagall*, Vermont, The Stephen Greene Press, nd, *c* 1968, p5. See also Walker, Colin S.K., *William McGonagall*, Edinburgh, Birlinn, 1993, p11; Nasmyth, Charles, *The Comic Legend of William McGonagall*, New Lanark, Waverley Books, 2007 (The Artist's Notes); Hunt, Chris (ed), *William McGonagall Collected Poems*, Edinburgh, Birlinn, 2006, Introduction pv.
5. National Census information on McGonagall is available from the Public Record Office, or online through scotlandspeople.org.uk. The pages referred to are listed in the bibliography below.
6. Watson, Norman, *Dundee: A Short History*, Edinburgh, Black & White Publishing, 2006, p96.
7. Walker, William, *Juteopolis, Dundee and its Textile Workers, 1885–1923*, Edinburgh, Scottish Academic Press, 1979, p117.
8. *Dundee Advertiser*, 16 December 1856.

9. The *Weekly News*, 19 March 1887; Willocks, *Lamentations*, 1885, and Anon. [Willocks, John], *This is the Book of Lamentations of the Poet McGonagall, Portraying in His Own Unapproachable Style His Birth and Parentage, Early Struggles, Miraculous and Hairbreadth Escapes, with a Graphic and Characteristic Account Setting Forth, How, By His Inspired Genius and Indomitable Pluck, He Passed From Penury and Persecution Through a Knighthood into an Immortality of Fame*, Dundee: John Durham, 1905.

10. Gray, J.T., *Maybole, Carrick's Capital*, Ayr, Alloway Publishing, 1982, p76.

11. Handley, James E., *The Irish in Scotland*, Glasgow, John S. Burns & Co., 1964, p47.

12. *The Imperial Gazetteer of Scotland, or Dictionary of Scottish Topography*, Edinburgh, A. Fullerton & Co., nd, *c* 1867, Vol III, p406.

13. Gray, p296. My thanks to the Maybole Historical Society.

14. Thanks to Dick Levens of Garth, South Ronaldsay, Orkney.

15. Orkney Archives, D31/3/3/3.

16. I am indebted to Sarah Maclean of Orkney Archives for this information.

17. Halkirk Parochial Records, Register of Poor admitted to Roll 1, 1865, p51.

18. Myles, James, *Rambles in Forfarshire*, Edinburgh, 1850, p14.

19. Handley, p90.

20. Knox, William, *A History of the Scottish People: Poverty, Income and Wealth in Scotland 1840–1940*, SCRAN website paper 2009, chapter 5, p3.

21. Handley, p98.

22. *Weekly News*, 10 November 1894.

23. Halkirk Parochial Records, Register of Poor admitted to Roll 1, 1865, p51; Westgreen Asylum Male Case Book, 1891–93, Dundee University Archives, THB7/8/9/36, p409.

24. Willocks, 1885, p2; the *Weekly News*, 21 November 1891.

25. Chalmers, James, *The History of Dundee, From its Origins to the Present Time*, Dundee, J. Chalmers, 1842, p73. See also, Devine, T.M. (ed), *Irish Immigrants and Scottish Society in the Nineteenth and Twentieth Century*, Proceedings of the Scottish Historical Studies Seminar, University of Strathclyde, 1989/90, Edinburgh, John Donald, 1991, p9.

26. Gauldie, Enid (ed), *The Dundee Textile Industry 1790–1885, From the Papers of Peter Carmichael of Arthurstone*, Scottish Historical Society, Edinburgh, T. and A. Constable, 1969, pxxiv and p75. See also Watson, Norman, *Dundee: A Short History*.

27. *Chapters in the Life of a Dundee Factory Boy*, p14. Christopher Whatley, who studied *Chapters*, commented '*Chapters* is certainly not worthless as a primary source. The descriptions of factory conditions owe much to

the findings of Sadler's 1832 parliamentary report on children in factories, which included evidence taken from workers in mills in and around Dundee.' Whatley, Christopher A., *The case of James Myles, the 'Factory Boy', and Mid-Victorian Dundee, in Victorian Dundee, Image and Realities*, Edinburgh, Tuckwell Press, 2000, p75.

28. Watson, Mark, *Jute and Flax Mills in Dundee*, Tayport, Hutton Press, 1990, p14.
29. Burgh of Dundee Marriage Register, 11 July 1846. Macrae, David, *George Gilfillan, Anecdotes and Reminiscences*, Glasgow, Morison Brothers, 1891, p43.
30. 'Recollections of a Stage-Struck Hero', *People's Journal*, 22 June 1872.
31. *The Statistical Account of Scotland*, Dundee, 1833.
32. Quoted in Watson, *Dundee: A Short History*, p120.

CHAPTER TWO

1. Gauldie, Enid (ed), *The Dundee Textile Industry 1790–1885, From the Papers of Peter Carmichael of Arthurstone*, Scottish Historical Society, Edinburgh, T. and A. Constable, 1969, p190. See also Phillips, David, *No Poets' Corner in the Abbey*, Dundee, David Winter & Son, 1971, p39; Myles, James, *Rambles in Forfarshire*. Edinburgh, 1850, p86.
2. Watson, Norman, 'Gender and Representation', PhD thesis, Open University, 2000.
3. Most anthologies provide one of McGonagall's autobiographies and say little on his pre-poet life.
4. Black, Aileen, *Gilfillan of Dundee 1813–1878*, Dundee, Dundee University Press, 2006, p154.
5. Thom, William, *Rhymes and Recollections of a Hand-Loom Weaver*, London, Smith, Elder & Co., 1845, p14; Gilmour, David, *Reminiscences of the Pen Folk: Paisley Weavers of Other Days*, Paisley, Alex Gardner, 1879, p39; *Dundee Literary and Scientific Institute Journal*, 1846, Dundee Central Libraries, D22022.
6. Robertson, Alec, *History of the Dundee Theatre*, London, Precision Press, 1949, p20; 'Dundee Theatricals I', *People's Journal*, 28 February 1891; 'Dundee Theatricals III', *People's Journal*, 14 March 1891.
7. Boyd, Frank, *Records of the Dundee Stage*, Dundee, W. & D.C. Thomson, 1886, p37; Robertson, p13
8. McGonagall, William, *Shakespeare Reviewed*, Dundee, 1878. Although this slim booklet is clearly inscribed 'composed 1878' and may well have been written that year, it was not published until 1892.
9. Quoted in Robertson, p23. Dundee Central Libraries holds copies of the short-lived *Comet*, first published in 1862.

10. 'Dundee Theatricals V', *People's Journal*, 28 March 1891.

11. 'Recollections of a Stage-Struck Hero', *People's Journal*, 22 June 1872. Although Old Stager does not mention McGonagall by name, his reminiscences in 1872 identify Dundee's poet-in-waiting. There is no doubt that Old Stager was referring to William McGonagall as he continued to comment on his poetical contributions to Dundee newspapers for many years, repeating his 1872 anecdotes in the *Weekly News* of 15 January 1876, in which he names McGonagall as the person under discussion.

12. idem.

13. idem.

14. Boyd, pp41–42; Smith W. J. (ed), *James Chalmers, Inventor of the Adhesive Postage Stamp*, Dundee, David Winter & Son, 1970, p14.

15. Myles, p92.

16. Gauldie, p153–4.

17. Dundee Central Libraries, Lamb Collection, 329 (1).

18. 'Recollections', *People's Journal*, 22 June 1872.

19. 'Lines on A Well-Known Local "Tragedian" (!),' Anon., signed 'Old Stager', *People's Journal*, 15 January 1876.

20. Norrie, William, *Norrie's Hand Book to Dundee, Past and Present*, Dundee, W. Norrie, 1876, p118.

21. Gauldie, p177; Whatley, Christopher A., 'The Case of James Myles, the "Factory Boy", and mid-Victorian Dundee', in Miskell, Louise; Whatley, Christopher A.; Harris, Bob (eds), *Victorian Dundee, Image and Realities*, Edinburgh, Tuckwell Press, 2000, p91.

22. Poor Relief Roll, Parish of Halkirk, Book 1, 1865. See also Phillips, p43.

23. Boyd, p69.

24. McGonagall Collection; Phillips, p57.

25. Valuation Roll for the Burgh of Dundee, 1871–72 Folio 77, Dundee City Archives.

26. 'A High Compliment to an Actor', *Dundee Advertiser*, 31 May 1872.

27. *People's Journal*, 12 January 1876.

28. Walker, *Juteopolis*, p54.

29. *Weekly News*, 7 July 1877.

30. *Weekly News*, 11 August 1877.

31. William McGonagall to Ex-Provost Cox, letter, 1 September 1877, Dundee University Archives.

32. Phillips, p69. The comment about Glasgow poets came after another bad storm had hit Scotland. Both were reported in the *Weekly News*, 30 December 1893.

33. *Weekly News*, 22 September, 1877. McGonagall was telling interviewers as late as 1893 that he was blamed for the fall of the bridge, the *Weekly News* of 30 December that year suggesting that Glasgow poets in particular had placed the calamity on his shoulders.

34. 'Old Stager' letter to *Weekly News*, 29 September 1877, and to the *People's Journal*, 29 September 1877.

35. The requisition and Sir Thomas Biddulph's reply are with Dundee Central Libraries' McGonagall Collection. Magnus Magnusson wrote in his *Weekend Scotsman* article, 'The Dignity Within the Absurd McGonagall' (23 January 1965), 'He had been hoaxed by a forged letter with some sort of seal into thinking that the Queen wanted to see him.'

36. *Weekly News*, 27 September 1877.

37. *Weekly News*, 6 October 1877.

38. *Weekly News*, 13 October 1877, 1 December 1877, 29 December 1877.

39. *Weekly News*, 4 May, 18 May, 8 June 1877; *People's Journal*, 6 October 1877.

CHAPTER THREE

1. *Dundee Advertiser*, 17 June 1875; Gauldie, p219.

2. Lenman, Bruce, 'McGonagall's Dundee', in the *Scots Magazine*, May, 1969, pp175–184; Gauldie, pp223–4.

3. Thom, pp9–10.

4. Norrie, p167; *Evening Telegraph*, 28 June 1878.

5. Anon. [James Myles], *Chapters in the Life of a Factory Boy*, p40.

6. Johnson, Ellen, *Poems and Songs of Ellen Johnson, The Factory Girl*, Glasgow, 1867. Preface by George Gilfillan, dated Dundee, 21 July 1866.

7. Thom, p19.

8. Idem, p36.

9. *Weekly News*, 26 May and 2 June 1877.

10. *Weekly News*, 9 June 1877.

11. *Weekly News*, 19 January 1878.

12. Letter headed 19 Paton's Lane, signed and dated 19 January 1878, in *Weekly News*, 26 January 1878.

13. *Weekly News*, 26 January 1878.

14. *Weekly News*, 23 March 1878.

15. Although uncatalogued, both copies were located in 2009 in the McGonagall Collection, Dundee Central Libraries.

16. *Evening Telegraph*, 6 May 1878.

17. *Weekly News*, 4 May 1878.

18. *Evening Telegraph*, 4 June 1878.
19. Phillips, p43.
20. George Gilfillan to William McGonagall, 16 July 1878.
21. Bambrick, Gordon, 'The Heroic Warrior: Sir William Topaz McGonagall, Poet and Tragedian, Knight of the White Elephant, Burmah', MA thesis presented to The Faculty of Graduate Studies of the University of Guelph, Canada, 1992; Smith, William, 'The McGonagall Story', undated notes for a McGonagall talk, *c* 1980, private collection.
22. McGonagall to Alex Lamb, 7 November 1889.
23. *Weekly News*, 16 November 1878.
24. *People's Journal*, 7 June 1879.
25. 'Poet McGonagall's Holiday Tour, Ill Requited Genius', *People's Journal*, 21 June 1879.
26. The *Comet*, Third Series, November 1877.
27. 'Poet McGonagall's Holiday Tour'.
28. 'Grand Entertainment by Mr McGonagall', *Weekly News*, 5 July 1879.
29. 'Grand Entertainment by Poet McGonagall', *Weekly News*, 5 December 1879.
30. idem.

CHAPTER FOUR

1. *Weekly News*, 15 March 1879.
2. *People's Journal*, 25 May 1878; *Weekly News*, 15 March 1879.
3. *Weekly News*, 12 July 1878.
4. 'Poet McGonagall's Tour Through Fife', *People's Journal*, 11 October 1879.
5. 'McGonagall at Blair's Hall', *Weekly News*, 25 October 1879.
6. Idem.
7. Macartney, Lowden, *Select Poems of McGonagall*, Glasgow, J. & D.R. Burnside, nd, (1934), p18; 'Miss Carrie's Memories of MacGonagall' (sic), *People's Journal*, 16 February 1980.
8. McGonagall to James Laskie, 21 October 1886.
9. Auchterhouse School Board Minutes, 1873–1895, E/SB/AU/1/1 Angus Archives.
10. *Evening Telegraph*, 29 December 1879.
11. Phillips, pp93–4.
12. *People's Journal*, 17 January 1880.
13. 'The Poet McGonagall Interviewed', unattributed cutting, 24 April 1880, McGonagall Collection.

14. McGonagall, William, copy of poster, Dundee Central Libraries, Map Room, Poster Drawer; *People's Journal*, 1 September 1877; *Weekly News*, 1 December 1877.
15. Macartney, p13.
16. Macartney, p26; *Edinburgh Evening Despatch*, 7 December 1967.
17. 'The Bards of Avon and the Tay Bridge, Honour and Glory to McGonagall', *Weekly News*, 5 June 1880.
18. idem.
19. 'The Bards of Avon', *Weekly News*, 5 June 1880.
20. *People's Journal*, 17 March 1894.
21. 'The Bards of Avon'.
22. 'Cruel Hoax on McGonagall', unattributed cutting, 12 June 1880, McGonagall Collection.

CHAPTER FIVE

1. 'McGonagall's Farewell to Dundee, Grand Valedictory Entertainment', *Weekly News*, 26 June 1880.
2. 'McGonagall at the Argyll Hall', unattributed cutting, Dundee Central Libraries, 22 June 1880.
3. idem. See also the report of his performance at Ancell's Restaurant in Glasgow described by the *Courier*, 4 April 1888.
4. 'McGonagall's Return From London', *Weekly News*, 20 July 1880.
5. idem.
6. idem.
7. idem.
8. McGonagall to A.C. Lamb, 28 September 1886 and 13 February 1888; *Weekly News*, 16 October 1880.
9. 'McGonagall at the Thistle Hall', *People's Journal*, 9 October 1880. See also 'McGonagall at the Thistle Hall, Rough Reception of the Poet', *Weekly News*, 16 October 1880.
10. 'McGonagall at the Thistle Hall'.
11. Phillips, p217.
12. idem.
13. Advert for Trades Hall performance, unattributed and undated cutting, McGonagall Collection.
14. *Weekly News*, 27 November 1880; Hall, 12 February 1881.
15. McGonagall to Mr Gardener, Brechin, 24 May 1887, copy letter in McGonagall Collection.
16. McGonagall at Arbroath, unattributed cutting, 12 February 1881.
17. 'McGonagall' by 'R.N., Arbroath', *Weekly News*, 28 May 1881.
18. *Brechin Advertiser*, 28 April 1881.

19. Unattributed cutting, 28 April 1881, McGonagall Collection.
20. McGonagall to Mr Balfour, Montrose, 5 May 1881.
21. McGonagall to Mr Balfour, Montrose, 17 July 1881.
22. McGonagall, William, *Biographical Reminiscences by the Author*, preface to *Poetic Gems* (Second Series), 1891.

CHAPTER SIX

1. *Biographical Reminiscences.*
2. Ponsonby to McGonagall, 17 October 1881.
3. *Edinburgh Evening Despatch*, 7 December 1949; 'The Real McGonagall', unattributed, undated cutting which details a reader's personal memory of McGonagall in Spence, Lewis, 'The Great McGonagall', in *Scotland's SMT Magazine*, April 1947, p52.
4. Wolseley to McGonagall, 13 November 1882.
5. Wolseley to McGonagall, 3 March 1885.
6. These letters, too, are with the McGonagall Collection.
7. Quoted by Jim Crumley in the *Courier*, 6 May 2008. See also Crumley's *The Winter Whale*, Edinburgh, Birlinn, 2008.
8. McGonagall to a friend, quoted in Phillips, p217.
9. McGonagall to Alex Hutcheson, 20 January 1885.
10. Lenman, Bruce, 'McGonagall's Dundee', *Scots Magazine*, May 1969, p180.
11. McGonagall to Alex Hutcheson, 20 January 1885.
12. *Dundee Advertiser*, 4 February 1885.
13. Anon. [Willocks, John], *This is the Book of the Lamentations of the Poet McGonagall, An Autobiography, Dedicated to Himself, Knowing None Greater*, Dundee, nd, (1885), p16.
14. Willocks to John Thomson, 8 December 1885. Willocks wrote the spoof autobiography in black ink in a lined notebook. The printer, A. Mitchell of Seagate, provides the estimate: type 30 shillings, 300 books 25 shillings and labour 10 shillings, total 65 shillings.
15. Hunt, Chris, 'Introduction', *William McGonagall Collected Poems*, Birlinn, 2006, p565.
16. These letters are with the McGonagall Collection.
17. Phillips, p155.3
18. McGonagall's diaries are reported in 'Poet McGonagall on the Atlantic', *Weekly News*, 9 April 1887, and 'Return of McGonagall The Poet, To Scotland', *People's Journal*, 21 May 1887.
19. For US antagonism see, Szasz, Ferenc M., 'Scots Poet William McGonagall Visits America', 1887, in *Scotiz*, Volume XVII, 1993, p29, although this account uses only McGonagall's 1901 autobiography.

20. The *Courier*, 4 April 1888.
21. The manuscript programme is bound with broadsides in the McGonagall Collection.
22. MacDiarmid, Hugh, *Scottish Eccentrics*, London, Michael Joseph, 1936, (1972 reprint), p72; Campbell, James, 'Bard of the Silv'ry Tay', the *Guardian*, 21 January 2006.
23. Phillips, p168.
24. *Courier*, 25 May 1886.
25. *Courier*, 15 June 1887.
26. *Courier*, March 1888, various dates.
27. *Dundee Advertiser*, 11 May 1888.
28. Dunsmore, Alan, 'It All Began with a Threepenny Theatre', *People's Journal*, 23 March 1968.
29. 'The "Poet" Under Fire, McGonagall at the Nethergate Circus', *Dundee Advertiser* 29 December 1888.
30. *Dundee Advertiser*, 7 February 1889.

CHAPTER SEVEN

1. *Courier*, 21 August 1889.
2. Phillips, pp172–3.
3. William McGonagall to A.C. Lamb, 7 November 1889.
4. Phillips, pp175–6.
5. *Weekly News*, 20 October 1877.
6. *Weekly News*, 26 April 1890.
7. A facsimile of *Poetic Gems*, McGonagall's first proper book, was created by David Winter & Son in 1938.
8. *Weekly News*, 10 May 1890. The *People's Journal* of 10 May also gave the publication a short review.
9. *Weekly News*, 7 June 1890.
10. *Weekly News*, 28 June 1890.
11. Phillips, pp178–9.
12. Phillips, p181. McGonagall's letter to the Marquis of Lothian was displayed in an exhibition marking the centenary of the first Scottish Secretary at Inverleith House, Edinburgh in 1985.
13. National Archives of Scotland, HH1/109 5522/1.
14. National Archives, HH1/1109, 5522/1–2; Phillips, p182.
15. Phillips, p183.
16. idem, p185.
17. idem, p190.
18. idem, p191.
19. Burgh of Perth Land Valuation Roll, 1888–93, MS 8/3/86.

20. McGonagall to A.C. Lamb, 21 May 1891. See also Phillips, pp191–2.
21. *Weekly News*, 3 October 1891.
22. *Weekly News*, 31 October 1891.
23. 'Shakespeare Reviewed' was probably backdated to 1878 by McGonagall.
24. *Courier*, 20 February, 1892.
25. *Weekly News*, 1 and 8 October 1892.
26. MacDiarmid, Hugh, *Scottish Eccentrics*. London, Michael Joseph, 1972 (reprint of 1936 edition), p72.
27. 'Poet McGonagall in Perth', *Weekly News*, 19 March 1892.
28. *Weekly News*, 2 April 1892.
29. *Weekly News*, 27 October 1892.
30. *Courier*, 5 January and 24 February, 1892.
31. *Weekly News*, 28 January 1893 and 21 February 1893; *People's Journal*, 4 March 1893.
32. *Dundee Directory 1894–1895*, p83.
33. *Weekly News*, 4 February 1893.
34. *Weekly News*, 28 January 1893; Phillips, p197.
35. *Weekly News*, 23 September 1893.
36. *Weekly News*, 25 March 1893.
37. *Weekly News*, 13 May 1893.
38. *Weekly News*, 21 January 1893.
39. idem.
40. *Weekly News*, 28 January 1893.
41. 'McGonagall in Arbroath, Lively Proceedings', *Weekly News* 13 May 1893.
42. *Weekly News*, 12 and 16 September, 1893.
43. William McGonagall to A.C. Lamb, 14 May 1894.
44. William McGonagall to A.C. Lamb, 18 May 1894.
45. William McGonagall to Sir John Leng, 21 June 1894.

CHAPTER EIGHT

1. 'Poet McGonagall's Plaint', *People's Journal*, 25 February 1893.
2. 'Poet McGonagall Disgusted with Dundee', *Weekly News*, 13 May 1893.
3. McGonagall's four troubled performances were recorded by both the *Courier* and *Weekly News*.
4. *Weekly News*, 5 May 1894; Phillips, p191.
5. *People's Journal*, 22 April 1893.
6. 'McGonagall and Sheriff Campbell Smith, A Tragic Disposition', *People's Journal*, 29 April 1893.

7. Westgreen Asylum, Male Case Book No. 35, Dundee University Archives, THB 7/8/9/35; Joseph McGonagall certificate of death, 1901.

8. *Weekly News*, 7 April 1894.

9. *Weekly News*, 5 May 1894.

10. *Weekly News*, 10 November 1894.

11. *Weekly News*, 1 September 1894.

12. *Weekly News*, 8 September 1894; *Courier*, 26 September 1894.

13. *People's Journal*, 13 October 1894.

14. Burgh of Perth Land Valuation Rolls, 1894–95, Perth City Archives, MSS 8/3/97.

15. *The Autobiography of Sir William Topaz McGonagall, Poet and Tragedian, Knight of the White Elephant, Burmah*, Part 5, 'A Hearty Highland Welcome'.

16. *Weekly Scotsman*, 29 September 1894.

17. *Courier*, 4 December 1894.

18. *Weekly News*, 11 July 1895.

19. *Weekly News*, 27 October 1895.

20. Undated cutting, Edinburgh Cuttings Wallet, McGonagall Collection.

21. Undated cutting, Edinburgh Cuttings Wallet, McGonagall Collection.

22. *Edinburgh Evening News*, 15 November 1950.

23. *Edinburgh Evening Despatch*, 5 & 18 January 1935.

24. *Edinburgh Evening Despatch*, 18 January 1935.

25. Phillips, p217.

26. *Weekly News*, 15 June 1895 and 12 October 1895.

27. *Weekly News*, 11 July 1896 and 3 July 1897.

28. *Weekly News*, 22 January and 3 December 1898.

29. *Weekly News*, 22 July 1898.

30. *Weekly News*, 3 December 1898 and 20 May 1899.

31. *Weekly News*, 18 March 1899.

32. *Weekly News*, 24 June 1899.

33. *Weekly News*, 16 July 1899.

34. 'McGonagall on the War. Attacks Rudyard Kipling.' *Weekly News*, 18 November, 1899.

35. *Weekly News*, 18 November and 9 December 1899. See also *The Kipling Journal*, Vol. 82, No. 34, June 2008, pp40–49.

36. The Shand letters, McGonagall Collection.

37. *Weekly News*, 15 June 1901.

38. *Weekly News*, 20 August 1901.

39. *Weekly News*, 13 September 1902.

CHAPTER NINE

1. Gibson, Colin, 'The Poet's Box', in the *Scots Magazine*. Broadsides on pink paper have been seen, but none on green paper.
2. Macartney, Lowden, *Select Poems of McGonagall*. Glasgow, J. & D.R. Burnside, nd (1934), pp18/19.
3. idem, Preface.
4. Munro, Neil, *The Brave Days, A Chronicle from the North*, Edinburgh, Porpoise Press, 1931; Power, William, *My Scotland*. Edinburgh, Porpoise Press, 1934, pp 285, 290.
5. MacDiarmid Hugh, *Scottish Eccentrics*, London, Michael Joseph, 1972, reprint of 1936 edition, pp 64–64 and p70.
6. *Edinburgh Evening Despatch*, 22 Jan 1935. For further information on this series of articles see Newspaper Cuttings Book 1, Edinburgh Room, Edinburgh City Libraries.
7. 'The Real McGonagall', proof of unpublished book, David Winter & Co., 1985, pp117–118.
8. idem.
9. Spence, Lewis, 'The Great McGonagall', in *SMT Magazine*, April 1947, also repeated in *The Angus Fireside*, Vol. 1, No. 7, Spring 1949.
10. Brown, Mike, 'McGoonagall – the Man, the Poet', in *The Goon Show Preservation Society Newsletter*, No. 125, December 2008.
11. *Sunday Express*, 10 July 1977.
12. *Edinburgh Evening News*, 28 April 1947; *Scotsman*, 3 May 1947.
13. *Courier*, 19 August 1971.
14. *Scotsman*, 15 July 1972.
15. Sir John Betjeman to William Smith, 10 August 1977; Lord Thomson to K. Malcolm, 12 July 1977.
16. The William McGonagall Society (Japan) Information Bulletin, No. 2, undated, c 1978.
17. Smith and McGonagall, in 'The Real McGonagall', draft of unpublished book, David Winter, 1985, pp115 and 117.
18. *Courier*, 30 March 2003.
19. *Evening Telegraph*, 17 December 2002.
20. *Evening Telegraph*, 12 July 2002.
21. *Courier*, 13 July 2002.
22. *Courier*, 16 and 17 July 2002.
23. *Courier*, 6 November 2006. Dr Carruthers' comments were also contained in the BBC website article, 'Critics pan play by "worst poet"', 6 November 2006.
24. Bill Crabb to author, 28 May 2009.
25. *Courier*, 25 October 2001.

26. *Courier*, 15 April 1982.
27. Councillor Ian Luke to Henny King, (private collection).
28. Cherry Strange, letter to *Courier*, 20 May 1995.

CONCLUSION

1. Wade, Shamus O.D., 'Who was the Better Poet? Kipling or William McGonagall?', in *The Kipling Journal*, Kipling Society, London, Vol. 82, No. 327, June 2008, p44; *Scotland on Sunday*, 20 February 1991.
2. *Weekly News*, 29 September 1894.
3. *Weekly News*, 19 March 1892.
4. Henderson, Hamish, 'McGonagall and the Irish Question', in *New Edinburgh Review*, No. 14, August–September 1971, p41; *People's Journal*, 31 July 1971; Disch, Thomas M., 'Inverse Genius: on the Greatness of William McGonagall', in *Parnassus, Poetry in Review*, Vol. 24, No. 1, New York, 1999, p211.
5. *Edinburgh Evening Despatch*, 22 January 1924.
6. Spence, Lewis, 'The Great McGonagall', in *Scotland's SMT Magazine*, April 1947.
7. Wittig, Kurt, *The Scottish Tradition in Literature*, Edinburgh, Oliver and Boyd, 1958, p253.
8. *Weekly News*, 31 March 1900 and 9 November 1901.
9. BBC website, 'Health, Inflammation Link to Autism', 2004 (http://news.bbc.co.uk/1/hi/4004075.stm).

BIBLIOGRAPHY

PRINCIPAL SOURCES

The best source for the study of William McGonagall's life and work is the McGonagall Collection at Dundee Central Libraries. This comprises an internationally important archive of correspondence, manuscript poems, letters, broadsides, pamphlets, books, photographs and related works. It also contains two manuscript autobiographies. Where items from the collection have been consulted in the text it is referenced as 'McGonagall Collection'.

A significant archive of McGonagall's printed broadsides is housed in the National Library of Scotland, while major libraries with contemporary material include Edinburgh Central Libraries, the National Archives of Scotland and the British Library. The Dundee newspapers, of course, provide the best contemporary comment. Where newspaper articles are used, they are mentioned in footnotes.

The website www.mcgonagall-online.org.uk is an excellent start point for an overview of his poems.

PUBLICATIONS BY WILLIAM MCGONAGALL

In probable date of issue:

A Summary History of Poet McGonagall, undated manuscript, four pages, *c* 1878

Original Manuscript of an Autobiography by William McGonagall, undated manuscript, 15 pages, *c* 1880. (This document is untitled, but is bound in a folder labelled 'Original Manuscript of an Autobiography by William McGonagall', in the McGonagall Collection.)

Poems and Song, by William McGonagall, Poet to Her Majesty, nd [1878] (pamphlet with four poems)

The Complete Poetical Works of Poet McGonagall, Dundee, 1879. 'With a Copy Letter from the Queen to the Poet'. (Pamphlet with 17 poems and two letters.)

The Authentic Autobiography of the Poet McGonagall, Written by Himself. Dundee, Luke, Mackie & Co., Printers, nd *c* 1885 (printed version of Original Manuscript, *c* 1880)

The Autobiography and Poetical Works of William McGonagall, Dundee. Dundee, Charles Mackie & Co., Printers, 1887

Poetic Gems, Selected from the Works of William McGonagall, Poet and Tragedian, Dundee, Winter, Duncan & Co., 1890

Poetic Gems (Second Series), Selected from the Works of William McGonagall, Poet and Tragedian. Dundee, Winter, Duncan & Co., 1891

Shakespeare Reviewed, by William McGonagall 'composed 1878', nd (four-page prose pamphlet, apparently first published in 1892)

Poet McGonagall's Masterpieces, First Time Published. Dundee, John Pellow, nd [post-1894]

Poet McGonagall's Masterpieces, Second 5000th, Second Edition, Dundee, John Pellow, nd (post-1894)

The Autobiography of Sir William Topaz McGonagall, Poet and Tragedian, Knight of the White Elephant, Burmah, published in parts by the *Weekly News* in 1901 and reissued as an 18-page pamphlet the same year, apparently by McGonagall himself

PRIMARY SOURCES

Auchterhouse School Board Minutes, 1873–1895, Angus Archives E/SB/AU/1/1

The Boucicault Collections, Templeman Library, University of Kent, Canterbury, UKC/CALB/BIO: F205520

Burgh of Dundee Valuation Rolls, Liff & Benvie Parish, Dundee City Archives

Grampian Television, 'The Ups and Downs of William McGonagall'. Script of a biography recorded by Alastair Borthwick, 1965, Dundee Central Libraries, Lamb Collection 438 (3)

Kett, David, 'William McGonagall, Actor and Poet Extraordinary'. Text of lecture, 2009

Marwick, Ernest, 'McGonagall and His Teacher', also, 'William McGonagall's Alma Mater'. Unpublished typescript articles, nd, *c* 1970, Orkney Archives, D31/3/3/3

McGonagall, William, letter to Ex-Provost [James] Cox, 1 September 1877, Dundee University Archives, MS 6/2/4/140

McGonagall, William, copy of poster, 'Macbeth', Theatre Royal, Dundee, 2 December 1858. Dundee Central Libraries, Map Room, Poster Drawer

National Census. Various dates. The most valuable entries relating to McGonagall can be found at:
 1841, District 37, p4;
 1851, Vol. 215, Register 76, p11
 1861, Vol. 138, District 28, pp25–6
 1871, Vol. 282, Book 4, p23

1881, Vol. 282, Book 5, p14

1891, Vol. 282, Book 16, p17

Perth & Kinross Land Valuation Rolls, 1891–95, Perth & Kinross Council Archives

St John's Free Church, Dundee, Communion Roll and Baptismal Register December 1845. Dundee City Archives

School Wynd U.U. Church, Communion Roll and Library Register, c 1840s, Dundee City Archives

Trust, Peter, 'A View from William McGonagall'. Typescript handout to accompany Peter Trust's exhibition at the Dundee Festival, 1981

Westgreen Asylum Day Books, Dundee University Archives

Willocks, John, manuscript of *The Book of the Lamentations of the Poet McGonagall, An Autobiography, Dedicated to Himself, Knowing None Greater.* McGonagall Collection, nd (1885)

Winter, David & Son, sale ledger, 1894. Dundee City Archives, MS 29/3

NEWSPAPERS

William McGonagall's activities in Dundee were best covered by the Dundee edition of the *Weekly News, c* 1872–1902 (D.C. Thomson & Co.), and the Dundee edition of the *People's Journal, c* 1872–1902 (John Leng & Co.), both of which had heavily subscribed correspondence columns devoted to amateur poetry. The *Dundee Advertiser* (John Leng & Co.) and the *Courier* (D.C. Thomson & Co.) paid less attention to the poet, leaving it to their populist sister weeklies to highlight his activities. For example, one contemporary index of *Advertiser* contents shows only two mentions of the poet in the 1880s and one in the 1890s. The *Dundee Evening Telegraph* offered occasional mentions. McGonagall's seven years in Edinburgh drew little comment from the *Scotsman*, but featured occasionally in the *Edinburgh Evening Despatch. The Comet,* also mentioned McGonagall occasionally – see its third series, 1877.

The McGonagall Collection in Dundee City Library has a wallet of Edinburgh newspaper cuttings detailing the poet's activities in the capital, while recent articles are held in its bound Cuttings and Special Collections volumes. Edinburgh City Council library has newspaper cuttings books with late nineteenth- and early twentieth-century articles concerning the poet's life in the capital (Edinburgh Room).

JOURNAL AND INTERNET ARTICLES

BBC, Critics Pan Play by 'Worst Poet', BBC News/Scotland website article, November 2006: http://news.bbc.co.uk/1/hi/scotland/tayside_and_central/6120910.stm

Brown, Mike, 'McGoonagall – the Man, the Poet', in *GSP*, the Goon Show Preservation Society Newsletter, No. 125, December 2008, pp13–16

Disch, Thomas M., 'Inverse Genius: on the Greatness of William McGonagall', in *Parnassus, Poetry in Review*, Vol. 24, No. 1, New York, 1999

Gibson, Colin, 'The Poet's Box', in *Scots Magazine*, March 1977, pp601–648

Grossman, Allen, 'Inquiry into the Vocation of Sir William Topaz McGonagall, Poet and Tragedian: The Poetics of Derision and the Epistemic Nobility of Doggerel'. TriQuarterly, Fall 1990, pp239–258

Hay, Robert, 'McGonagall, Perhaps He Had The Last Laugh', *Scots Magazine*, Dundee, July 1956, pp276–281

Henderson, Hamish, 'McGonagall and the Irish Question', in *New Edinburgh Review*, No. 14, August–September 1971, pp38–44

Henderson, Hamish, 'William McGonagall and the Folk Scene', in *Chapbook*, Vol. 2, No. 5 [1965], pp3–35

Holroyd, James Edward, 'Whit about McGonagall?', unattributed cutting, Dundee Central Libraries, Lamb Collection 268 (28)

Knox, William, *A History of the Scottish People: Poverty, Income and Wealth in Scotland 1840–1940*, SCRAN website paper 2009

Lenman, Bruce, 'McGonagall's Dundee', the *Scots Magazine*, Dundee, May 1969, pp175–184

Rogers, Tony, 'Inadvertent Doggerel', internet article, www.bikwil.com/Vintage05/Inadvertent-Doggerel.html

Szasz, Ferenc M., 'Scots Poet William McGonagall Visits America, 1887', in *Scotiz*, Volume XVII, 1993, pp25–33

Spence, Lewis, 'The Great McGonagall', in *Scotland's SMT Magazine*, April 1947

Stiven, W., 'The Importance of Cultivating a Taste for Literary Pleasure', in *Magazine of the Dundee Literary and Scientific Institute*, 1846–7

Wade, Shamus O.D., 'Who was the Better Poet? Kipling or William McGonagall?', in *The Kipling Journal*, Kipling Society, London, Vol. 82, No. 327, June 2008, pp40–49

Watson, George, 'Sixth Sense for Poetry', *Times Higher Education Supplement*, 19 January 1996

THESES AND DISSERTATIONS

Bambrick, Gordon, 'The Heroic Warrior: Sir William Topaz McGonagall, Poet and Tragedian, Knight of the White Elephant, Burmah', MA thesis presented to The Faculty of Graduate Studies of the University of Guelph, Canada, 1992

Watson, Norman, 'Gender and Representation', PhD, Open University 2000

PUBLISHED WORKS

Anon. *The Imperial Gazetteer of Scotland, or Dictionary of Scottish Topography*, Edinburgh, A. Fullerton & Co., nd, *c* 1867

Anon. 'Proceedings at the Unveiling of the Burns Statue in Dundee', *Dundee Advertiser*. Dundee, John Leng, nd, [1880]

Anon. *The Real McGonagall*. Glasgow. D.R. Burnside, 1945

Anon. *The Real McGonagall*. Dundee, David Winter & Son, 1985. Unpublished proof

Anon. *The Second Statistical Account of Scotland*, Dundee, 1833

Anon. [James Myles], *Chapters in the Life of a Dundee Factory Boy: An Autobiography*. Dundee, William Kidd, 1887

Anon. [John Willocks], *This is the Book of the Lamentations of the Poet McGonagall, An Autobiography, Dedicated to Himself, Knowing None Greater*. Dundee, nd, (1885)

Anon. [John Willocks], *This is the Book of Lamentations of the Poet McGonagall, Portraying in His Own Unapproachable Style His Birth and Parentage, Early Struggles, Miraculous and Hairbreadth Escapes, with a Graphic and Characteristic Account Setting Forth, How, By His Inspired Genius and Indomitable Pluck, He Passed From Penury and Persecution Through a Knighthood into an Immortality of Fame*. Dundee, John Durham, 1905

Anon. *William McGonagall Collected Poems*, Omnibus Edition, Edinburgh, Birlinn, 1992

Anon. *Wm McGonagall, Omnibus Edition*, Dundee, David Winter and Son, 1969

Barry, George, *The History of the Orkney Islands*. Kirkwall, William Peace, 1867

Black, Aileen, *Gilfillan of Dundee 1813–1878*. Dundee, Dundee University Press, 2006

Boyd, Frank, *Records of the Dundee Stage*. Dundee, W. & D.C. Thomson, 1886

Chalmers, James, *The History of Dundee, from its Origins to the Present Time*. Dundee, J. Chalmers, 1842

Cooke, A. J. (ed), *Baxters of Dundee*. Dundee, University of Dundee, 1980

Devine, T.M. (ed), *Irish Immigrants and Scottish Society in the Nineteenth and Twentieth Century*, Proceedings of the Scottish Historical Studies Seminar, University of Strathclyde, 1989/90. Edinburgh, John Donald, 1991

Etty, Ross, and others, *The Moc Gonagall*. Dundee, Valentine & Sons, nd (1960)

Gauldie, Enid (ed), *The Dundee Textile Industry 1790–1885, from the Papers of Peter Carmichael of Arthurstone*. Scottish Historical Society, Edinburgh, T. and A. Constable, 1969

Gifford, Douglas and Riach, Alan, (eds), *Scotland's Poets and the Nation.* Carcanet/Scottish Poetry Library, Manchester and Edinburgh, 2004

Gilmour, David, *Reminiscences of the Pen Folk: Paisley Weavers of Other Days.* Paisley, Alex Gardner, 1879

Gray, James T., *Maybole, Carrick's Capital.* Ayr, Alloway Publishing, 1982

Handley, James E., *The Irish in Scotland.* Glasgow, John S. Burns & Co, 1964 [1967]

Hunt, Chris (ed), *William McGonagall Collected Poems.* Edinburgh, Birlinn, 2006

Jamieson, Jane (ed), *Family History, A Guide to Ayrshire Sources.* Ayrshire Archaeological and Natural History Society, 1984

Johnson, Ellen, *Poems and Songs of Ellen Johnson, The Factory Girl.* Glasgow, William Love, 1867

Kinsey, James (ed), *Scottish Poetry: A Critical Survey.* London, Cassell & Co., 1955

Macartney, Lowden, *Selected Poems of William McGonagall.* Glasgow, J. & D.R. Burnside, nd, [c 1934]

MacDiarmid, Hugh, *Scottish Eccentrics.* London, Michael Joseph, 1972 (reprint of 1936 edition)

Macrae, David, *George Gilfillan, Anecdotes and Reminiscences.* Glasgow, Morison Brothers, 1891

Maloney, Paul, *Scotland and the Music Hall 1850–1914.* Manchester, Manchester University Press, 2003

Martin, George M., *Dundee Worthies, Reminiscences, Games, Amusements.* Dundee, David Winter & Son, 1934

Metcalfe, W.M., *A History of Paisley.* Paisley, Alexander Gardner, 1909

Munro, Neil, *The Brave Days, A Chronicle of the North.* Edinburgh, The Porpoise Press, 1931

Murray, Janice, and Stockdale, David, *The Miles Tae Dundee, Stories of a City and its People.* Dundee, Dundee Art Galleries & Museum, 1990

Murray, Norman, *The Scottish Handloom Weavers 1790–1850.* Edinburgh, 1978

Myles, James, *Rambles in Forfarshire.* Edinburgh, 1850

Nasmyth, Charles, *The Comic Legend of William McGonagall.* New Lanark, Waverley Books, 2007

Norrie, William, *Norrie's Hand Book to Dundee, Past and Present.* Dundee, W. Norrie, 1876

Perkins, John, *The Tay Bridge Disaster.* Dundee, Dundee City Council, 1975

Phillips, David, *No Poets' Corner in the Abbey, The Dramatic Story of William McGonagall.* Dundee, David Winter & Son, 1971

Phillips, David, *McGonagall and Tommy Atkins.* Dundee, David Winter & Son, 1973

Power, William, *My Scotland*. Edinburgh, Porpoise Press, 1934

Robertson, Alec, *History of the Dundee Theatre*. London, Precision Press, 1949

Smith, James L. (ed), *The Great McGonagall, Poetical Pearls from the Pen of William McGonagall*. Vermont, The Stephen Greene Press, nd, *c* 1968

Smith, Robin, *The Making of Scotland*. Edinburgh, Canongate, 2001

Smith W.J. (ed), *James Chalmers, Inventor of the Adhesive Postage Stamp*. Dundee, David Winter & Son, 1970

Strawhorn J., *Ayrshire, The Story of a County*. Ayr, Ayrshire Archaeology and Natural History Society, 1985

Swinfen, David, *The Fall of the Tay Bridge*. Edinburgh, Mercat Press, 1994

Swinfen, Whatley etc, *The Life and Times of Dundee*. Edinburgh, John Donald, 1993

Thom, William, *Rhymes and Recollections of a Hand-Loom Weaver*. London, Smith, Elder & Co., 1845

Thomson, William, P.L., *History of Orkney*. Edinburgh, Mercat Press, 1987

Walker, Colin S.K., *William McGonagall*. Edinburgh, Birlinn, 1993

Walker, William, *Juteopolis, Dundee and its Textile Workers 1885–1923*. Edinburgh, Scottish Academic Press, 1979

Watson, Norman, *Dundee: A Short History*. Edinburgh, Black & White Publishing, 2006

Watson, Robert A. and Watson, Elizabeth S., *George Gilfillan, Letters and Journals, with Memoir*. London, Hodder and Stoughton, 1892

Watson, Mark, *Jute and Flax Mills in Dundee*. Tayport, Hutton Press. 1990

Whatley, Christopher A., *The case of James Myles, the 'Factory Boy', and Mid-Victorian Dundee*, in Miskell, Louise; Whatley, Christopher A.; Harris, Bob (eds), *Victorian Dundee, Image and Realities*, Edinburgh, Tuckwell Press, 2000

Winter, David & Son, *Last Poetic Gems*. Dundee, 1968

Winter, David & Son, *More Poetic Gems*. Dundee, 1962

Winter, David & Son, *Poetic Gems*. Dundee, 1938 (facsimile of 1890 edition)

Wittig, Kurt, *The Scottish Tradition in Literature*. Edinburgh, Oliver and Boyd, 1958

WILLIAM McGONAGALL GAZETTEER

Pre-1841 Uncertain

1841   Hawkhill, Dundee (possibly 199 Hawkhill)

1851   44 West Port, Dundee

1857   Roseangle, Dundee (precise location uncertain)

1860   24 Mid Wynd, Dundee

1863   Pennycook Lane, Dundee (precise location uncertain)

1870   39/41 Step Row, Dundee, until around 1875

1873   Smiths Buildings, 19 Paton's Lane, Dundee

1885   31 Paton's Lane, Dundee (the move along the street took place in March 1885)

1887   48 Step Row, Dundee

1891   41 Paton's Lane, Dundee (possible census error as living at 48 Step Row in March 1891)

1891   Perth (possibly lodged at 74 South Street, Perth for a few months)

1891   48 Step Row, Dundee (until eviction in September 1894)

1894   57 South Street, Perth (from late September until June 1895)

1895   Temporary lodgings in Leith, Edinburgh (location unknown)

1895   12 Grove Street, Edinburgh (from autumn 1895 to about May 1898)

1898   21 Lothian Street, Edinburgh (from around May to about April 1899)

1899   Munro & Sons Buildings, Potter Row, Edinburgh (May–June only)

1899   Union Buildings, 26 Potter Row, Edinburgh (from June 1899 until April 1901)

1901   1 Cotts Union Building, 5 South College Street, Edinburgh (from August until death in September 1902)

CHRONOLOGY OF WILLIAM MCGONAGALL'S POEMS AND SONGS

This is the first time William McGonagall's poems have been placed in order of composition. Around 270 poems and songs and one play are listed. Where they have not appeared in any book either by McGonagall or since his death, they are marked as unpublished. The poems are recorded from various sources, including manuscripts, broadsides, newspaper reviews and McGonagall's publications. Poems known by title only, but which have not been seen, are not included. These include, for example, 'Lines on a Dog or Something in the Shape of One', mentioned in the *Weekly News* in November 1878, but not published, and poems such as 'Glamis Castle' and 'Beautiful Craighall, Blairgowrie', which are known to have been written by McGonagall, but have not apparently survived.

MS – Manuscript version survives
BS – Broadside version survives
* – Unpublished

1877
'To A Local Star' (fragment) *
'Address to the Rev George Gilfillan', July 1877 MS
'The Railway Bridge of the Silvery Tay', August 1877 MS, BS
'The Testing Day of the Bridge of Tay' (fragment), September 1877, *
'Immortal Robert Burns of Ayr', September 1877 BS. (Later, 'Ode to the Immortal Bard of Ayr, Robert Burns', contributed to the *Ayrshire Post* by Sir William Topaz McGonagall, 24 April 1897)
'An Address to Shakespeare', September 1877 MS
'An Ode to The Queen', September 1877 MS

'The Bonnie (Broon Hair'd) Lass o' Dundee', September 1877 (song) MS
'Bruce at Bannockburn', September 1877 (also, 'The Battle of Bannock-burn') MS, BS
'A Requisition to the Queen', September 1877 (poetic verse accompanying poems) MS
'A Summary History of Sir William Wallace', October 1877 MS, BS
'A Descriptive Poem on the Silvery Tay', 1877 MS

1878

'Bonnie Dundee in 1878', January 1878 MS
'Genius' (fragment), March 1878 *
'Bonnie Mary', March 1878 *
'The Sorrows of the Blind', May 1878 BS
'The Castle of Mains', May 1878 BS
'An Address to Prince Leopold, Written in Anticipation of his coming to open the Railway Bridge over the Silvery Tay', May 1878 BS
'Loch Ness', June 1878 MS, BS
'The Newport Railway', June 1878 MS, BS
'A Descriptive Poem on the Scenery While Journeying to Balmoral', July 1878
'A Descriptive Poem on the Spittal of Glenshee', July 1878 MS
'Balmoral Castle', July 1878 (pre-1879, probably written on his return from the Highlands) BS
'Lines in Memoriam of the Late Rev George Gilfillan', August 1878
'The Burial of the Rev George Gilfillan', August 1878 BS
'The Rattling Boy from Dublin', October 1878 BS
'Dedicated to Mr Barry Sullivan, Tragedian, Without Permission' (fragment), November 1878 *
'Mary, the Maid o' the Tay', November 1878
'The Christmas Goose', December 1878 BS
'The Beautiful Moon', December 1878 (also, 'Address to the Moon') MS, BS
'Little Jamie', 1878 MS
'The Irish Convict's Return', 1878 MS
'The Inauguration of the Hill o' Balgay', 1878 MS
'The City of Perth', 1878 MS

1879

'The Flower Called Forget-Me-Not', March 1879 (also, 'Forget-Me-Not') BS
'Here We Are Met, A Very Merry Set' (fragment), March 1879 *

'The Convict's Return to Scotland', April 1879 BS
'The Death of the Old Mendicant', June 1879 MS, BS
'A Tribute to the Rev Mr Macrae', October 1879 BS (possibly first printed
    broadside) *

1880
'The Tay Bridge Disaster', January, 1880 BS
'Stirling Castle', March 1880 BS *
'Farewell Address to Dundee', June 1880
'Jottings of London', June 1880 BS, (also, 'Descriptive Jottings of London')
'Burns Statue' (fragment), October 1880

1881
'Bonnie Montrose', April 1881 (also, 'Beautiful Montrose') MS
'Glasgow', July 1881 (also, 'Beautiful Glasgow') BS
'The Royal Review', September 1881
'The Wreck of the "Thomas Dryden" in the Pentland Firth, Belonging to
    Newcastle, which I was an Eye-Witness of', October 1881 BS
'Beautiful Edinburgh', 1881

1882
'A Tribute to Mr Murphy and the Blue Ribbon Army', January 1882 BS
'The Attempted Assassination of the Queen', May 1882 BS
'The Wreck of the Steamer "London" while on her way to Australia',
    November 1882 BS
'The Battle of Tel-el-Kebir', (subtitled, 'The Latest Laurel of the British
    Army, Dedicated expressly to Sir Garnet Wolseley and the British
    Army under his Command'), October, 1882 (A later broadside, c 1896,
    was further subtitled, 'Published by Particular Request of the Friendly
    Citizens of Edinburgh') MS, BS
'The Den o' Fowlis', 1882 MS, BS

1883
'Saving a Train', February 1883 BS
'The Death of John Brown', March 1893
'The Beautiful Sun', June 1883 BS
'The Sunderland Calamity', June 1883 BS
'The Death of Captain Webb', August 1883
'The Inauguration of University College, Dundee', October 1883 BS
'Beautiful Glasgow', 1883 (song), (A broadside with the same title was
    issued in September 1889, with the amendments 'Late of Dundee' and

'Published by Particular Desire'. It contains two extra verses to the 1883 version to satisfy Glaswegian tastes.)

1884

'The Famous Tay Whale', January 1884 MS, BS

'Saved by Music', January 1884 BS

'The Battle of El-Teb', March 1884 MS, BS

'The Clepington Catastrophe', March 1884 BS

'The Death of Prince Leopold', (subtitled, 'Dedicated Expressly to the Memory of the Late Prince Leopold'), April 1884 BS

'The Beautiful River Dee', April 1884 BS *

'The Battle of Waterloo', June 1884 MS, BS

'The Battle of Flodden Field', August 1884 BS

'The Great Franchise Demonstration, Dundee 20 September 1884', (subtitled, 'Expressly Dedicated to the Right Hon W. E. Gladstone MP, The "Grand Old Man"'), September 1884 BS

'Women's Suffrage', October 1884 BS

'A Christmas Carol', December 1884 BS

1885

'The Battle of Abu Klea', (subtitled, 'Fought in 1885'), (further subtitled, 'Respectfully dedicated to Sir Herbert Stewart')', February 1885 BS

'The Battle of the Alma, Fought in 1854', January 1885 MS, BS

'General Gordon, the Hero of Khartoum', (subtitled, 'Dedicated Expressly in Memory of'), March, 1885 MS, BS

'The Capture of Lucknow', April 1885 BS

'The Rebel Surprise Near Tamai, (subtitled, 'Dedicated Expressly in Praise of General McNeill and the British Army under his Command')', April 1885 BS

'The Battle of Alexandria, or The Reconquest of Egypt', June 1885 MS, BS

'Jack o' the Cudgel, A New Recitation', June 1885 BS

'Jack o' the Cudgel, The Hero of A Hundred Fights' (play)

'Jack o' the Cudgel, or the Battle of Cressy, A New Poem, Canto Second', July 1885 BS

'Jack o' the Cudgel, or the Battle of Calais , Canto Forth (sic)', August 1885 BS

'A Tribute to Dr Murison', August 1885

'Bill Bowls, the Sailor', September 1885 BS

'Bill Bowls the Sailor, Second Canto', September 1885 BS

'A New Temperance Poem, in Memory of my Departed Parents, Who were sober living and God-Fearing people', October 1885 BS

1886

'The Wreck of the Barque 'Lynton' while bound for Aspinall, Having on board 1,000 tons of coal', January 1886 BS

'The Wreck of the 'Columbine', March 1886 BS

'The Wreck of the Barque 'Wm Paterson' of Liverpool', April 1886 BS

'A Horrible Tale of the Sea', May 1886, (also, A Tale of the Sea) BS

'Greenland's Icy Mountains', May 1886 BS

'Beautiful Oban', June 1886 (also, Oban and Descriptive Beautiful Oban) BS

'Loch Katrine', July 1886 (song), (also, Beautiful Loch Katrine) MS, BS

'Young Munro the Sailor', July 1886 BS

'The Queen's Visit to the Exhibition', August 1886 BS *

'The Dundee Flower Show, (subtitled, 'Dedicated to the Rt Hon Earl of Dalhousie')', September, 1886 BS

'The Battle of the Nile', September 1886 BS

'Hanchen, the Maid of the Mill', October 1886 BS

'An Autumn Reverie', November 1886 BS

'Baldovan Mansion', December 1886 (also, Baldovan) BS

'Loch Leven', December 1886 BS

'Broughty Ferry', December 1886

1887

'The Wreck of the Schooner "Samuel Crawford"'', January, 1887 BS

'Lines Dedicated To Mr James Scrymgeour, Dundee, By His Kind Permission', January 1887 BS *

Voyage Poems, April 1887 (McGonagall's 'diary' of his visit to New York contained around 20 stanzas, mostly describing his voyage) *

'Jottings of New York', May 1887 BS

'An Address to the New Tay Bridge', June 1887 BS

'An Ode to the Queen on her Jubilee Year', June 1887 BS

'The Adventures of King Robert the Bruce', July 1887 MS, BS

'Grace Darling or, The Wreck of the 'Forfarshire Steamer,' August, 1887 BS

'Little Pierre's Song', August 1887 BS

'The First Grenadier of France', August, 1887 MS, BS

'Grif, of the Bloody Hand', September 1887 BS

'The Burning of the Exeter Theatre', September 1887 MS, BS

'The Demon Drink', October 1887 BS

'An Adventure in the Life of King James V of Scotland', November, 1887 MS, BS

'The Black Watch Memorial', November 1887 BS

'The Death of Lord and Lady Dalhousie', December, 1887 MS BS
'The Tragic Death of the Rev. A. H. Mackonochie', December 1887 BS

1888

'The Death of The Rev Dr Wilson', January 1888, (subtitled, 'Dedicated to Mr James Scrymgeour, By His Kind Permission', January 1888') MS, BS
'The Burning of the Steamer 'City of Montreal'', January 1888 MS, BS
'John Rouat the Fisherman', February 1888 MS, BS
'Annie Marshall, the Foundling', February 1888 BS
'The Great Yellow River Inundation in China', March 1888 BS
'The Funeral of the German Emperor', April 1888 BS
'The Wreck of the Whaler 'Oscar'', April 1888 BS
'Jenny Carrister, the Heroine of Lucknow-Mine', May 1888 BS
'The Death of Fred Marsden, the American Playwright', June 1888 BS
'Beautiful Nairn', June 1888 BS
'An Excursion Steamer Sunk in the Tay', July 1888 BS
'The Horrors of Majuba', August 1888 (reprinted 'By Request' c 1896) BS
'The Drowning of the Rev Wm Horne, Late of Dundee', August 1888 BS *
'The Queen at the International Exhibition, Glasgow', September 1888 BS *
'The Miraculous Escape of Robert Allan, the Fireman', October 1888 BS
'The Battle of Shina, in Africa, (subtitled, 'Fought in 1800')', October, 1888 BS
'The Collision in the English Channel', November 1888 BS
'The Funeral of the Late Ex-Provost Rough, Dundee', December 1888 BS
'The Storming of the Dargai Heights', 1888

1889

'The Destroying Angel or The Poet's Dream', January 1889 MS, BS
'The Wreck of the Steamer 'Storm Queen,' January 1889 MS, BS
'Richard Piggot, The Forger', April 1889 MS, BS
'No More: A Tale of Elsinore', May 1889 BS
'The Pennsylvania Disaster', July 1889 MS, BS
'The Poacher and His Family', August 1889 BS
'Lines in Protest to the Dundee Magistrates', September 1889
'Jack Honest, or the Widow and Her Son', November 1889 BS
'The Sprig of Moss', December 1889 BS

1890

'The Prize Poem; A Tribute to Henry M. Stanley, 'The Great African Explorer', (subtitled, 'By Particular Request'), June 1890 BS

'The Crucifixion of Christ' (subtitled, 'Composed by Special Request, 18 June 1890') June, 1890 BS
'Beautiful Monikie', July 1890
'William Fly, the Pirate', September 1890 BS *
'The Nithsdale Widow and Her Son', December 1891 BS
'A Tribute from Zululand', 1891

1891
'The Battle of Langside', April 1891 BS *
'Tributes in Praise of Poet McGonagall from Glasgow University, Christmas, 1891', December 1891 BS

1892
'The Death of Black Beard The Pirate', April 1892 (also, Captain Teach alias 'Black Beard') BS
'The Bonnie Lass o' Ruig', April 1892 MS, BS
'The Wreck of the 'Abercrombie Robinson,' May, 1892 MS, BS
'The Bonnie Sidlaw Hills', August 1892 (song) MS
'Beautiful Newport on the Braes o' the Silvery Tay', August, 1892 BS
'Beautiful Rothesay', August 1892 MS
'Too Late', August 1892 BS *
'The Troubles of Matthew Mahoney', August 1892 MS, BS
'Bonnie Callander', September 1892 (song) MS
'Bonnie Kilmany', September 1892 (song) MS
'The Life Boat Demonstration', October 1892 BS *
'The Death and Burial of Lord Tennyson', October 1892 BS
'Hawthornden', November 1892 BS *
'Royal Visit of Princess Louise and the Marquis of Lorne', November 1892 BS
'The Foundering of the Steamer 'Spree' while on her way to New York', December 1892 BS

1893
'A New Year's Resolution to Leave Dundee', January 1893
'Lines in Reply to the Beautiful Poet who Welcomed News of McGonagall's Departure from Dundee', January 1893
'A Soldier's Reprieve', January 1893 MS BS
'The Ancient City of St Andrews, March, 1893 MS
'Beautiful Aberfoyle', March 1893 MS, BS
'Lines in Praise of Mr J. Graham Henderson, Hawick', March 1893 BS
'A Tribute to Mr J. Graham Henderson, The World's Fair Judge', March 1893

'Saving a Train', May 1893 BS
'The Faithful Dog Fido', June, 1893 BS *
'The Loss of the 'Victoria,' June, 1893 BS
'Lines in Praise of the Royal Marriage', June 1893 MS *
'The Horse Parade: or Demonstration, In Respect of the Royal Wedding',
    July 1893 *, MS BS
'The Blind Girl', October 1893 BS
'Little Popeet – The Lost Child', November 1893 BS
'The Terrific Cyclone of 1893', December 1893 BS
'Lost on the Prairie', December 1893 BS
'Lines in Memoriam Regarding the Entertainment I Gave in Reform
    Street Hall, Dundee on the 31 March, 1893'

1894

'The Little Match Girl', January 1894 BS
'Saved by Music', January 1894 BS
'The Kessack Ferry-Boat Fatality', February 1894 BS (broadside incor-
    rectly dated – occurred March 1894)
'St Andrews University Liberal Association and their Famous Dinner',
    February 1894 *
'Lines in Praise of Sunlight Soap', February 1894 BS
'The Lakes of Kilarney, or Norah and Barney', March 1894 MS, BS
'The Beautiful City of Perth, A New Version', April 1894 BS
'A Tribute to the Rev Alexander C. Henderson, (Subtitled, 'Previous to
    his leaving for Australia')', May 1894 BS *
'The Village of Tayport and its Surrounds', BS July 1894
'Lines in Praise of the Lyric Club Banquet, held at Queen's Hotel, Perth,
    5 September, 1894', September 1894
'The Hill of Kinnoull', September 1894 *
'The Fair Maid of Perth's House', October 1894
'The Heather Blend Club Banquet', October 1894
'A Wonderful Medicine – Lines in Praise of Beecham's Pills' (fragment),
    1894 *

1895

'Lines in Praise of Professor Blackie', April 1895 BS
'Edinburgh', June 1895 BS (new version)
'The River of Leith', September 1895 BS
'An Address to the Members of the Phunological Society', 1895 BS *

1896

'New North Bridge Ceremonials', May 1896 BS

'Colinton Dell and Its Surroundings', August 1896 BS, Unpublished

'The Burning of the People's Variety Theatre, Aberdeen', 1896 BS

'Lines in Defence of the Stage', 1895 BS

1897

'The Military Review by Lord Wolseley; in the Queen's Park, Edinburgh, 5 Dec 1896'. February 1897 BS

'Ode to the Immortal Bard of Ayr, Robert Burns: contributed to the 'Ayrshire Post' by Sir William Topaz McGonagall, 24 April 1897 (See also 1877)

'The Queen's Diamond Jubilee Celebrations', May, 1897 BS (also, 'An Ode to the Queen on Her Sixty Years Rein')

'The Beautiful Sun', June 1897 BS (sister poem to 'The Beautiful Moon')

'The Storming of Dargai Heights', November 1897 BS

'The Fearful Calamity in Paris, 1897' BS (subtitled, 'Fire in a Charity Bazaar')

'The Military Review in the Queen's Park by the Duke of Cambridge', 1897 BS

1898

'Calamity in London', January 1898 BS (subtitled, 'Family of Ten Burned To Death')

'The Battle of Atbara', April 1898 BS

'The Burial of Mr Gladstone', May 1898 , (subtitled, 'The Great Political Hero') BS

'The Albion Battleship Calamity', June 1898 BS

'The Disastrous Fire at Scarborough', June 1898 BS

'The Battle of Omdurman', September 1898 BS

'The Wreck of the Steamer Mohegan', November 1898 BS

'Beautiful Balmerino', 1898

'The Execution of James Graham, Marquis of Montrose', 1898 BS

1899

'Saving a Train', January 1899 (new version)

'(Henry Hook) The Hero of Rorke's Drift', February 1899 BS

'Beautiful Crieff', April 1899 BS

'The Ancient Town of Leith', May 1899 BS

'The Wreck of the Steamer "Stella" ', May 1899 BS

'A Summary History of Lord Clive', June 1899 BS

'Beautiful Comrie and Its Surrounds', June 1899 BS
'Beautiful North Berwick and Its Surrounds', June 1899 BS
'The Last Berkshire Eleven', July 1899 BS
'A Humble Heroine', September 1899 BS
'The Hero of Kalapore: or, An Incident of the Indian Mutiny', August
    1899 BS
'The Wreck of the 'Indian Chief', October 1899 BS
'Lines in Praise of Tommy Atkins', November 1899 BS
'The Battle of Glencoe', November 1899 BS
'The Battle of Modder River', December 1899 BS

1900
'The Relief of Ladysmith', April 1900 BS
'Beautiful Village of Penicuik', May 1900 BS *
'Beautiful Balmoral', May 1900 BS
'The Relief of Mafeking', June 1900 BS
'Lord Roberts' Triumphal Entry into Pretoria', June 1900 BS
'The Capture of Havana', July 1900 BS
'The Battle of Corunna', August 1900 BS
'Lord General Roberts in Afghanistan', August 1900 BS
'The Burning of the Ship "Kent"', September 1900 BS
'The Death of Carl Springel', October 1900 BS
'A Tale of Christmas Eve', December 1900 BS
'The Funeral of the Late Prince Henry of Battenberg', 1900 BS

1901
'The Death of Captain Ward', January 1901 BS
'The Death of the Queen', January 1901 BS
'The Siege of Seringapatum', March 1901 BS
'The Downfall of Delhi', April 1901 BS
'A Tale of Elsinore', June 1901 BS
'An All-Night Sea Fight', June 1901 BS
'The Battle of Gujrat', August, 1901 BS

1902
'The fall of Coomassie' (subtitled, 'The Ashantee War'), January 1902 BS
'McGonagall's Ode to the King', June 1902 (subtitled, 'Extracted from the
    Weekly News, July 5, 1902') BS
'Beautiful Torquay', 1902 BS
'The Battle of Inkermann', 1902 BS
'Drogheda and its Surroundings', 1902 BS *

'The Battle of Toulouse', 1902 BS
'The City of Sligo and its Adjacent Surroundings', 1902 BS *
'The Coronation of the King', September 1902 *

Unknown dates
'The Late Sir John Ogilvy'
'The Battle of Culloden', pre 1891
'The Battle of Sheriffmuir', pre 1891
'The Capture of Lucknow'

INDEX